MW01164983

TRIBUTE TO OCTAVIO PAZ

TRIBUTE TO OCTAVIO PAZ

MEXICAN CULTURAL INSTITUTE OF NEW YORK
MEXICAN CULTURAL INSTITUTE OF WASHINGTON
OCTAVIO PAZ FOUNDATION

Contents

PRESENTATION

The texts that are gathered here are the result of a tribute to one of the greatest poets of the last century: Octavio Paz. Organized by the Mexican Cultural Institutes of Washington and New York, along with the Hispanic Division of the Library of Congress and the Metropolitan Museum of Art in New York, the tribute brought together poets, artists and friends of the poet who joined their voices in celebrating the interior richness and vast achievements of the acclaimed writer.

The lamentable death of Octavio Paz, on April 19, 1998, left behind an intellectual and creative void in Mexico, impossible to fill. As Dr. Ernesto Zedillo Ponce de León stated during the funeral services offered at the Palacio de Bellas Artes: "...starting today, we will miss the courage and clarity of his thought, the vastness of his knowledge and the dignity of his unyielding defense of liberty". The evocation of the themes that always interested him, and the readings of his most celebrated poems on behalf of his friends, added a further dimension to the tributes rendered to him in his country, celebrating the achievements of a whole lifetime.

Octavio Paz was one of the great poets of the xx^{th} century. His poetic genius and his acute judgements as an art critic should be considered along with his unparalleled intellectual character. Perhaps the absolute independence of his criteria and his open honesty stand above everything else. In his writings concerning art, love, India, eroticism, politics and Sor Juana Inés de la Cruz, or Colonial Mexico, Octavio Paz always displayed an attitude that was at the same time critical and passionate towards each object of his study, shedding new light on each occasion and on a wide variety of themes of capital importance. Never in his life was he interested in the passing fashion of a moment. His conscience was his only guide and he vigorously opposed dogmatism, nationalism and any other form of authoritarianism always in benefit of the defense of humanism and the unrestricted defense of the liberty and dignity of the individual. Founder and contributor of innumerable cultural enterprises, Octavio Paz culminated his editorial work with the creation of *Vuelta*, a monthly publication that for more than twenty years was dedicated to expounding and defending the ideas of liberty and democracy throughout essays and articles written by the most creative and independent writers of Mexico, Latin America and the world.

Many persons and institutions contributed to the complete success of the *Tribute to Octavio Paz* that was held in Washington, D.C. and New York between the 20th and the 24th of October, 1999. Mrs. Marie José Paz heads the list: her generosity and support were unlimited, and her presence in both cities highlighted the successful event. Georgette Dorn, Director of the Hispanic Division, and Barbara Tenenbaum, specialist in Mexico, both from the Library of Congress, as well as Mr. Phillipe de Montebello, Director of the Metropolitan Museum of Art in New York, gladly supported the realization of this tribute. The orientation and suggestions of Mr. Eliot Weinberger, translator of Octavio Paz's poetry into English, as those of Mr. Guillermo Sheridan, formerly Director of the Octavio Paz Foundation, were in every moment generous and opportune. Additionally, we gratefully acknowledge other prestigious institutions that willingly joined this endeavor, particularly the Cervantes Institute, the American Poets Society and the Poetic Society of America. We also thank Álvaro Rodríguez Tirado and Juan García de Oteyza, who were Directors of the Mexican Cultural Institutes at the time of celebration of this tribute.

We would also like to mention the support of our sponsors: the MexAm Cultural Foundation, the Artención Cultural Foundation, the Magowan Family Foundation, Mr. Plácido Arango, Mrs. Marieluise Hessel, Aeroméxico, Continental Airlines, Cervecería Modelo and the Mexico-United States Cultural Trust Fund, an organization integrated by the Rockefeller Foundation, the Bancomer Cultural Foundation and the Fondo Nacional para la Cultura y las Artes.

Finally, we would like to express our gratitude to the Organization of American States and, particularly, to its Secretary General, Mr. César Gaviria, and Mrs. Sara Meneses, Director of Cultural Affairs of said organization, for the invaluable support in the publication of this memoir.

The figure of Octavio Paz was not only unique in its kind within Mexico, due to the intrinsic value of his work and the profoundness of his legacy, but also had an international impact that is impossible to exaggerate. Thanks to the works of Octavio Paz the world knows Mexico better and appreciates more deeply the profoundness of its cultural legacy as well as the immense flow of its artistic patrimony. We are sure that the *Tribute to Octavio Paz*, as well as the publication of this book, will greatly contribute in this noble deed.

IGNACIO DURÁN
Executive Director
Mexican Cultural Institute
Washington, D.C.

HUGO HIRIART
Executive Director
Mexican Cultural Institute
New York

Part I. Symposium

TESTIMONIALS

CHOICE AND CHANCE:
RECALLING OCTAVIO PAZ

CHARLES TOMLINSON

In thinking about this appreciation of Octavio Paz and our affectionate relationship as poets, I became aware that two words kept recurring in my mind —choice and chance. All human life seems to be divided between these two. And sometimes it's unified by them— when, that is, we consent to chance and choose to accept what it gives us, something accidental becoming an event that weaves itself into the texture of our lives.

I first met Octavio by chance on the concourse of the Rome Airport. We were both traveling from separate places to a poetry reading at Spoleto, and, though we were already corresponding with each other, neither of us had foreseen this first meeting in these surroundings. Indeed, I might well have missed him, but I suddenly caught sight of a lady whose appearance was quite unlike that of any woman I had met before. The thought darted into my head, "Suppose this were the wife of Octavio Paz ..." She was moving fairly swiftly, so I rapidly followed, in a rather Groucho Marx-like fashion, secretive but purposeful. And sure enough, the man who was changing money in front of a counter and towards whom she was directing her steps, was Octavio, instantly recognizable from his photographs. So we traveled together by train to Spoleto beginning the first of the very many conversations that occurred in our friendship during the next thirty years.

Behind this event were a number of earlier conjunctions of chance and choice. In 1963, passing through Mexico City, I had happened to find in a bookshop a copy of *Salamandra*, the first collection of Octavio's that I had seen. I was fascinated by many of these poems and set about translating some of them. On my return to England, I published the translations in a then well-known magazine of literature and politics, *Encounter*.

Slowly but ominously, it dawned on me that I had done nothing about obtaining rights to these texts. When they appeared, I had distressing intimations of a lawsuit and ruination. One day there arrived by post a large brown package from the Mexican Embassy in New Delhi, where Octavio was ambassador at the time. This was it! This was the beginning of my downfall. I nervously prised open the envelope. Octavio had not thought about rights either, but was delighted that a fellow poet had decided to translate him. This was another fresh beginning for both of us, as we continued to translate each other's poems and even went on to write collaborative poems together in imitation of the Japanese collaborative form, the renga. We also passed ideas back and forth. In his long poem, *Sunstone*, Octavio numbers Trotsky among the many victims of the violence of politics, along with Montezuma, Robespierre and Lincoln. This poem led me ultimately not only to visit the house where Trotsky was assassinated in Mexico City, but also to write a poem entitled *Assassin*, with an epigraph taken from *Sunstone:* "Trotsky's death rattle and his howl like a boar." In turn, when *One Earth, Four or Five Worlds: Reflections on Contemporary History*, the English version of Octavio's examination of revolution and its aftermath, appeared, he had added two new essays to the original Spanish text: one had for its title a phrase from my poem *Assassin*, "The contaminations of contingency," the other, entitled "The Assassin and Eternity", was a profound meditation on that same poem. All this is a measure of the way friendship between two poets can lead, not merely to imitation, but to a new lease of creative life for both of them. It is also a measure of Octavio's generosity of spirit that he was open to the relationship with a much younger poet, writing in another language and tradition, and that he would willingly translate my poems, putting all his artistry at another's disposal.

To return to my opening theme and to our chance meeting at Rome airport. Our friendship ripened through chance and we chose it also. Chance is —well— chancy and it requires human fidelities that survive the flux of time by transforming what is random in experience into what is lasting, into an experience that takes place on a different level from mere chance. Something similar happens in the composition of poetry: you begin with perhaps a random instance, something caught sight of accidentally, then you embody that instance in language and in a certain poetic form. A poem is also rather like taking a walk. You may know pretty well the direction you will go in, but you do not know in advance all the things you will see along the way or all the things that may pass through your mind as you continue to write. Somehow, accident and form have got to be reconciled in the finished poem.

This thought brings back many walks with Octavio over the years — in Mexico City, Paris, Cambridge, Spoleto, New York. I remember in particular a cool bright spring afternoon on Fifth Avenue. Manhattan possessed that quality which Matisse especially admired there— the crystalline. The cold air seemed to endow everything with a sharpness of angle, an impinging presence. Suddenly Octavio said, as if the reflection had all at once surprised him, "You know, they made something beautiful by accident here." We are back with our theme of the relation of chance to achievement. Octavio was thinking of the original grid pattern mapping out New York, which determined the shape of the city before New York had arrived there, so that when it did arrive, here was this underlying form that so marvelously chimed with the tall buildings, the light and air. They had indeed made something beautiful by accident there. If on that spring afternoon, the city had become endowed with speech, what we would have heard was (in Octavio's phrase) "the other voice" —the voice that somehow exceeded the chance of which it was a part, that reconciled and transcended the disparate elements in a sort of aria of light and space. The aria, with its melody, would have gone beyond and yet contained the individual separateness of street corner, facade, side street, doors, windows, of people walking like us.

The union of the seemingly arbitrary element —the grid, the abstract pattern— with the busy particulars of daily life, struck me again when Octavio and I wrote together a sequence of poems called *Airborn*. This composite poem was basically following out an ancient Japanese form, the renga, a poem written by a group of poets who continue one another's work. Renga is thus a form where chance and choice are often brought into startling relationship, Renga thrives —it can only go on— when it develops and exploits the faculty of making fortunate discoveries by accident. You never quite know what theme governs the poetry you're going to be asked to continue, so you never quite know in what direction you will be forced or, most happily, will choose to go.

Years before composing *Airborn*, at Octavio's suggestion, four of us —Octavio, an Italian, a French poet, and myself— had experimented

together with the renga form. It is typical of Octavio's openness to possibility that he should have had the idea of transplanting renga to Europe
—to Paris, where we all assembled to write the first European renga. It is
typical, also, in the later case of *Airborn* that he should further refine the
form as something that could be written by two poets and conducted by
airmail since he was about to return to Mexico. More chance intervened.
We had set out from our house, Brook Cottage, to put Octavio and
Marie-José on the London train at our local station. That day the train
didn't run, so we retired to a nearby pub to get a snack and await the next
connection. It was there that Octavio suggested we take two very basic
words, house and day, and collaborate in using them in a poem, a renga— in sonnet form like that first European renga. The choice of "house"
was prompted by Brook Cottage, that of "day" by the fact that the day was
suddenly so typically English, with Constable-like clouds scudding excitingly before the wind. I wrote the first four lines of "house" and sent it
to Octavio to continue; Octavio wrote the first four lines of "day" and sent
it to me to continue likewise. We wrote eight sonnets, four to each word,
and then translated them into our own languages.

So this preconceived form, the sonnet, like New York's grid pattern,
was there to support and to be transformed by all the elements that
would flow through it. This transformation of the given must be the
work of the imagination, and the imagination must bring to birth
something beyond the merely given and beyond our mere daily selves:
it must make us and our readers hear "the other voice." Of that voice
Octavio had once written: "The 'other voice' is my voice. Our being already contains that other we wish to be ..."[1] And he concludes: "Inspiration is that strange voice that takes us out of ourselves to be everything
that we are..."[2] So the work of the poetic imagination is to subsume
and to integrate all that is seemingly arbitrary in poetic form —those
pre-existing fourteen lines, for example.

If, in poetic composition, the other voice is the enemy, or rather the
vivifier of what is simply given, in history it is the voice always opposing historical determinism, refusing the staleness of fate and the dead-

---

[1] [*The Bow and the Lyre,* trans. Ruth L. C. Simms (Austin: University of Texas Press, 1973)].
[2] *Ibidem.*

ends that our lives can too easily be led into. Octavio puts it this way: "Every poem is an attempt to reconcile history and poetry for the benefit of poetry", so that "Poetry is the other voice. Not the voice of history or of anti-history, but the voice which in history, is always saying something different."

When the other voice makes itself heard, it tends to leave our attempts to pontificate on "the future of poetry" looking rather foolish. Where would you look or listen during the *fin-de-siècle* —that of the nineteenth century and also our own— to find that voice? One of the places to seek it out in the last century would have been the unlikely city of Alexandria in Egypt, where two very different poets, Cavafy and Ungaretti, were both born. Amid the leftovers of Oscar Wilde and late Swinburne, who would have thought of listening for that other voice in "a half-savage country" (Pound's phrase), the United States of America? In other words, the arrival of Pound and Eliot and their particular poetries were wholly unforeseen. Similarly, who would have supposed that (only yesterday, so to speak) in a decaying house in Mixcoac, just outside Mexico City, the other voice was preparing to make itself heard in the person of Octavio Paz, a voice born out of and yet transcending the complex fate of being a Mexican and of seeking an identity for oneself and one's country.

"Inspiration," as I have already quoted from Octavio, "is that strange voice that takes us out of ourselves to be everything that we are ..." In our age of conceptual art and other gimmicks, we hesitate even to talk about inspiration and yet, in one form or another, it is this power, not disdained by Paz, that unites very different kinds of poets and poetry, and can link together in a more vivid consciousness the entire human race. Inspiration extends from the Bible to the poetry of what we used to call the American Indians; it overrides distinctions between classicism and romanticism; it can inform the "disciplined kind of dreaming" T.S. Eliot attributes to Dante and the (apparently) undisciplined overflow of the unconscious the Surrealists felt themselves to be tapping. Basically, the address to the Muse from Homer to Milton and the waiting on a vision —frequently that of some animal— by the Hopi and the Navajo have this in common, a respect for the unpremeditated, for that which lies beyond merely conscious purposes and merely voluntary intentions.

One speaks of inspiration, the Muse and the unforeseen. But at the same time, one must also stress that poetry —the act of writing poetry— is a practical and not essentially a mystical act. It is tied to the given nature of language itself. Poetry is not a sudden explosion of truth, but a step-by-step, sound-by-sound, word-by-word creation, structured by connections of sound, syntax and grammar. It is rooted in the physical act of speaking and its music is that of the human voice and the human mind on a journey of auditory discovery. Different poets dramatize the steps of this auditory journey in different ways, as they trace the essentially concrete relationships between the words they use. What they all have in common is that they make us hear that "other voice" of which Octavio speaks. The other voice is the human voice rescued from history by poetry.

In the person of Octavio Paz, I salute a poet of the tradition of inspiration and of the tradition of the new.

It would be an over-simplification if I did not stress the human factor in this poetic unity. The strength of Octavio's poetry surely derives from and celebrates the constant companionship of Marie-José and her fine intuitive understanding of what Octavio was doing, from the time they met and married.

The reception of the other voice has to be prepared for, and Octavio's unmistakably twentieth-century poetry, a poetry appearing in the aftermath of Eliot's *The Waste Land*, owes much of its accuracy and tonality to his knowledge of earlier poetries —to medieval and seventeenth-century Spanish, nineteenth-century French (Mallarmé in particular), to the Nahuatl poetry of his native land. In Paz we have a clear instance of the way the other voice is nurtured by the past and by past forms— even that most traditional of forms, the sonnet. So a poet has this in common with a city —out of the given, both create the unforeseen, out of the apparently fated they release new possibilities for life itself.

My thoughts go back to New York —a relatively recent city by European standards, but one that has long established and developed its own traditions and outgrown its earlier self. New York, on a brisk spring day, can persuade us, like the poetry of Octavio Paz, that humankind can achieve a vision of the crystalline and the miraculously renewable.

RIGHTS OF POETRY

ENRICO MARIO SANTÍ

We celebrate the life and work of a most extraordinary man: a Nobel laureate poet who also wrote about history and challenged states and governments; an intellectual who cared deeply about freedom, in particular the freedom to think and create; a man who sang endlessly about love but also analyzed loneliness, the modern world's as well as his own; a Mexican who sought to place his country in particular, and Latin America in general, on a moral par with other countries. It is of course impossible to summarize adequately Octavio Paz's sixty-year career: his complete works span fourteen volumes, each of which contains an average of 500 pages, and deal with subjects ranging from poetics and literary theory to art criticism and anthropology. It is equally difficult to find parallels for Octavio Paz. Like Alfonso Reyes, his fellow Mexican, or Jorge Luis Borges, his contemporary, he was a wide-ranging humanist, poet, and essayist. But Paz's work surpassed the limits of Reyes' and Borges' thematic repertoire through his extensive writings about the visual arts, for example, or by constantly engaging debates on history and politics. If Paul Valéry and T.S. Eliot, to take two other examples from outside Latin America, were fundamentally poets and literary essayists, and their cultural criticism was relatively limited, Paz's own meditations on history and culture persisted since at least 1931. Both Unamuno and Ortega y Gasset, to take examples from within the Hispanic realm, produced a vast amount of work within a broad philosophical spectrum. But again, neither displayed the kind of sensibility towards the visual arts of their time that was one of Octavio Paz's greatest contributions. Neither Unamuno nor Ortega ever reflected upon the Orient, our great Other, in the creative and sustained way that Paz did. But neither did Pablo Neruda, the one 20th-century poet from Latin America closest in importance to Paz, who did spend time in the Orient, but hated it.

Few works, few people, have had Octavio Paz's power of convocation, in the precise sense of "calling to one's side." Throughout the course of his career, Paz founded no less than six magazines, in which he wrote about everyone around him whom he believed worth spotting, and thus promoted the careers not only of poets and writers, but also of painters, sculptors, literary critics, philosophers, and cultural figures. His influence has reached well beyond the Hispanic world, and touched virtually all of the countries of Europe and many in Asia. That influence is due, in large measure, to the highly unusual thematic variety of Paz's work, the kind of variety that allows readers all over to identify readily with his voice. Our so-called "global culture" finds in Octavio Paz its own global spokesman. In his work, cultures, times, spaces, languages, and traditions all converge. Borges said once that Quevedo, arguably Spain's greatest poet, had been so compendious that he had ceased to be a writer and became a literature. No less can be said of Octavio Paz.

Why Octavio Paz became this kind of writer can be explained, in part, by historical circumstance. Paz was present at the major historical events of this century —from the Mexican Revolution, in the midst of which he was born, to the Spanish Civil War, in which he participated; from post-war Paris and Tokyo, where he lived as a diplomat, to 1968, when he resigned his post as ambassador in protest over his government's massacre of 300 students; from the Cold War to the fall of the Berlin Wall, about which he wrote extensively. And yet, throughout all of these numerous and sometimes terrible events, what remained distinctive about the work of this Mexican writer was the primacy of poetry.

It is no exaggeration to say that all of Octavio Paz's work constitutes a vast and powerful defense of poetry. Few times in Western intellectual history, and rarely in the Spanish language, had a writer treated poetry with such prominence, and in ways that went beyond the narrow limits of literary or art criticism. Indeed, Paz made poetry the foundation of culture in general, and argued for poetry's former status in relation to all other discourses or modes of knowledge, including religion in its various forms, and even the religious instinct itself. According to Paz, the experience of Poetry, which is the experience of otherness or of strangeness of being, is previous to the experience of the Sacred. What this meant, for

Paz and for us, is that the historic Western polemic between poetry and philosophy became decentered or displaced. To quote Paz:

> Poetry, like Philosophy, is an amphibian activity which partakes of both the moving waters of History and of the transparency of Philosophy, but which is neither History nor Philosophy. Poetry is always concrete, it is singular; Poetry is never abstract, it is never general.

No other work of a poet, no other reflection on poetry within Western intellectual history that I know of has been able to articulate the most fundamental questions regarding human nature. Paz wrote:

> Between Revolution and Religion, Poetry is the other voice. Its voice is Other because it is the voice of the passions and of visions; it is otherworldly and this-worldly; of days long gone and of this very day, an antiquity without dates.[1]

Anyone even mildly familiar with the work of Octavio Paz is immediately struck by the overall tension in his work between what, for lack of a better description, one could call aesthetic purity and social contamination. Paz himself often told the story of a luncheon in Mexico City in the late 1930s where the poets of the *Contemporáneos* group —Xavier Villaurrutia, José Gorostiza, Carlos Pellicer, Jaime Torres Bodet— an older and certainly canonical group, pointed out to him the disturbing contradiction in his work: his poetry, heir to the Symbolist tradition, dealt with the traditional themes of nature, desire, and the self in the most traditional language, whereas his political views, close to anarchists and Marxists alike, argued for a social revolution in the most strident terms. After this luncheon with his mentors —perhaps as a result of it— Octavio Paz did write a number of political poems, some of which, like the Spanish Republican ode "¡No pasarán!", he included in his *Complete Works*. But this was to be the exception, and Paz remained throughout his career a Janus-like figure in regard to the relationship between History and Poetry. This is perhaps one of the

---

[1] *The Other Voice: Essays on Modern Poetry*, trans. Helen Lane (New York: Harcourt Brace Jovanovich: 1991), 151.

least known links between Paz and French Surrealism, or at least the
kind of Surrealism that was espoused by André Breton and Benjamin
Péret, among his strongest influences: society's revolution ought not to
be confused with the poem's, or for that matter with the mind's. Edward Hirsch, the distinguished American poet, who wrote one of the
most moving pieces on the occasion of Paz's death, has given us an eloquent summary of this split:

> Paz had a keen sense of the civic responsibilities of the poet. He eagerly en-
> tered the political fray —as a foreign diplomat, as the founding editor of
> many magazines, as an outspoken critical thinker... Paz's reputation as a
> man of letters, his books on the history and politics of our time, threatened
> to overshadow his work as a poet, though all of his writing grew out of his
> commitment to poetry.[2]

Paz defended, sometimes against his critics, this split or double attitude toward poetry and history. He cared deeply about both but felt that
each had its own genres, modes and, above all, its own occasions. In this,
he reacted strongly to his heritage, the recent history of modern poetry,
whose reaction to the century's political convulsions had polarized poetic representation. While poets like Yeats, Valéry, Juan Ramón Jiménez,
Rilke, or Eliot had prolonged the Romantic-Symbolist tradition of
alienation from society and non-involvement, attempting to isolate the
imagination from everyday barbarity through poetic impersonality, other poets like Pound, Neruda, and Brecht had gone to the other extreme,
reclaiming a civic role for the language of poetry and for the poet's social and political involvement. Paz was one of the very first in his generation, taken in its broad sense of a trend rather than a narrowly
Hispanic group, to realize the dangers of an alienating isolation as well
as the corruption of poetic language through a pedestrian politics. That
is why as a young poet Paz soon abandoned the early and conflicting
models of Xavier Villaurrutia and Pablo Neruda —the one, an introspective poet of death and pure language, the other, a passionate bard of

---

[2] Edward Hirsch, "Octavio Paz: In Defense of Poetry," *The New York Times Book Review*, June 7,
1998, VII: 39: 1.

physical love and civic duty— for other poets whose use of everyday language for intimate meditation resonated more closely with his goals: poets like Luis Cernuda and Antonio Machado, for example, or Robert Frost, each of whom he met during stays in Spain and the United States, and about whom he wrote telling essays in the early forties. Like Machado and Frost, Paz set out to approximate language to human experience, but without betraying language either to abstract imagination or to an all-too-concrete sectarian politics. In 1979, long after he had absorbed and surpassed these two models, among others, Paz summarized this uneasy balancing act in a statement that I at least find very powerful:

> Between the more or less real person and the figure of the poet the relationship is, at once, intimate and circumspect. If the fiction of the poet swallows up the real person, then all that remains is a literary character: the mask eats up the face. If on the other hand the real person overpowers the poet, then the mask evaporates and with it the poem itself, which then stops being a work in order to become a document. This is what has happened to most of modern poetry. All my life I have struggled against this misunderstanding; the poem is neither a confession nor a document. To write poems is to walk on a tightrope between fiction and reality, between the mask and the face. The poet must sacrifice the real face in order to make his mask more living and credible; at the same time he should care that the mask will not petrify: it should have the mobility— and liveliness— of his face.

By thus choosing this particular "poetics of the tightrope," so to speak, poetry being neither a confession nor a document, and while recognizing the precarious nature of poetic language, Paz realized, towards the end of the forties, that his Faustian curiosity had to be channeled through parallel tracks, poetry and the essay. He could not, however, keep them completely apart, and against all rational or geometric imperatives he slowly and subtly brought together those two parallel lines. "Poetry and philosophy," he once wrote, "are like two houses next to each other connected by secret passageways." That is why, as we progress through Paz's poetry— from the introspective reflections of *Libertad bajo palabra*, to the desperate passion of *The Violent Season*, and from the Oriental meditations of *East Slope* to the historical consciousness of *Return* and *A Tree Within*, we find a growing incorporation of philosophical speculation and historical commentary, as if poetic perception had to be increasingly sustained through discursive reasoning. We find somewhat less of the opposite, that is, the incorporation of poetic or lyric procedure into his prose, in the development of his essays, though I would argue that there comes a time in Octavio Paz's work, after his definitive return to Mexico in the early seventies, when there occurs a gradual fusion of his poetic and political personae.

What remains crucial, however, is that, whether he wrote verse or prose, whether he wrote about himself or about history, the experience that Octavio Paz invariably invoked was poetry, a literally higher ground from which contemporary debates on society and culture could be clearly discerned and judged. Since for Paz poetry was not merely the writing of verse but rather the fleeting but nevertheless trenchant access to the human condition, poetic discourse assured for him a timeless moral authority that transcended history itself. This is precisely the argument of *The Bow and the Lyre*, his 1956 book and the centerpiece of his poetics, although some of the book's basic arguments were already present in his work as early as the thirties and forties. For Paz, poetry was the fulcrum around which all of human culture rotated, and therefore was the privileged center from which human activity could be read.

> My ambition was to be a poet and nothing but a poet. In my books in prose it was my intention to justify and defend it, to explain it to others and to myself. I soon discovered that the defense of poetry, scorned in our century, was inseparable from the defense of freedom. That is the source of my interest in the political and social questions that have convulsed our time.[3]

One of the tragic misunderstandings that haunted Octavio Paz in life, and I would argue even after his death, was the view that his discovery and construction of poetry as a platform to judge human affairs was an attempt to erect himself as a divine authority, a kind of modern Mexican oracle. It is important to understand, however, that Paz always spoke about "the defense of poetry," not the defense of the poet. Unlike Shelley,

---

[3] *The Other Voice...*, op. cit., 61.

who claimed that poets were the "unacknowledged legislators of mankind," Octavio Paz felt that there was a greater and more accurate legislation:
poetry itself. And yet, how can one tell, as Yeats once enigmatically
asked, the dancer from the dance? How can one possibly separate the
poet's interested and personal views from the disinterested, impersonal
requirements of a poetic morality? Paz answered this question simply:
"The false poet speaks of himself, almost invariably, in the name of others. The true poet speaks with others as he speaks to himself." The
proof of the legitimacy of a poetic citizenship, so to speak, lies not so
much in the poet's personal enunciation as in its collective inclusive-
ness, that is, its uncanny ability to include the others who lie beyond
the poet's immediate experience or personal statement even as the poet
only speaks, like a madman or a child, to him or herself.

In turn, yet another conviction, or sequence of convictions, requires
courage and self-sacrifice: more than the poet, there is the poem; more
than the poem, there is poetry; more than poetry, there is language;
more than language, there is nature and, of course, Time. Just as poetry speaks through the poem, Octavio Paz will say time and again, language speaks through the poem and through each and every one of us.
For Paz, poetry and language are, ultimately, two ontological horizons,
that, like Nature and Time, circumscribe human experience and expose
the limits of the subject. As the subject does not construct language,
but rather it is language that constructs the subject, so does poetry in
relation to the poem and the poet: poetry speaks through them. One
can identify, in a statement like this, a hidden polemic between Paz and
the greatest philosophical presence of this century, namely Martin Heidegger. Heidegger indeed believed that Time was the ultimate ontological horizon; but he privileged language, and particularly poetic
language as handled by the figure of the lyric poet, someone like Hölderlin, because poetry disclosed Being, therefore making of the Poet
what Heidegger called "the Shepherd of Being": *der Hirt des Seins*. Paz
distances himself from Heidegger and comes close to Wittgenstein, that
other philosophical presence in our century, to claim, ultimately, that the
Poet is a servant, not a shepherd, and that Poetry's ultimate goal is not
language or Being, but rather Silence. About language Paz wrote, shortly
before he died:

The writer says literally the unsayable, the unsaid, what nobody can or will say. Therefore, all great literary works are high-tension cables, not electrical but moral, aesthetic, and critical.

About poetry he also wrote, when he was living in India:

No one is a poet unless he has felt the temptation to destroy language or to create another one, unless he has experienced the fascination of non-meaning and the no less terrifying fascination of meaning that is inexpressible.[4]

Language and Poetry thus lie beyond the poet, but the poet nevertheless has access, profound yet fleeting, that can be shared with others. Thus, the proof of the poet's authenticity will lie, for Paz, in the uncanny ability to become the servant of Language and Poetry, rather than to use them for his or her own personal or political use. The extant critical canon on Paz has often read these ideas, with every good reason, in the context of Paz's exposure to Eastern thought, particularly Buddhism and its abolition of the subject. I would argue, however, that for all the importance Buddhism and Eastern thought had in general for Octavio Paz, he would still prefer us to view the experience of Poetry, rather than any particular religious experience, as the ultimate conditioner of subjective limits. What was interesting and valuable for Paz about the Buddha was the conjuring of silence as a horizon of meaning and therefore as a model for the understanding of poetics.

Equally tragic was the misunderstanding regarding Octavio Paz's politics, particularly after his definitive return to Mexico in 1971. It is perhaps an irony that for the longest time after his arrival, Paz became better known in Mexico for his political views than for his poetry, a situation that was the diametrical opposite abroad, particularly in France and the United States. These are the years after Paz's resignation of his ambassadorship to India, and thus his repudiation of the Mexican government's one-party system, his so-called "critique of the pyramid" and his onslaught against the Mexican and Latin American left, mostly

---

[4] *Alternating Current*, "Recapitulations", trans. Helen R. Lane (New York: Viking, 1973), 65.

through his editorship of the magazines *Plural* and *Vuelta*. At home, Octavio Paz's enemies, most of whom came from the privileged class and whose interests his critique of the PRI was questioning, branded him as a reactionary, a rabid anti-communist who had abandoned his true origins in the Mexican Revolution and had sided with the neo-liberal schemes of the PRI, particularly the government of Salinas, and of American imperialism. When in 1984 Octavio Paz dared to criticize publicly the violent trend of the Sandinista Revolution, an organized mob burned him in effigy in front of the American embassy in Mexico City to the tune of "*Reagan, rapaz, tu amigo es Octavio Paz.*"

Time passed, and in a few years the Soviet Union and the entire socialist bloc collapsed under the weight of their own incompetence and authoritarianism. Paz himself was awarded the Nobel Prize in 1990, was given a hero's welcome in Mexico, complete with mariachis and barrels of tequila. But even after such evident triumphs, even after the recent opening of the Mexican political system, even after Octavio Paz's death, it has not occurred to anyone that a public apology is owed to this visionary of Mexican history and society. Even here in the United States, where Paz is revered as a poet and as a thinker, many of his political and historical essays go unread and his figure is often scorned, particularly in the American academy. In many California university campuses, for example, Octavio Paz's name remains anathema, determined in part by the misplaced resentment of a few Mexican-American students and professors, who refuse to read his works and even forbid others to discuss them. And yet, if we only look carefully, what Paz advocated and finally celebrated during this turbulent period, from the seventies on, was not so much the defeat of the left or the fall of Communism as much as the triumph of freedom. Shortly before the Nobel Prize award, he wrote:

> Freedom is Man's historical dimension, because it is an experience in which the Other always appears. In saying yes or no, I discover myself and, upon discovering myself, I discover the others. Without them, I am not I. But this discovery is also an invention: upon seeing myself, I see the others, my peers; upon seeing them, I see myself. An exercise of the active imagination, freedom is an endless invention.

Yes: poetry does have rights. It has the right to question power from the vantage point of a greater power, the marginality to which modernity has displaced poetic discourse because it does not produce anything valuable, except perhaps the questions that poetry always asks: who am I, why am I here, whom do I love, and who loves me? Poetry has the right to invent me as I write it, just as I invent the other in the other's reciprocal invention of myself. But then Poetry is not just a right, but also a *rite*, a ritual or ceremony that begins in mutual recognition and ends in the experience we call love. One of the great poems of his later years says:

Memory, a scar:
—from where were we ripped out?
                              a scar,
memory, the thirst for presence,
                              an attachment
to the lost half.
                    The One
is the prisoner of itself,
                    it is
it only is,
            it has no memory,
it has no scars:
                    to love is two,
always two,
            embrace and struggle,
two is the longing to be one,
and to be the other, male or female,
                              two knows no rest,
it is never complete,
                    it whirls
around its own shadow,
                    searching
for what we lost at birth,
the scar opens:
            fountain of visions,

two: arch over the void,
bridge of vertigoes,
two:
mirror of mutations.[5]

Poetry has the right to name freedom in the name of language, and to name itself in the name of freedom. It has the right to question language, and even the right to question itself, indeed to destroy itself along with language, in the name of life and love.

The last time I saw Octavio Paz was on April 1, 1998. I had gone to the Casa Alvarado in Coyoacán, the huge, gorgeous colonial house that was his last home, now the site of the Octavio Paz Foundation, to deliver flowers that I had bought for him and his wife Marie-José. I had flown to Mexico City the day before to attend that night a special event honoring Paz's 84th birthday, but was saddened that he had been too weak to appear at the ceremony, and none of his friends who had gathered there got to see him. I returned to Coyoacán hoping to see him, and perhaps to say good-bye before returning to Washington.

That day was sunny. Spring was in the air. Flowers, birds, and insects ran amuck. But as soon as I arrived, Marie-José Paz told me that her husband was feeling weak and that, sadly, he could not come out to see me. April is indeed the cruelest month.

I had lingered at the house chatting with Guillermo Sheridan, the Foundation director, and my friend Eliot Weinberger, Paz's American translator, for close to an hour, when suddenly Marie-José Paz appeared again to say that Octavio Paz had awoken and had asked to be brought out to the inner patio, where the sun was shining and a water fountain flowed. We saw Marie-José slowly pushing out the wheelchair where her husband sat still. He was wearing a heavy sweater, and a blanket covered his lap. However weak and emaciated he may have looked then, I was thrilled to see him again, that man with whom I had spoken so often in life but who now was close to death. I remember jumping up, walking up to him, and grabbing both of his thinned hands.

[5] Octavio Paz, "Letter of testimony", *The Collected Poems of Octavio Paz, 1957-1987*, ed. Eliot Weinberger, (New York: New Directions, 1991), 631.

Lost in silence, he looked down at mine and then looked up beaming, all teeth, baby blue eyes, with the same boyish face as always, and yet resoundingly silent. "Es sonrisa de amigo", said his wife, as if forced to translate his courtesy. For he and I knew then that there was nothing left to say, except of course the unsayable, which we left unsaid, because we both knew it already.

Friends of mine arrived to pick me up. I awkwardly mumbled good-bye to the group and, as I always did, gave Octavio Paz a big *abrazo*. As I walked out the door of that colonial house, with its flowing water fountain and its colorful gardens, I could not help but look back at him and think that that was surely the last time I would see him. The sadness I felt at that moment has not left me. I often wonder if it ever will. But I do know that Octavio Paz's smile, the look on those beaming blue eyes, and especially his magnificent silence, will protect and sustain us, his readers and friends, for the next thousand years. Maybe more.

THE LANGUAGE OF PASSION

MARIO VARGAS LLOSA

Upon André Breton's death, Octavio Paz said in his tribute that it was impossible to speak of the founder of Surrealism without using the language of passion. The same might be said of Paz himself, given that throughout his life, and especially over the past few decades, he lived within controversy, unleashing enthusiastic adherence or ferocious abjuration all around him. Polemics will continue to surround his work as a whole, imbued as it is by the century in which he lived, torn by ideological confrontation and political inquisitions, cultural guerrilla warfare and intellectual wrath.

He lived his 84 long years splendidly, submerged in the maelstrom of his time by a youthful curiosity that accompanied him to the end. He participated in all the great historical and cultural debates, aesthetic movements, and artistic revolutions, never failing to take sides and explain his preferences in essays that often shone with the excellence of his prose, the lucidity of his judgment, and the vast expanse of his information. He was never a dilettante or mere witness, but always played a passionate role in whatever took place around him. He was a rare bird among those in his line of work, one of the few who weren't afraid to go against the grain or confront unpopularity. In 1984, shortly after his effigy was burned in response to his criticism of the Sandinista government, during a protest in Mexico City (staged by perfect idiots who chanted, outside the United States Embassy, *Reagan, rapaz, tu amigo es Octavio Paz!* ["Rapacious Reagan, your friend's Octavio Paz"]), our paths crossed: one might have expected him to be depressed, but he was as happy as a schoolboy. Three years later, I was not a bit surprised in Valencia, during a fistfight that broke out at the International Writers' Congress, to see him advance towards the brawl, rolling up his sleeves. Was it appropriate to want to throw punches at age seventy-three? "I couldn't let them gang up on my friend Jorge Semprún," he explained.

To review the themes of his books produces vertigo: the anthropological theories of Claude Lévi-Strauss and the aesthetic revolution of Marcel Duchamp; pre-Hispanic art, Basho's haiku, and the erotic sculpture of Hindu temples; poetry from the Golden Age of Spain and Anglo-Saxon verse; the philosophy of Sartre and that of Ortega y Gasset; the cultural sphere under the Viceroyalty of New Spain and the baroque poetry of Sor Juana Inés de la Cruz; the meanderings of the Mexican soul and the mechanisms of authoritarian populism established by the Institutional Revolutionary Party (PRI); the evolution of the world following the collapse of the Berlin Wall and the disintegration of the Soviet empire. The list, if we add prefaces, lectures, and articles, could go on for many pages, to such an extent that it is by no means an exaggeration to say of him that all the great cultural and political events of his time stirred his imagination and kindled stimulating reflections. Because, while never renouncing the passion that swells between the lines of even his most moderate pages, Octavio Paz was first and foremost a thinker, a man of ideas, a formidable intellectual agitator in the tradition of Ortega y Gasset—perhaps the most lasting influence among the many he assimilated.

Doubtless he would have liked posterity to remember him above all as a poet, because poetry is the prince of all genres, the most creative and the most intense, as he himself demonstrated in his beautiful readings of Quevedo and Villaurrutia, of Cernuda, Pessoa, and so many others, or in his admirable translations of English, French, and Oriental poets. And he was unquestionably a magnificent poet, as I discovered while still at school, reading the radiant verses of *Sunstone,* one of the poems I kept by my bedside in my youth and always return to with immense pleasure. But I have the impression that a good deal of his poetry, mainly the experimental variety (*Blanco, Topoems, Renga,* for example) succumbed to that thirst for novelty he described in his lectures at Harvard (*Children of the Mire*) as subtle venom against the endurance of works of art.

In his essays, on the other hand, he was perhaps more audacious and original than in his poems. Having touched on such a wide range of topics, he could not give an uniformly well-versed opinion of them all. He was superficial and inconstant at times. But, even in what seem to be lightly-penned pages on the subject of India or love with nothing too personal or profound to offer, what he does say is expressed with such elegance and clarity, with such intelligence and polish, that it is impossible to brush them aside. He was a splendid writer of prose: one of the most suggestive, clear, and luminous ever produced by the Castilian tongue, a writer who modeled the language with superb assurance, making it say everything that struck his intellect or fantasy —veritable intellectual delusions at times, like the ones that sputter in *Conjunctions and Disjunctions*— with a wealth of tones and subtleties that turn his pages into an overwhelming spectacle of rhetorical sleight-of-hand. But unlike Lezama Lima, not even when he abandoned himself to wordplay did he succumb to the *jitanjáfora* (the term invented by Alfonso Reyes for pure verbalism, lacking bone or sinew). Since he loved conceptual significance as much as the music of words, these, when passed through his pen, always had to say something in order to appeal to the intelligence of the reader, while at the same time reaching one's sensitivity and one's ears.

Since he was never a Communist (nor a fellow-traveler) and never had any qualms about criticizing those intellectuals who, because of conviction, opportunism or cowardice played the accomplice to dictatorships —that is to say, four-fifths of his colleagues— those who envied his talent, the awards showered on him, his constant presence in the spotlight of current events, were the ones who constructed the conservative, reactionary image that, I'm afraid, will not be dispelled in the near future: the vultures have already set about their merciless task with his remains. But, the paradoxical truth of the matter is that, in political terms, from his first book of essays in 1950, *The Labyrinth of Solitude*, to the last one he dedicated to the subject in 1990 (*Pequeña crónica de grandes días*), Paz's thinking was much closer to the democratic socialism of our time than to conservatism or even liberal doctrine. Marked by Surrealism, he evolved from the Trotskyist and anarchist sympathies of his youth towards the defense of political democracy, that is to say, of pluralism and lawful government. But the free market always inspired an instinctive distrust in him —he was convinced that wide sectors of culture, for example poetry, would disappear if their existence depended solely on the interplay of supply and demand— and for the same reason, he declared himself in favor of prudent State interventionism in the economy in order to correct —the eternal argument of the social democrats— any imbalances or excessive social inequalities. That someone who thought this way, and who had firmly condemned all the acts of the United States forces in Latin America, including the invasion of Panama, was placed on a par with Ronald Reagan and victimized by an inquisitorial act staged by "progressives," speaks volumes about the degree of phoniness and stupidity attained by political debates south of the Río Grande.

However, it is true that his political image was somewhat tainted in his final years by his relations with the PRI's administrations, towards which he moderated his critical stance. This change was not gratuitous, nor are people right in saying he backed down in response to a groundswell of flattery and homage rendered by those in power in hopes of bribing him. It was due to a conviction that Paz defended with coherent arguments, —although I found it misguided— and the cause of the only disagreement to cast a fleeting shadow over our friendship of many years. Since 1970, in *The Other Mexico: Critique of the Pyramid*, his splendid analysis of the political reality of Mexico, he sustained that the ideal form of democratization his country so badly needed was not revolution, but evolution: gradual reform brought about from within the Mexican system, something that, according to Paz, began to take place with the government of Miguel de la Madrid and was later irrevocably hastened with that of his successor, Salinas de Gortari. Not even the great scandal of that administration's corruption and crimes moved him to revise his theory that it would be the PRI itself —symbolized anew by former President, Zedillo— that would put an end to the political monopoly of the governing party and bring democracy to Mexico.

Many times over the years I have asked myself how the Latin American intellectual who had most insightfully anatomized the phenomenon of dictatorship (in *The Philanthropic Ogre*, 1979) and the Mexican brand of authoritarianism, could have displayed such naiveté on this particular point. One possible answer is as follows: Paz upheld such a theory not because of his faith in the aptitude of the PRI to metamorphose into a genuinely democratic party, but rather because of his pugnacious distrust of Mexico's alternative political forces, the National Action Party

(PAN) and the Revolutionary Democratic Party (PRD). He never believed that these configurations were fit to carry out the political transformation of Mexico. To him, the PAN seemed to be a provincial party of Catholic lineage, far too conservative; and the PRD, a hodgepodge of former members of the PRI and ex-Communists, a party lacking in democratic credentials that in all likelihood, upon rising to power, would reestablish the authoritarian sell-out tradition it was supposed to combat. Let us knock on wood in the hope that reality will not confirm his somber prediction.

Since everyone else says so, I also feel compelled to say that Octavio Paz, a poet and writer open to all of the spirit's tempests, a citizen of the world if ever there was one, was also Mexican to the core. And yet, I confess I haven't the slightest idea of what that might actually mean. I know many Mexicans and no two are alike; therefore, with respect to national identity, I fully subscribe to the statement Octavio Paz himself made: "The famous search for identity is an intellectual pastime, or even a business opportunity for idle sociologists."

Unless, to be sure, being Mexican to the core is tantamount to an intense love for Mexico —its scenery, its history, its art, its problems, its people— which, by the way, would mean Malcolm Lowry or John Huston were Mexicans to the core as well. Paz loved his country and dedicated a great deal of time to reflection on the subject of Mexico, studying its past and debating its present, analyzing its poets and painters, and in his vast body of work, Mexico shines with a fiery light, as reality, as myth, and as a thousand metaphors. The fact that this Mexico is surely fantasized, much more a product of the imagination and the pen of an outstanding creator than just plain Mexico —without literature, the product of an impoverished reality— is irrelevant. If there is something we can be sure of, it is that, with the inexorable passage of time, the gap will close and the literary myth will go on enveloping and devouring the reality while, sooner rather than later, from the outside and from within, Mexico will be seen, dreamed, loved and hated, in the version written by Octavio Paz.

Translated by Tanya Huntington and Álvaro Enrigue

THE POETIC WORKS
OF OCTAVIO PAZ

READING PAZ IN PEACE?*

TOMÁS SEGOVIA

When I decided on the title of these pages, long before I actually began
to write them, what I had in mind was the way one always attempts to
rescue poetry from petrification at these official ceremonies, either from
being congealed and digested by official wisdom, or even from institutional exaltation and consecration. It is therefore imperative to surrep-
titiously carry the poems off to some peaceful corner, because in an
institution there is no real peace, despite appearances. Every institution
is by definition a triumphant institution, given that it was founded by
a war of some kind, albeit a civilized war, and more specifically by victory, the most unsightly aspect of war. Fleeing from these triumphant
ceremonies is, of course, another ceremony, but with an intent that is
more or less contrary: not so much in that it is a solitary ceremony, but
rather because of its solitary nature, for in a certain sense he who is left
out is never left alone: here on the outskirts, we are legion. Yet in another
sense, he who is left out clearly stands alone. The only community in
which he forms part is that of solidarity, and everyone knows there is
nothing less solid than solidarity. Camus once made a pun on "solitary"
and "solidarity." True solidarity can only be extended to one who is left
out, that is to say, to a solitary man. It is clear that solidarity with the
triumphant is not solidarity at all, at any rate not in the noble sense of
the word, which no one is willing to surrender, least of all those who
have need of that noble sense as an alibi. Because it is clearly in the institution where solidarity becomes solidity, and where solidarity with
power or with the powerful is the only profitable choice. One could
immediately conclude that if solidarity works there, it is only because
it was never real solidarity to begin with. But it would be better to avoid
coming to any conclusions just yet.

---

* All footnotes are by the translators and do not appear in Tomás Segovia's original Spanish text.

One of the consequences, undoubtedly a terribly insignificant one, of this solid lack of solidarity is that an institution can impose on a solitary writer like myself, the requirement to decide far in advance what I will say many months later. It is one of the innumerable insignificant, or gigantic, tensions between the institution and those being institutionalized. My time, of course, is not that of the institution, and when the time has come to make them meet, there are inevitable maladjustments. In the meantime, for example, I have added a question mark to my title, which had originally taken the form of a statement. I have had time to doubt, an activity strictly unheard of at any institution. What started as a proposal is now a question. I ask myself: is it truly possible to read in peace, or at any rate to read Paz in peace?

For I've had time to recall something I said before (and even wrote something about already) regarding another Mexican poet, Ramón López Velarde. Poetry tells us what happens. But that which happens only really happens if it happens to me. If the poet speaks in the first person, it is because all persons are by definition first. His "I" is not that of psychology, but rather of language. López Velarde has no need for the uncertain teachings of linguistics or of the philosophy of language to be perfectly lucid in this sense:

> Yet my faith never failed
> if I said "I".[1]

He knew very well that the I who says "I" is not that of psychology, the ego described by language, be it psychological or of any other kind; it is not the I being said, but rather the I who says. The other, the ego, is perhaps in the flesh or perhaps, in the spirit or perhaps both; it is a thing at any rate, and as such is swallowed or capable of being swallowed by words:

> If I say spirit or flesh
> it seems to me the devil
> is laughing at the word.[2]

---

[1] "Mas nunca vaciló / mi fe si dije 'yo'." There is no English translation available of this poem. See Ramón López Velarde, "Zozobra," *Obras* (Mexico: Fondo de Cultura Económica, 1979) 172-173.

[2] "Si digo carne o espíritu / paréceme que el diablo / se ríe del vocablo." Ramón López Velarde, *ibid.*

That is to say, I am not a word. The I who speaks is not a word but an act. I will not discuss whether or not there is another or there are other fundamentals of language, but it is clear to me that this act, if not fundamental, is undoubtedly the foundation of language.

But this does nothing more than introduce the drama or tragedy of language, in other words, of history. López Velarde also knew with complete lucidity that any language which truly says what happens transforms it for that very reason in what remains. Language is also an institution. The anguished attempts of López Velarde to escape this destiny are useless: in the end a disgraceful title, that of the nation's poet, will seek him out and devour him.

Just now I am not thinking of López Velarde, but of Octavio Paz, and this spontaneously transports me to another time, a time shared rather than merely evoked, a time I can still feel as if it were today. And as I retrace the steps of the drama of language from López Velarde to the present, I cannot help but feel, upon entering its atmosphere, that it smacks of nihilism. Therefore, I have asked myself whether it is worthwhile to savor in any other way the unwavering drama of faith of someone like López Velarde.

The confiscation of meaning by an institution can be seen as nihilism, at least from the perspective of living, germinal meaning. To be sure, Hegel indoctrinated us in the faith that this confiscation is the only true salvation of meaning, but it is also true that afterwards, Nietzsche vociferously insisted that Hegel had lied to us. Neither one nor the other, in any case, could predict the abysmal refinements, knots, circles, contradictions, and perversions that the institution has attained today. The poet born in the country of the "institutional revolution," who coined the no less vertiginous phrase "the tradition of rupture," knew exactly what he was talking about. If an institutional nihilism lies within the confiscation of meaning and the monopoly of its collective worth, it is a nihilism capable of encompassing all of history. The latter is well suited to a time that we may judge to be lesser or greater in scope, but that we all call our own.

It isn't that the institution hasn't always been ambiguous, but never before had we arrived at this uncontrollable osmosis of the values that have characterized our century, especially at its peak. All contaminants are filtered in a disorderly fashion through membranes that are increasingly lax as they become more complex, and increasingly fallacious as they become more flexible. It is characteristic of our time that no one is more conservative than the innovators, more tyrannical than the liberators, more academic than the avant-garde, more institutional than the revolutionary, more traditional than the professionals of disruption, more obedient than the rebel. No matter how much we celebrate an end to certain polarizations and simplifications, to certain authoritarianisms and repressions, it is difficult not to feel at the same time nostalgia for a time when we could recognize the face of our enemy, when we knew what we were fighting for. Although that fight may have threatened us with defeat or death, it was by no means senseless. To be sure, it is terrible that the bourgeois allowed Van Gogh to die of hunger and madness, but it is not out of bounds to think that it is far worse for them to adorn the walls of their offensive office buildings with his paintings today. Nor is it out of bounds to suspect that this nihilism is the worst of all. How could we not dream of a world in which socialism would be the opposite of Margaret Thatcher's policy, democracy the opposite of financial dictatorship, rebelliousness the opposite of uniformity, free choice the opposite of middle-of-the-road indoctrination? A world where, for example, loving Van Gogh would be the opposite of loving official programs on the history of art, where defending the freedom to create would be an attack on the MOMA, where writing subversive poetry would be a refusal to act as the subject of academic theses or compete for the Nobel Prize.

Such a world has become radically utopian. In the meantime, the institution became completely impervious once it learned the supreme astuteness of cannibalizing any attacks, a marvelous genetic adaptation that our time perhaps acquired, subconsciously I assume, from the abysmally slippery defensive technique of those viruses we find so fascinating today. Nietzsche could not have imagined, naturally, that his transmutation of values would take the form of vertiginous viral mutations. Transmuting values turns out to be the most naive of utopias, once these values enter into perpetual mutation and once crafty osmotic exchanges between the baring of the senses and the institutionalization of those senses —and of the baring process itself— completely elude our grasp.

Whoever has seen or believes to have seen this aspect of our time must inevitably ask himself: is there no escape from this nihilism? But there is another question that must come first: do we want to escape? Shortly over a century ago, it was crystal-clear that a painter like Van Gogh did not intend in any way, shape, or form to accept the national award for painters or be invited to the equivalent of our ostentatious biennials. When Rimbaud said, "We must be absolutely modern," what he wanted was to deal a blow to those academics who frowned upon the modern. But what to do when academics are the ones who pawn modernity among themselves, excluding and subduing those whom they have decided are not modern enough? Then again, let us also ask ourselves: didn't Van Gogh think or at any rate feel that being excluded from museums, galleries, and official recognition was an injustice? After all, wasn't it in museums where he could see some of the paintings that were as basic to him as food and drink? Then, if museums have mutated to the extent of bitterly disputing the property of a Van Gogh, is this not a victory for Van Gogh, even supposing that it is an involuntary victory? That is what I was thinking about when I proposed earlier on that it was better not to come to hasty conclusions. As I have already said, this is not a lie, but a tragedy.

What I am attempting to clarify for my own benefit are some peculiarly modern traits of this tragedy of meaning, or of language, or of history. And I hope it is clear that I have not for one moment stopped talking about Octavio Paz, although I haven't named him. In any case, I have not stopped thinking about him. It seems to me that the most generally shared view of Octavio Paz is that he embodies his time as few other writers have. To embody one's time, in good philosophy, does not necessarily equate to positive or negative value. But it is precisely in our time that we wholeheartedly believe this value is positive by definition, and specifically, in some fields —for example, in art, in thought, and even in politics— that it is the supreme value. In modernity, the term "modern" does not describe, it glorifies. Whoever embodies this exact time must also share that faith. The work of the thinker, critic, and analyst Octavio Paz has undoubtedly contributed to the configuration of this mid-century of modernity, and furthermore to its clarification, interpretation, and diffusion. But when I proposed, many months ago now, to carry out a reading of this work in peace, I was thinking that poetry should always be read in peace. Meanwhile, I have had enough time to suspect it is not always that simple.

It seems clear, in effect, that the poetry of Octavio Paz also embodies his time. However, does it do so in the same way? Let us be clear: in one sense, a work always, inevitably, embodies its time. It can be sustained that the critics of a given time, even in their outright struggle against it, form as much a part of that time as their panegyrics and alliances, just as the opposition forms part of the government, or minorities form part of society. If indeed we can make any distinctions, it will have to be on more specific terms. For instance, by attempting to think about what the specific language of poetry implies in this field. Or in my own case, by going back to what I had already thought about López Velarde, but carrying this time the fresh taste of our nihilism on my tongue.

It occurs to me then that there is a possible reading of the poetry of Octavio Paz with this same taste in my mouth. But I should quickly clarify that I do not believe for a moment that this reading is the only one, or the best one, or the most basic. I am far from tempted to consider myself capable of providing the key, or even of accomplishing that which is carelessly referred to as an analysis, or of coming to any conclusions. I am simply reflecting, but the temptation I have surrendered to with this reflection, as you have probably noticed by now, is that of escaping, to some degree, from some of the constraining habits of these institutional ceremonies. In this sense, I am in fact reading in peace. I would like to come as close as possible —which likely will not amount to much— to speaking here of this poetry as it would speak to me in the peace of my solitary reading. I know the risk I run, and I also know that singling it out beforehand has never given anyone insurance against that risk. I will say only that I accept it, because the tribute I want to give, to the point of agreeing to give it on infidel territory —and by that I mean territory alien to that of poetry— is not to the Octavio Paz of these official consecrations that already abound in good will, more than anyone could want, and can therefore do without my rather dubious authority: rather, it is to the Octavio Paz I knew, with whom I worked, argued, and learned the great lessons of poetry, who encouraged and supported me, and who also chided and judged me, who revealed absolute essentials to me, and with whom I was at times in absolute disagreement.

But let us get back, peacefully or not, to poetry, and back once again to López Velarde. One might imagine that López Velarde's strategy manifests itself in *La suave Patria* as an attempt to escape the drama of poetic language. In this poem, we clearly perceive that the poet has already understood he will not escape his destiny as the national poet: "Today, at center stage, I raise my voice..."[3] Therefore, it seems clear enough that his strategy is one of sweet irony, amicable playfulness, deceptively naive style, and irreproachably disarming candor. This is coherent with everything essential about López Velarde, who always knew how to be candid, even in the darkness, and who always triumphed through heroic ingenuousness. It may seem surprising that the emblematic poem of a nation could be so candid and playful, but then again, it is not uncommon for great, fundamental texts to be filled with such antics; to find one we need look no further than the *Quijote*. This would undoubtedly give us food for thought if we had time for it now. In any event, it would be hard to doubt the effectiveness of this strategy in López Velarde.

But irony and humor are not characteristics of the poetry of Octavio Paz. Toying with the themes he has proposed or adopted is not suited to his style, which always takes itself seriously, and even the Surrealist or neo-avant-garde games he once played are infused with gravity and even solemnity. Of course, a poet unable to take them seriously would not have been as representative of his time. Even his changes in perspective are the changes central to modernity, in other words, to the leading perspectives of our modernity, and in few writers can one so closely follow a trajectory through that central modernity, without making any detours, but also without taking any shortcuts. If there is something entirely absent from his work, it is indubitably marginality. On the other hand, all the remaining steps are clearly there, from the fervor of innovation and the revolutionary rebelliousness of a young century to the resigned, globalized diversity of the end of a millennium,

[3] Ramón López Velarde, "Suave patria / Sweet Land," *Song of the Heart: Selected Poems*, trans. Margaret Sayers Peden, (Austin: University of Texas Press, 1984), 79.

having passed through an epidemic of schematized manifestos, pheno-menological ruminations, existentialist shocks, the institutionalization of the avant-garde, neo-rebellious rumblings, the assault on language, dogmatic formalisms, neo-liberal restoration, and all the rest.

If indeed his work has fully documented much of the century, it must have also documented what I have called our peculiar brand of nihilism. I will explain once more what I refer to: our peculiar osmosis of values, which means that today, when we come up against a star-tlingly radical text, it is impossible for us to know without additional information whether it is the manifesto of a clandestine or even terrorist insurrection, or the sedate declaration of some respectable academic ins-titution, or perhaps part of the official program of the most obsequious agency of a more or less manipulative government. What is truly unique about this century is not the fact that academic studies and scholarship programs end up including any project that poses itself as either inno-vation, revolt, insolence, or insurrection, but rather that these perspec-tives continue to regard themselves (or continue in their attempt to have us regard them) as avant-garde, innovative, and subversive, despite the fact that they are obviously protected and encouraged by official culture. It is not the institutionalization of meaning that is new but the technique of viral mutations I previously described, the new virulence of an institution that disarms us as antibodies and leaves us no choice beyond affiliation or marginal resignation.

And poetry? Naturally, poetry is not immune. But in the radical na-ture of its language, it has its own nihilism. Poetry is among the lan-guages made to go on speaking in the first person. In that sense, it is language itself, because as López Velarde already told us, real language, the kind that merits our unwavering faith, rests entirely on the first per-son. It is also language itself, for two reasons: because even languages that do not internally distinguish the first person assume its existence, and because poetry does not remain on the tongue but transforms the tongue into language, and makes the first person intrude into it. I can-not go on at great length about this just now, but believe me, I do not speak lightly.

Language has, therefore, its nihilism which, in a certain sense (but not in every sense) is opposite and complementary to that of the institution.

The nihilism of language lies within its originating existence. The place from which meaning flows obviously borders on the meaningless —or Nothingness, as we shall see. If the nihilism of the institution threatens to derail meaning (and also if it is saved by this means, as Hegel tells us), it makes a doctrine of the truth, a lesson of revelation, an understanding of knowledge, a transaction of desire, and even a contract of love and friendship; in a word, taming the germinal violence of meaning through a pact established by society. The nihilism of language, on the other hand, threatens to tear down all instituted certainties, including those of language itself. Because, as I have already said, language is also an institution. But it is a very peculiar institution. On one level, it is an institution like any other, but on another, it is the institution of all institutions. Other institutions are contiguous to each other and, in the end, with the institution of language as well. However, language borders these institutions on one extreme, and nothing —or Nothingness— on the other, it borders cosmic lack of meaning. I personally believe that there is still something between that black hole and incipient meaning, something I call Desire, to use a Platonic and not Freudian term, but now is not the time to discuss this.

I believe that an inveterate reader of poetry, when he reads a poetic work —I refer to reading in a simple and direct sense, as one reads at home or in a park or on a bus, not in the sense of "doing a reading" or "giving a reading"— picks up every once in a while on the tensions between these two nihilisms: he is perceiving, or guessing, or he believes he's perceiving and guessing that which the poet has received and accepted from his culture, from his understanding, from his critics and from his own criticism, from his points of view, from what he knows is expected and can be expected of him and also, in a worst-case scenario, what he calculates will be most applauded or rewarded as well as, on the other hand, what the explosion of meaning —whose incendiary charge is always the detonator of truth— has imposed on his language. Once more, I am not saying this is how it must be read, or that this is what poems are about, or that it is possible to make a dual list of one and the other. But when I reread, for example, the poem "Immemorial Landscape" from *Vuelta*, I feel the evidence that has been imposed here on the poet borders on true nihilism:

One day
the streetlights will explode
from their iron stalks
                    One day
the bellowing river of engines
will stop
                    One day
these houses will be hills
once more
                    the wind in the stones
will talk only to itself
                    Aslant
among the shadows
                    unshadow
will fall
          almost blue
on the earth
                    The same as tonight
the million year old snow.[4]

I am not saying the language of truth must necessarily be nihilist. Rather, I believe this nihilism is never terminal. The language that tells what is meaningless continues to create meaning, since it tells. We may or may not doubt whether a language that is meaningless is actually possible, but it is clear that there has been no shortage of attempts, these having abounded at any rate in our century. To take into account the intent of these attempts independently of their nature is of course to pass judgment on that intent. But if ethical judgments are to make any sense at all, mustn't they act precisely as judgments of intent?

Nor is the nihilism of the institution terminal, but it can drain meaning by cutting it off at the roots and placing within the closed circuit of the instituted without ever allowing it to make contact with extrainstitutional reality, which is the only place where it can absorb the

4 "Immemorial Landscape," *The Collected Poems of Octavio Paz, 1957-1987*, ed. Eliot Weinberger (New York: New Directions, 1991), 353.

energy that gives it life. This situation has been many times described as the perverted language of power that George Orwell exposed for the first time, and which undoubtedly has infinite derivations, variations, and shades of meaning. The candid game of López Velarde is clearly one way to counteract this venom. Octavio Paz reacts in a very different way. It seems natural to me to feel that he reacts very violently at times to the osmotic institutional nihilism of the age, a violence that surely is directed at least partially against himself. The "Mexico City" section of *Vuelta* is written almost entirely in this vein, and the *San Ildefonso Nocturne* even more so:

> (. . .)
> We didn't lack integrity:
> > we lacked humility.
> What we wanted was not innocently wanted.
> Precepts and concepts,
> > the arrogance of theologians,
> to beat with a cross,
> > to institute with blood,
> to build the house with bricks of crime,
> to declare obligatory communion.
> > > Some
> became secretaries to the secretary
> to the General Secretary of the Inferno.
> > > Rage
> became philosophy,
> > its drivel has covered the planet.[5]

Given that I am nearly out of time, I will close with a few generalizations. This was not about carrying out a possible reading of Octavio Paz with a touch of nihilism. It is only a suggestion, and these pages clearly do not constitute a formal study. I had intended to carry some of his poems off to a peaceful corner, perhaps the *San Ildefonso Nocturne*,

---

[5] *San Ildefonso Nocturne, ibid.*, 419-421.

perhaps *Sunstone*, perhaps *The Monkey Grammarian*, and speak of them in hiding from his consecration as a great figure. I have not been able to avoid the fact that the abduction of sorts I promised myself has driven me to provide explanations with regards to its conditions and to go on at length, not so much about him as about his time. This time is especially well represented in him, but he is something more as well. My attempted abduction proposed to demonstrate that this other something is what is heard when his poetry is read in solitude. But after all, I am not even certain, although that wasn't how I imagined it at first, of not having perpetrated somehow in the end, with stops and starts and some imperfections, an effective attempt at abduction.

Translation by Tanya Huntington and Álvaro Enrigue

OCTAVIO PAZ:
IN SEARCH OF A MOMENT

EDWARD HIRSCH

Octavio Paz practiced poetry like a secret religion. He dwelt in its mysteries, he invoked its sacraments, he read its entrails, he inscribed its revelations. Writing was for him a primordial act, and he stared down at the blank page like an abyss until it sent him reeling over the brink of language. The poems he brought back are filled with ancient wonder and strangeness, hermetic wisdom, a dizzying sense of the sacred. They are magically —sometimes violently— uprooted from silence. They are drawn from a deep well. Here is his three-line poem *Escritura* (*Writing*): "Yo dibujo estas letras / como el día dibuja sus imágenes / y sopla sobre ellas y no vuelve":

> I draw these letters
> as the day draws its images
> and blows over them
> and does not return.

Paz started writing poems as a teenager and never let up until the end of his life. Lyric poetry was for him a core activity, at the root of being, and for nearly 70 years he was driven by invisible demons to try to connect to himself and to others through the sensuality —the rhythmic fervor— of words. Inspiration was for him not a static entity, but a forward thrust, an aspiration, the act of "going beyond ourselves to the encounter of ourselves."[1] Paz wrote poetry with a sharp awareness of being oneself and, simultaneously, someone or something else. He called this "the other voice."[2] He experienced the merging of voices as a submer-

---

[1] *The Bow and the Lyre*, trans. Ruth L. C. Simms, (New York: Mc Graw Hill, 1975), 161.
[2] *The Other Voice: Essays on Modern Poetry*, trans. Helen Lane, (New York: Harcourt Brace Jovanovich, 1991), 151.

sion, a type of flooding. "We still keep alive the sensation of some minutes so full they were time overflowing, a high tide that broke the dikes of temporal succession," he writes in *The Bow and the Lyre*, a sustained defense of poetry Shelley himself might have cherished. "For the poem is a means of access to pure time, an immersion in the original waters of existence."[3] He also defined the poetic experience as "an opening up of the wellsprings of being. An instant and never. An instant and forever."[4]

Paz was —and in his work remains— a seeker, and the quest for a moment to abolish linear or successive time is one of the driving forces of his aesthetic, a defining feature of his pilgrimage. Poetry is a wayward siren song calling him to a perpetual present, to an erotic consecration of instants, and to a superabundance of time and being. "Poetry is in love with the instant and seeks to relive it in the poem, thus separating it from sequential time and turning it into a fixed present," he says in his Nobel lecture, "In Search of the Present."[5]

The fixed present, the endless instant, the eternal moment —the experience is for Paz something to be attained, like reality, like being itself. "Door of being, dawn and wake me," he prays near the conclusion of his circular masterpiece *Sunstone*:

> allow me to see the face of this day,
> allow me to see the face of this night,
> all communicates, all is transformed,
> arch of blood, bridge of the pulse,
> take me to the other side of this night,
> where I am you, we are us,
> the kingdom where pronouns are intertwined,
>
> door of being: open your being
> and wake, learn to be…

If you can get to the present, there are presences, Paz suggests, and he trusts poetry's capacity to deliver those presences through images in-

---

[3] *The Bow and the Lyre, op. cit.*, 15.
[4] *Ibid.*, 139.
[5] "In Search of the Present: Nobel Lecture, 1990," *The Georgia Review* (Spring 1995), 259.

carnated in words, through words flowing in rhythm: "The instant dis-solves in the succession of other nameless instants. In order to save it we must convert it into a rhythm,"[6] he writes in *Alternating Current*, where he also defines rhythm as "the reincarnation of the instant." Rhythm serves the poet as a means of access —a reliable guide— to ori-ginary or pure time.

Paz needed lyric poetry as a primary mode of crossing, of rendering the self diaphanous, of becoming "a wind that stops / turns on itself and is gone" (*The Face and the Wind*). The words themselves become a way of seeking others that also links him back to the spaces opening up in-side himself. "Between now and now, / between I am and you are, / the word *bridge*," he declares in his short poem *The Bridge:*

> Entering it
> you enter yourself:
> the world connects
> and closes like a ring.

Language becomes a form of practical magic as the word becomes a bridge, a juncture, a span of connection. "Everything is a door / every-thing a bridge," he proclaims in *Sleepless Night*. Words are transfiguring and have a threshold power. They are portals to the other side. *Words are bridges*, he writes in a refrain that reverberates through his poetic cantata, *Letter of Testimony*. They are a form of a linkage, a way of reach-ing out, reaching across, that is also a means of reaching in:

> Let yourself be carried by these words
> toward yourself.

> (*Letter of Testimony*)

The words become the only way for him of attaining himself, at-taining a truer identity than social identity —a shadowy, psychic truth, a mode of being. "I'm not finished with myself yet," he declares in his

---

[6] *Alternating Current*, trans. Helen Lane, (New York: Viking, 1973), 65.

prose poem *The Besieged.* "I am the shadow my words cast," he concludes in *A Draft of Shadows.* It's as if he doesn't have that real self, that
hidden or shadow identity without the word, the syllable, the poetic
act. The word *bridge*, the wordbridge, becomes the site of a poetic
crossing into true being. As he puts it in *Pillars:*

> Between the end and the beginning,
> a moment without time,
> a delicate arch of blood,
> a bridge over the void.

I'm struck by how many of Paz's poems seem to unfold and take place
in liminal spaces, in pauses and intervals, odd crossings, interrupted
movements. He is poetically empowered not just by bridging, but also
by moments when bridges go up, by disconnection. He finds a poetic
space opening up in gaps and ruptures ("Poetry is the crack / the space
/ between one word and another," he announces in "Letter to León Fe-
lipe"), in the transitional realm of the betwixt and the between. Think
of the slippage in his well-known poem dedicated to the linguist Roman
Jakobson, *Between What I See and What I Say... ":*

> Between what I see and what I say,
> between what I say and what I keep silent,
> between what I keep silent and what I dream,
> between what I dream and what I forget:
> poetry.

Paz takes up the essential ambiguity —the elusive clarity— of such
marginal or liminal moments in his poem *Interval:*

> Instantaneous architectures
> hanging over a pause,
> apparitions neither named
> nor thought, wind-forms,
> insubstantial as time,
> and, like time, dissolved.

Made of time, they are not time;
they are the cleft, the interstice,
the brief vertigo of *between*
where the diaphanous flower opens:
high on its stalk of a reflection
it vanishes as it turns.

Never touched, the clarities
seen with eyes closed:
the transparent birth
and the crystalline fall
in the instant of this instant
that forever is still here.

Outside the window, the desolate
rooftops and the hurrying clouds.
The day goes out, the city
lights up, remote and near.
Weightless hour. I breathe
the moment, empty and eternal.

Paz is trying to nail down the cleft and interstice, the fissure in temporal process, the brilliant weightlessness of what Wordsworth calls "those fleeting moods / Of shadowy exultation."

It seems crucial to Paz to keep affirming that the real self is achieved in such intervals, luminous moments, fluid states. These states are utterly essential: they are perceptions of reality, modes of transparency. Moreover, it's as if we all exist most fully in these spacious intervals, these widening gaps and eternal pauses, which are perceived as a true condition of the world itself. What seems like a struggle attained in bridging over the self in some lyrics becomes a canny reconnaissance about the world in others. Such a perception seems to inhere in the poem *Between Going and Staying*:

Between going and staying the day wavers,
in love with its own transparency.

The circular afternoon is now a bay
where the world in stillness rocks.

All is visible and all elusive,
all is near and can't be touched.

Paper, book, pencil, glass,
rest in the shade of their names.

Time throbbing in my temples repeats
the same unchanging syllable of blood.

The light turns the indifferent wall
into a ghostly theater of reflections.

I find myself in the middle of an eye,
watching myself in its blank stare.

The moment scatters. Motionless,
I stay and go: I am a pause.

The lyric exploration is for Paz always epiphanic, always precarious. Such key or luminous moments (it is "Within a Moment: A Pulsation of the Artery," Blake writes, "When the Poet's Work is Done") are by definition sudden, unexpected, revelatory, unconscious. They are dangerous breakthrough experiences. Such "Moments of Being" (the phrase is Virginia Woolf's) are also transitory and difficult to pin down. They usurp the social realm and create their own sense of eternity. They also create ruptures in ordinary experience, pockets of emptiness, holes in time. They defy time-bound narratives. Think, for example, of the playful, paradoxical, quasi-philosophical way that Paz traces the struggle between temporal process and the atemporal instant in *Into the Matter*:

> it's not time now
> now it's now
> now it's time to get rid of time

> now it's not time
> > it's time and not now
> time eats the now

Paz structures and arranges his poems in such a way —in a non-narrative manner— to create disjunctions that deliver how epiphanies derange and rupture chronological time. I'm thinking of the spatial arrangements in his poems, the length of his lines and minimal use of punctuation, the associative drift of his surrealist attention, the sonorousness of his Spanish, his trust in circularities (*Sunstone*) and white spaces (*Blanco*), in presences that defy narrative closure. They are structured for immediacy, to approach and hold a moment. And they try to create a space in which "the present is motionless" (*Wind from All Compass Points*). Like Joseph Cornell boxes, they become "monuments to every moment" and "cages for infinity" (*Objects and Apparitions*).

Paz was a restless innovator, and he was continually seeking forms that would create a house for being, consecrating a stillness. That stillness was something he desperately sought, something he spiritually needed, and as a result he was willing, even eager, to cross thresholds and risk an annihilation he could embody in poems. At times he seems cut off from the moment itself, lost in a dire, chaotic, threatening form of inner exile. His lyric access produces a kind of terror. I suspect that's why so many of his poems are filled with shadowy tunnels and traps, elemental passageways, vertiginous heights. They move through endless "corridors terraces stairways" (*Wind from All Compass Points*). "I crossed through arches and over bridges," he writes at a key moment in "Coming and Going": "I was alive, in search of life." But the restless search for life also becomes, paradoxically, a search for death. "The sun of the high plains eats my remains," he concludes: "I was alive and went in search of death." Life and death are held together in a single weightless moment beyond time.

Paz's poems are filled with moments of bewildering quest, with a lost searching. He could at times "engrave vertigo" (*Tomb*). He vacillates between isolation and connection, solitude and communion, doubt and rapture. He had an uncanny feeling for the inner spaces that keep opening up in poetry, and his poems can induce a kind of mental slippage and dizziness, a sense of traveling down interminable corridors. "I follow my raving, rooms, streets, / I grope my way through corridors of time, / I climb and descend its stairs, I touch / its walls and do not move," he writes in *Sunstone*:

> I search without finding, I write alone,
> there's no one here, and the day falls,
> the year falls, I fall with the moment,
> I fall to the depths, invisible path
> over mirrors repeating my shattered image,
> I walk through the days, the trampled moments,
> I walk through all the thoughts of my shadow,
> I walk through my shadow in search of a moment,

What made Paz such a deep initiate of connection was the psychic truth that so much of his poetry was elaborated out of a radical sense of human estrangement and exile, a feeling of unreality. He considered the experience of being born "a wound that never heals" —it is "a fall into an alien land"[7]— and he sought through poetry to reunite with others, a way back toward the maternal Other. "I am living / at the center / of a wound still fresh," he writes in *Dawn*. Always he was seeking to heal a human cleft, an irreparable sense of division, a fissure in being. He universalized the experience ("The consciousness of being separate is a constant feature of our spiritual history,"[8] he said), but it was a generalization experienced on his pulse, in his own body, which is why it motivated, both consciously and unconsciously, so much of his poetic production.

The same lyric practice that gives us moments of annihilation also gives us moments of ecstatic union, fusion with the glorious Other. They salvage and deliver back to us the enormous moment when we glimpse "the unity that we lost" and recall "the forgotten astonishment of being alive" (*Sunstone*). Paz had a skeptical intelligence, but he was

---

[7] "In Search of the Present: Nobel Lecture, 1990" *op. cit.*, 257.
[8] *Ibid.*, 257.

never really a cerebral poet, as has often been suggested. Rather, his poems are driven by a sometimes anguished, sometimes joyous eroticism.
Most of his poems seem shadowed by the obscure absence or presence
of the beloved. When the beloved is absent from the poem, he feels
acutely cut off from nature and from himself, delivered back to his own
estranging desires and to the linear flow of time. But when the beloved
visits the poem, he feels the overflowing circularity of time, the dance
of being, the affirmation of an eternal moment. Poetry becomes a means
of attainment, the reconciliation of opposites, a way of participating in
an abundant universe. It becomes a form of creative love that moves beyond the duality of subject and object, annulling the temporal world,
offering up the mysteries of incarnation. Here the moment widens into
eternity:

> all is transformed, all is sacred,
> every room is the center of the world,
> it's still the first night, and the first day,
> the world is born when two people kiss,

And:

> the two took off their clothes and kissed
> because two bodies, naked and entwined,
> leap over time, they are invulnerable,
> nothing can touch them, they return to the source,
> there is no you, no I, no tomorrow,
> no yesterday, no names, the truth of two
> in a single body, a single soul,
> oh total being...

(from *Sunstone*)

"Being is eroticism,"[9] Paz affirms. In his splendid book on love and
eroticism, *The Double Flame*, he explicitly links the erotic act and the

[9] *The Bow and the Lyre, op. cit.*, 162.

poetic act through the agency of imagination. "Imagination turns sex into ceremony and rite, language into rhythm and metaphor," he writes. "The poetic image is an embrace of opposite realities, and rhyme a copulation of sounds; poetry eroticizes language and the world, because the operation is erotic to begin with."[10] I am moved by Paz's suggestion that love, like poetry, "is a victory over time, a glimpse of the other side, of the there that is a here, where nothing changes and everything that is, truly is."[11]

Paz's poetry of attainment fulfills the Sufi or mystical maxim, "The Beloved and I are One." He defines —he defends— the creative moment when two people merge and thereby protect their share of the eternal, our ration of paradise.

> To love:
> to open the forbidden door,
> the passageway
> that takes us to the other side of time.
> The moment:
> the opposite of death,
> our fragile eternity.

(from *Letter of Testimony*)

"The poet endeavors to make the world sacred,"[12] Octavio Paz declared in *The Siren and the Seashell*, and in his restless search for the present, the contemporaneous, he never lost sight of poetry's irrational power and sacred mystery, its archaic roots, its spiritual audacity. "Poetry is knowledge, salvation, power, abandonment,"[13] he declares at the outset of *The Bow and the Lyre*. He treated lyric poetry as a revolutionary emotional activity, a spiritual exercise, a means of interior liberation, a quest for

---

[10] *The Double Flame: Love and Eroticism*, trans. Helen Lane (New York: Harcourt Brace, 1995), 3.

[11] *Ibid.*, 264.

[12] *The Siren and the Seashell, and Other Essays on Poets and Poetry*, trans. Lysander Kemp and Margaret Sayers Peden, (Austin: University of Texas Press, 1976), 167.

[13] *The Bow and the Lyre, op. cit.*, 3.

transfiguration. His poems inscribe a quest and an attainment as they hold together what he calls "life and death in a single instant of incandescence."[14] Here is a poetry that seeks to return us —to restore us— to the totality of being. It is a living poetry that leaps over time and delivers inscriptions of timelessness, time without limit or measure, the emptiness and plenitude of a moment "forever arriving."

[14] *Ibid.*, 139.

OCTAVIO PAZ AND MODERN ENGLISH-LANGUAGE POETRY

ANTHONY STANTON

For Charles and Brenda Tomlinson

The dead don't die. They look on and help.

D. H. LAWRENCE

From an early moment, the work of Octavio Paz transcended national boundaries. Of all modern poets and essayists, few have established such wide-ranging dialogues with other traditions; few have built as many cultural and epistemological bridges between Mexico, Latin America and the world. In his exploration of modernity, in his "search for the present," Paz is a unique figure: an interpreter and architect of traditions. Little has been said of his long relationship with English-language poetry. I shall not speak here of his translations of John Donne and Andrew Marvell, nor can I dwell on the mediating role that poets, critics and translators such as Ezra Pound, Arthur Waley and Donald Keene had in Paz's passion for classical Chinese and Japanese literature. Instead, I shall sketch his relations with modern English-language poetry, what he received and what he gave, focusing on two moments in his evolution: his beginnings, in the thirties, and his full maturity in the sixties and seventies.

The first contact was undoubtedly indirect, through Spanish translations. Early readings are formative, and in some of his youthful prose and poetry there are allusions to the English Romantics, especially Blake and Keats, as well as to two modern writers: D.H. Lawrence and T.S. Eliot. In the thirties and early forties, Paz expresses his fascination with Lawrence, not so much the poet in verse as the narrator-poet and the polemical critic of Western rationalism. What could this defender of vitalism, spontaneity, the instinctive and intuitive, have meant to a young Mexican poet? Lawrence had been in Mexico, where he had invented the apocalyptic myth that locates the source of salvation for modern Western consciousness in the pre-Columbian religions. Before Artaud, Breton, and the Surrealists, Lawrence is the initiator of the primitivist myth of Mexico, especially in *The Plumed Serpent* (1926), the novel whose worldview haunts some of Paz's early poems and can even be felt years later in *The Labyrinth of Solitude* (1950).

To Paz, he seemed a visionary in 1941: "Quería fundar una religión que hincara sus raíces en lo más antiguo del hombre: el sexo."[1] Like Blake, Novalis, or San Juan de la Cruz, Lawrence identifies the poetic act with eroticism and religion. These are prophetic and apocalyptic writers whose sacred view of eroticism provoked accusations of heterodoxy, such as Eliot's attack on Lawrence in the book he later suppressed, *After Strange Gods* (1934), with its disturbing subtitle: *A Primer of Modern Heresy*. Lawrence proposes a return to the primitive world of sensations, to the harmony before the Fall: "Esto es el nuevo romanticismo, que busca, defiende y rescata no a la conciencia del hombre, no al individuo, no a lo que separa y aísla, sino a lo que liga."[2] It is impossible to reread Paz's early poems, such as *Raíz del hombre*, without thinking about Lawrence's belief in "blood-consciousness."[3] This was part of Paz's dream of a "poetry of communion" capable of reconciling us with a pre-personal past, accessible in the experiences of poetry, religion and love: "Aunque la obra de Lawrence no es un mito, la inspira un mito: el de la búsqueda de la inocencia primordial, el regreso al origen y al gran pacto con las bestias, las plantas, los elementos, el sol, la luna, los astros".[4]

"Poetry of Solitude and Poetry of Communion," a programmatic essay of 1943, ends by citing one of Blake's most subversive books. This totalizing poetic attempts to "unite the two parallel tendencies of the human spirit: consciousness and innocence, experience and expression, the act and the word that reveals it. Or, as one of those masters said:

---

[1] *Primeras letras* (1931-1943), ed. Enrico Mario Santí (México: Vuelta, 1988), 90.

[2] *Ibid.*, 91.

[3] *Obras completas, (OC):* 10 (Barcelona/México: Círculo de Lectores / Fondo de Cultura Económica, 1996), 101. I shall subsequently include references to Paz's complete works as follows: *OC*, volume and page numer.

[4] *OC*, 10:104.

The Marriage of Heaven and Hell.[5] I have shown elsewhere that this theory of the history of Spanish poetry as an oscillation between the two epistemological poles of solitude and communion, with Quevedo and San Juan as their respective exponents, is a theological scheme inspired directly by Eliot's famous 1921 essay *The Metaphysical Poets*, which develops the myth of a "dissociation of sensibility": a Romantic myth that Eliot uses against Romanticism.[6]

In the review *Contemporáneos*, Enrique Munguía published in 1930 his prose translation of *The Waste Land*. Years later, Paz would recall that this reading opened to him the doors of modern poetry.[7] He was to assimilate the radical innovations in later poems such as *Hymn Among Ruins* and *Sunstone*, personal appropriations of the lesson of Eliot and Pound: the poem as a fragmentary and discontinuous text that violently juxtaposes different times and spaces, opposing styles and languages, the work as a palimpsest in which past and present coexist. His later critical reading, in *Children of the Mire: Poetry from Romanticism to the Avant-Garde*, argues convincingly that Eliot and Pound's "method," the constructive principle of their texts, is already contained in the *collage* theories of Cubism. Their original contribution lies in having included history and the modern city within the epic and ironic possibilities of this new spatial form that allows for parodic parallelism between past and present. More perfect in its poetic results, Eliot's lesson overshadows that of Pound's *Cantos*, and although Paz usually privileges *The Waste Land* over the *Four Quartets*, this later composition leaves traces in *A Draft of Shadows*, Paz's long poem in which Eliot coexists with Wordsworth, the inventor in the English tradition of poetic autobiography on a grand scale in *The Prelude*. The opening lines of *A Draft of Shadows* ("Heard by the soul, footsteps / in the mind more than shadows, / shadows of thought more than footsteps / through the path of echoes / that memory invents and erases") recall the first movement of the *Four Quartets*: "Footfalls echo in the memory / Down the passage which we

---

[5] *The Siren and the Seashell, and Other Essays on Poets and Poetry*, trans. Lysander Kemp and Margaret Sayers Peden (Austin: University of Texas, 1991), 172.

[6] *Primeras letras, op. cit.*, 303.

[7] *OC* 2: 290.

did not take / Towards the door we never opened / Into the rose-garden. My words echo / Thus, in your mind."[8]

Echoes of mental steps, footfalls in the memory, words that take us in both poems to the inner garden of "our first world," childhood. The poet sees himself in the double mirror of language and memory. Eliot is a direct model because he builds his text on a much clearer structural pattern than Wordsworth did: the musical scheme of movements that constantly return to the starting point, variations that expand the theme, recurring motifs, phrases, images, and rhythms that give flexible form to meandering consciousness: the Romantic spiral. In *A Draft of Shadows*, as in *The Prelude* and the *Four Quartets*, past and present are superimposed in an attempt to seize Paz's "instants," Wordsworth's "spots of time," Eliot's "point of intersection of the timeless / With time [...] the moment in and out of time."[9]

Let me go back now to the two years during which Paz lived in the United Sates, from December 1943 to the end of 1945. It is not difficult to imagine the voracious reading of English and North-American poets in their own language. His poetry changes on contact with these traditions. If we compare the poems of *A la orilla del mundo*, published in 1942, before his move, with those of the first edition of *Libertad bajo palabra* (1949), it is easy to hear the more natural diction of the later texts which shed the high rhetoric and move closer to the ideal of "living speech" in their versification. Irony appears for the first time. In June 1945, he travels to Vermont to meet Robert Frost.[10] The impact of Frost, extraordinary example of the recreation of spoken language dramatized in the monologue of a character, offers Paz a model for the soliloquies that he writes at that time. The appropriation is again personal, although it could have been facilitated by the example of Luis Cernuda, the Spanish poet who delved into similar sources, specifically the dramatic monologues of Browning.

Another discovery is that of Walt Whitman, the founding father of North American poetry, introduced to the Spanish-speaking world in

---

[8] "Four Quartets," in *The Complete Poems and Plays of T. S. Eliot* (London: Faber and Faber, 1969), 171.
[9] *Ibid.*, 189-190.
[10] The visit was recorded in a chronicle, "Visita a un poeta," in *OC* 2: 277-281 with the title "Visita a Robert Frost."

1887 by José Martí. In an appendix to the first edition of *The Bow and the Lyre* in 1956, Paz expresses his perplexed fascination with this inventor of modernity who used the vast rhythms of Biblical verse. Whitman is seen as the exception because he reunites the warring terms of poetry and history. Like Blake, Novalis, Lawrence, and San Juan, Whitman is taken to be a poet of communion: his beliefs coincide with those of his world. Unlike the marginalized modern poet, Whitman has faith in democracy, progress and the utopian dream of America. Whitman fascinates Paz because he seems to be the negation of the Romantic and Symbolist myth of the modern poet: he is the negation of Poe, that archetype of the *poète maudit* for Baudelaire and the French Symbolists. Thus we have, in Spanish America, in addition to the Whitman of Martí, Darío, Borges and Neruda, the Whitman of Paz. More than forty years later this reading was described in Harold Bloom's *The Western Canon* as "beautifully mistaken,"[11] a phrase I take to be a compliment coming from the defender of misreading as the principal way of renovating traditions and opening up imaginative space.

At this time Paz begins to read Wallace Stevens, Hart Crane and e.e. cummings, whom he finally meets in 1956 and translates later. The typographical and syntactic experiments of cummings seem to have no influence on Paz at that time, but there is another poet who is vaster and more varied than cummings: William Carlos Williams, author of *Spring and All* (1923) and the modern epic *Paterson* (1946-1958). Williams was one of the first translators of Paz into English: around 1955, he translated *Hymn among ruins*, a poem that probably interested him on account of its *collage*-type construction that employs devices he himself had used in his Imagist and Cubist beginnings. In 1973, Paz wrote a short critical piece on Williams to accompany his translations of selected poems.

Certain analogies can be perceived between Paz's *Eagle or Sun?* (1951) and Williams' *Kora in Hell: Improvisations* (1920), an early book of strange, miscellaneous prose texts centered on the power of the imagination. I am not suggesting a direct influence: it is virtually impossible that Paz could have read *Kora* (a book whose small first edition of 1920 was

---

11 Harold Bloom, *The Western Canon: The Books and School of the Ages* (New York: Harcourt, Brace & Company, 1994), 485.

not reprinted until the late 1950s), and we know that the main model for *Eagle or Sun?* was the French tradition of the prose poem. Another of Williams' early prose books, *In the American Grain* (1925), anticipates Paz's exploration in *The Labyrinth of Solitude* of the roots of a national tradition grounded in history and myth. In both essays, the imagination charts the underground continuity between past and present.

Williams may well have influenced the sudden change in the poetic syntax and versification of Paz's poetry from *Salamander* (1962) onwards. In the Hispanic tradition I see no direct models for this spatial or visual syntax with its cellular isolation of words. It is true that Mallarmé's *Un coup de dés* inspires the form of *Blanco*, but the other texts in *East Slope* and some previous ones in *Salamander* are much closer to Williams peculiar lineation with its dominant triadic pattern or "three-step lines" that spread across the page descending from left to right. Williams justified his metrical theory and practice with the bewildering notion of the "variable foot," a relative, non-fixed form for an age of relativity.[12] Williams' influence can be clearly seen in his Objectivist disciples such as Zukofsky and Oppen, but it is possible to see a similar practical influence in Paz's poetry.

A case of reciprocal relations can be established with Elizabeth Bishop, the strict and highly original poet whose work is dominated by what Paz calls "the power of reticence".[13] In the 1970s, when both coincide in Cambridge at Harvard University, Bishop translates some of Paz's recent poems,[14] and in 1974 Paz translates some of her texts, among them one inspired by her visits to St. Elizabeths, the asylum where Pound was locked up.[15] Paz's interest in Bishop at such a late mo-

---

[12] Williams thought he had first perfected this new measure of versification in "The Descent," intense lines included in *Paterson II* (1948). He used the same lines, now with the title, as the opening poem of *The Desert Music* (1954). It is interesting to note that this was one of the poems that Paz chose to translate in the 1970s: it was subsequently published in William Carlos Williams, *Veinte poemas* (México: Era, 1973) with a prologue by Paz, "La flor saxífraga."

[13] *OC* 2: 313-323.

[14] Bishop translates *La llave de agua* from *East Slope* and four texts from *Return: Por la calle de Galeana, La arboleda, Primero de enero,* and *Objetos y apariciones,* this last one dedicated to Joseph Cornell, an artist dear to both Paz and Bishop, and who acted as a stimulus on the artistic career of Marie-José Paz. Bishop's translations can be found in *The Complete Poems. 1927-1979* (New York: Farrar, Straus and Giroux, 1993), 269-276.

[15] Paz's translations are reproduced in *OC* 2: 315-323.

ment of his own career is due, I think, to her reaction against the loose rhetoric of much poetry in the 1960s and to her preference for simplicity, clarity, emotional and intellectual distance that permits precise and minute observation of the world: "no detail too small," she says in *Sandpiper*.[16] A cosmopolitan like Paz, Bishop represents the same kind of technical expertise at the service of a highly individual and almost ascetic worldview.

Let us now move to the other side of the Atlantic. As far as I know, nobody has explored the parallels between the linguistic, cultural and psychological excavation of the past in *The Labyrinth of Solitude*, *The Other Mexico*, or certain Paz poems and the unearthing and exorcising of a past laden with violence in *North* (1975) by Seamus Heaney, one of the greatest living poets writing in English. Perhaps we should not be surprised by the analogies between an Irish poet, obsessed with buried maternal traditions that distinguish Ireland from the dominant English tradition, and a Mexican poet determined from the beginning to bring to the surface of the present all the mutilated threads of a heterogeneous and non-Western past that gives Mexico its unique cultural identity. Poetry, then, as a *Door into the Dark* (to use the title of Heaney's second collection) or as the voice of otherness. In both poets, there is a strong tendency towards geological metaphors derived from the peculiar landscapes of their places of origin. The "black butter" of Heaney's Northern Ireland bog and the petrified volcanic lava of the central Valley of Mexico are vacuum chambers in which one can strip off layers or crusts to find the past preserved intact in the present: archeological finds. The poet only has to excavate below turf and peat or volcanic rock. Verbs from this semantic group are common in both: "digging" in Heaney (title of the poem with which his first book symbolically opens);[17] *desenterrar* ("unearth") in Paz. Excavation as a way of discovering and inventing the continuity of a tradition, even if this tradition implies atavistic barbarism and sacrificial violence: "We have dug up Rage," writes Paz in *The Petrifying Petrified*.

---

[16] Collected in *The Complete Poems, op. cit.*, 131.

[17] Seamus Heaney, *Digging*, in *Death of a Naturalist* (London: Faber and Faber, 1966), 13-14. In a Later essay, Heaney acknowledges that this first poem is also the beginning of his initiation.

In the case of Heaney, it is impossible to speak of influence, as I have no idea if the Irish poet had actually read Paz before writing his own poems, but there is one example of brotherhood that signals the illuminating power of Paz's mature work. I refer to his close friendship with the English painter-poet Charles Tomlinson. Tomlinson is the editor of *The Oxford Book of Verse in Translation* (1980), and his anti-provincial mentality soon opposed him to the insular attitudes of the members of "The Movement," among them Philip Larkin. Of few English poets can it be said that they are direct descendants of Pound, Stevens and Williams. Not surprisingly, his poetry was first recognized in America and by critics like Hugh Kenner, author of *The Pound Era*. Tomlinson is a poet of landscape, that of his native country, but also that of the places he has visited, such as the United Sates and Mexico. His clear and precise visions of the external world involve a sort of erasure of the Romantic subject and a foregrounding of concrete sensation.

The two poets meet in 1967, and in 1979 Tomlinson edits in England a bilingual anthology of Paz's poetry, with his own translations and those of Williams, Bishop, and Eliot Weinberger, among others.[18] We should remember the critical essays that each has written on the other and their reciprocal translations. Their two works of collaboration are interesting experiments: *Renga* (1971) and *Airborn / Hijos del aire* (1979).[19] The renga is a traditional Japanese form of collective chain poetry governed by strict rules that permit programmed chance. In 1969, four poets write in four different languages the first Western renga: Paz, Tomlinson, Jacques Roubaud, and Edoardo Sanguineti. Adapted to Western conventions, the Japanese tanka becomes the sonnet with no rhyme or fixed measure. As languages alternate, penetrate, and rebound off one another, the reader glimpses themes: criticism of the self, polyphonic intertextuality, creation as multiple translation, combinatory art,

---

[18] *Octavio Paz. Selected Poems*, ed. Charles Tomlinson (Harmondsworth: Penguin, 1979).

[19] The first quadrilingual edition of *Renga* (with a complete translation to French) was published in France in 1971 (Gallimard). Two more editions were published in 1972 (both reproduce the original quadrilingual version), one with a complete translation to English (New York: George Braziller) and the other to Spanish (Mexico: Joaquin Mortiz). A far as I know, there has not been an Italian edition. *Airborn / Hijos del aire* was published for the first time in Mexico (Taller Martín Pescador, 1979). The English edition was published by Anvil Press, London, 1981.

open work, Lautréamont's and Breton's dream of collective poetry. A game that recalls the "exquisite corpse" of the Surrealists, *Renga* is a Western appropriation of an Eastern form and proposes for modern poetry something similar, on a reduced scale, to what Joyce had attempted in *Finnegans Wake*: the possibility of a new language.

Perhaps inevitably, the theory of infinite potentiality was more enticing than the concrete result of this poem of poems. I think this awareness of not having achieved the original goals explains why Paz and Tomlinson looked for a stricter and more intimate form of experimentation. The result was *Airborn / Hijos del aire*, two sequences of four sonnets, each based on a pre-established theme: House and Day. The title alludes to a curious fact: the different parts were written in different continents and sent by airmail. At the end, as in *Renga*, each poet translated the other's stanzas into his own language. As a product of mutual understanding and shared tastes, *Airborn* is noteworthy for the quality of the poems (and I include as poems the translations). Less ambitious than *Renga*, this two-way creation is also less disperse and more intimate: what it loses in polyphonic extension it gains in vertical depth.

In Tomlinson's *Collected Poems*, the reader will find several compositions directly linked to Paz. *Landscape* is a precise and compact translation of *Paisaje*. *Variation on Paz* builds on part of a verse from *El cántaro roto*: "Hay que soñar [...] hacia dentro y también hacia afuera." *Assassin*, an extraordinary poem in the form of the interior monologue of Trotsky's assassin, is inspired by one and a half hendecasyllables from *Sunstone*: "Trotsky's death rattle and his howl / like a boar." This vivid psychological recreation is also a reflection on a certain vision of history. The subtitle of "In the Fullness of Time" declares that it is a "letter to Octavio Paz." It meditates on the following lines from *Wind from All Compass Points*:

> the present is motionless
> At the top of the world
> Shiva and Parvati caress
> Each caress lasts a century
> for the god and for the man

Tomlinson's eloquent poem begins thus:

The time you tell us is the century and the day
Of Shiva and Parvati: imminent innocence,
Moment without movement. Tell us, too, the way
Time, in its fullness, fills us
As it flows: tell us the beauty of succession
That Breton denied: the day goes
Down, but there is time before it goes
To negotiate a truce in time...[20]

Word-play, density of sound patterns and constant rhythmic variation distinguish this plea for a "truce in time." It is interesting that Tomlinson opposes Paz's vision of time to Breton's, perhaps projecting his
own doubts about Surrealism. These encounters with the man and his
work motivated the following declaration by Tomlinson: "Para mí, aún
permanecen en formas muy profundas y secretas las reverberaciones de
aquellos encuentros, formas difíciles de articular o de explicar. Estoy se-
guro de que han tenido como resultado cambios en el énfasis de mi obra
poética."[21] And with this testimony to the liberating energy that Paz's
poetry and thought have had on one of the major English poets of our
time, we can put a provisional end to a story that is, of course, endless.

[20] Charles Tomlinson, *Collected Poems* (Oxford & New York: Oxford University Press, 1985), 163.
[21] Charles Tomlinson, "Un juego libre de pensamiento," in *Octavio Paz*, ed. Pere Gimferrer (Madrid: Taurus, 1982), 32.

PAZ, ANTHROPOLOGY
AND THE FUTURE OF POETRY

NATHANIEL TARN*

Not a Paz Scholar. Not a piece about Paz
but inspired by Paz's spirit & enquiry

I take as my text today a passage from Octavio's *Alternating Current:*

> If imitation becomes mere repetition, the dialogue ceases and tradition petri-
> fies; if modernity is not self-critical, if it is not a sharp break and simply con-
> siders itself a prolongation of 'what is modern,' tradition becomes paralyzed.
> This is what is taking place in a large sector of the so-called avant-garde. The
> reason for this is obvious: the idea of modernity is beginning to lose its vitality.
> It is losing it because modernity is no longer a critical attitude but an accepted,
> codified convention...it has become an article of faith that everyone subscribes
> to...all this raking of the coals can be reduced to a simple formula: repetition at
> an ever-accelerating rate. Never before has there been such frenzied, barefaced
> imitation masquerading as originality, invention, and innovation.[1]

If this is a correct reading, it has deep implications for the future of
poetry. I will look at this question in my habitual persona as anthropologist. Be warned, gentle audience, that the social sciences do not often console. I offer a hypothesis in the form of a reduced model of an
extremely complex situation: there is no time for more. The reason for
a sociological approach? It is nonsense to talk about poetry, as most poets and critics today continue to do, without accounting for the socio-
economic context of poetry production and reception.

Let us suppose that the ancient art of poetry reposes on certain ancient foundations, which are being eroded or destroyed with ever increasing rapidity. Let's take three such foundations:

---

[1] *Alternating Current*, trans. Helen R. Lane, (New York: Viking, 1973), 18-19.

1) Non-Human Natural Species
2) Human Natural Species
3) What I shall call "Cultural Exemplars"

First: Now that we are environmentally conscious, we hear every day of disappearing species, many unknown to science —in the dwindling forests of the Amazon, or Southeastern Asia, or Africa. Likewise in the oceans, suffering to their very depths by over-fishing, pollution and global warming. Second: Those of us who care hear every day of underfed, poverty-stricken, culturally-deprived endangered and oppressed indigenous, "primitive," archaic, or traditional peasant peoples, whether in the Americas—the Amazon again; among the Maya of Central America; among our own Northern Native Americans or in other continents: in other words, genocide and ethnocide. After managing two world wars of unparalleled proportions, our century continues on its merry way with the horrors of Guatemala, Tibet, Kurdistan, Rwanda, Nigeria, Sierra Leone, the Congo, Kosovo, Burma, East Timor. The truth is that, whether of the Left or Right politically, elites need land and will kill to get it. Thirdly, along with the effects of the World Wars (I think of Dresden and Warsaw, for instance), there is unparalleled looting and destruction of cultural exemplars, whether at Angkor, or Egypt, or in the northern forests of Guatemala —or, equally, there are the various renovations and the drowning of historical centers by high-rises and bulk projects of every description. Belonging to both 2) and 3), there is the destruction of and backyarding of languages.

Nature Poetry is as old as mankind; so is that regarding human species: think of Homer or the *Mahabharata*. For the poetry of cultural exemplars, we evoke Dante's Florence or, more recently, Wordsworth's London and Baudelaire's Paris. It is my hypothesis that poetry consciously or unconsciously anchors itself in, and is nourished by, the existence of these traditional natural and cultural treasures, and that when these latter suffer as much as they are doing, poetry needs to become purely elegiac or turn to other forms of accomplishment. What it turns to, I'll argue, is no longer poetry but something which is increasingly being called, simply, "writing."

I am not unfamiliar with many of the internal arguments for this: those, for instance, attending to the changing mutual relations of poetry

79

and prose; the evolution of genres, and so forth. Here I continue to focus on the external and, because we are here and this is where we live, I focus on our country. Let me also stress, once and for all, that there are always exceptions in any theory or hypothesis.

O.K. As I have stressed many times before, the end of World War II witnessed the insertion of the creative arts into the academic universe with extraordinarily dramatic and transformative results. Let me go on dealing with creative writing, leaving aside music and the visual arts —while adding in passing a footnote to the effect that the sovereign reign of "installations" in the latter seems to me, for many reasons, to parallel the accession of "writing."

The transformation has proceeded along many different lines. The sheer *danger* and life-shaking, lifelong risks inherent in being a producer of poetry; the interminable alchemical process of conjugating intellect and emotion, head and heart, in order to produce a life-work in poetry, an opus if you will, has become in these institutions, since the head develops faster than the heart, one of the *fabrications* of a product known as "writing," using academic "theory" rather than life experience to, as they say so elegantly nowadays, write off of. This, I have found, often gives rise to bodies of theory from young practitioners infinitely exceeding in interest and value their actual writing production. The normalization of "poetry" production (I now use the word poetry in inverted commas) has led to the transformation of a vocation into a career, into a profession.

Our young student practitioners do not follow their life-experience, meager as it is; they follow their guru teachers. When all is said and done, it is impossible for the teacher not to assume that anyone in a class can become a writer (a variant of the Napoleonic "every soldier has a general's baton in his backpack"); impossible for it not to foster competition —first for the guru's favor, next for achievement in reading, publications, grants, awards, and the like. Competitiveness, reducing the writing career to a simulacrum of other late-capitalist careers, ensures a stultifying and extreme degree of unpleasantness, rudeness, irresponsibility, lack of community and mutual help in the writing population. Above all, the result is a terrifying overproduction of writers in a society which, in part because of the nature of "writing" as opposed to that of poetry, is under-producing readers, is in fact losing readers by the droves every day. I have described this in Lévi-Straussian terms as a prevalence of incest (the relation of poet as producer to poet as consumer) over marriage (the age-old relation of poet to common-or-garden reader). Regular incest, as we know, is not particularly good for any species. Yet another aspect of this population pressure is generation-related. In the Age of Information, the fashions and fads of culture move extremely fast (as a new book's title has it, *The Acceleration of Just About Everything*): one's creations may be out of date more than once in a lifetime. How does the average writer survive while aging?

Let me dwell for a moment on the question of difficulty and obscurity. While it is true that the great discoveries of modernism preceded the academization of "creative writing," my sense is that the progression of "writing" towards unreadability has been helped by that academization. Many have commented on the disappearance of a true avant-garde and its replacement by avant-gardism. Remember my quote from Octavio at the beginning. I see this as a prolongation of experimentation usually leading further on from collage and montage into ever-increasing fragmentation and eventually into a disease which, adapting an already common usage, I call "disjunctivitis." The argument, used by some producers who, correctly locating the seats of available power in the academy, have ensconced themselves therein every bit as much as the establishment mainstream, to the effect that the disruption of the common linguistic coin is part of a war against late-capitalist discourse, is singularly inept: I do not see oppressed workers of any kinds devouring the products of avant-gardism. The death-of-the-author thematic, as commonly adapted, is another inanity: when society does its very best to homogenize us, what is wrong with a strong, knowledgeable ego crying in the darkening wilderness? The expectation of exegesis in an ever backward-oriented academy (I am salaried to explain the previous generation; the next generation explains me but no generation explains itself) fosters a belief that significant writing is writing that needs explicating by critics, thus ever strengthening the hold of "theoreticians" and canon-formulating critics over the one-time freedom of the one-time poet. As for life among the incestuous, it hardly matters if a consumer truly understands a producer: we are all brothers and sisters under the skin and have to pretend to stick together.

A word also on competitiveness. "Mankind cannot stand very much reality," a poet once intimated, and I would add that it cannot stand very much writing. Bored to death on the one hand by the interminable repetitions of the MFA clones of their MFA teachers and, on the other, by the unreadable so-called "writing" of the reigning avant-gardisms, the public or the last common-or-garden readers left, faced in addition with this lemming-like overpopulation, have a desperate need of selection. This leads straight into the terminus of competitiveness: the winner-take-all syndrome, another familiar late-capitalist life-enhancing marvel. The award system is the crowning glory of this syndrome. It is deleterious not because it is unjust (nothing human is perfect), but because it inflicts an apparently consensual body of opinion on a public not usually aware of its options. The money-bags, playing it even more safely than the universities, select a group of trustworthy canonizers and trustworthy mainstream writers conveniently gathered in a number of *Academies* —a group in whom the public can be induced to trust since they are already so trustworthy— and regularly disburse large sums... almost always into the pockets of the already fortunate. The consensus established by this system is an appalling fraud but it is supported by a host of established colleges, universities, institutions, foundations, magazines, and publishing houses so large that it is never questioned. As I pointed out during Octavio's 80th birthday celebrations, the name of "poet" is now so poverty-stricken that it has been abolished. What you now have is the "poet-who-has-had-more-than-three-poems-published-in-recognized-peer-judged magazines;" the "published-poet;" the "esteemed-poet;" the "recognized-poet;" the "famous poet;" the "feted-poet;" the "awarded-poet;" the "much-awarded poet" —and who knows whether the State of Kansas, *inter alia*, will not come up with the "saved-poet" or the "much-redeemed-poet" by the time we have all finished? Without lacking in respect, I would point out that even our esteemed hosts here did not describe Mr. Paz, the subject of our celebration, in the first version of their program through anything else but a list of his awards. This, thankfully, has now been corrected. In short, there is a devaluation of the poet here as the poet disappears behind the award. The award is frantically crying out for an attention no longer granted to the poet: *society pretends* to value poetry by throwing sops to Cerberus.

It is immensely hard for the true innovator to remain outside the pale. In effect, he or she may be seriously said to face extinction: the law that there are no mute, inglorious Miltons has for some time been stifled under the weight of the over-producers. In the triumph of quantity over quality, it is now axiomatic that the indifferent and the sheerly lousy can stifle the interesting and the good. An additional factor is being witnessed in the last couple of years or so: rather like what happens with ecumenical efforts among churches when the world seems little inclined to be religious, there is an ever-increasing banding together of producers, a great deal of fraternization among individuals and groups recently antagonistic, for valid theoretical reasons, to one another. This, by the process of co-opting freelancers into establishment institutions, is leading to a blurring of the last few lines subsisting between differing schools of writing. We thus approach at ever gathering speed that state so beloved of the New Age in which "everything is happily, even deliriously, everything;" and all is for the best in the best of worlds. I have noticed yet another development: *The New York Times* reported, last August 12th, that those who made money after the Sixties and would now like to flesh out their youthful dreams can attend poetry-writing camps in environmentally choice surroundings, with healthy diets and no doubt much yoga, meditation, and hand-holding counseling to hoot. Democracy is undoubtedly the only valid form of government, but when "everybody is a poet" in a society which does not want poets, it certainly has massive drawbacks.

Is it any wonder that, added to the deliquescence of any sense of responsibility whatsoever in most parts of the publishing world, including allegedly progressive publishing, the deteriorations I speak of have led to a mass migration of so-called major publishers away from poetry? Is it credible that an American firm which has published a major American poet all his life suddenly decides that it will not bring out his Collected Works? This perhaps will be the crowning factor in my oncoming revelation: namely the proposition that Anglo (I use a New Mexican term but of course imply "Caucasian") elitist poetry, as we know it in these United Mistakes, is either dead or dying. If you take the figures of the Pound-H.D-W.C. Williams lineage; adding, let us say, the likes of Crane, Stevens, Eliot, Oppen, and other Objectivists; if you continue with the New Americans as anthologically defined between Donald Allen in the Sixties and Eliot Weinberger in the Nineties, you have a basic picture of the beauteous graveyard as we approach the so-called Millennium. Doubtless, there will always be names to add, and there can be similar lists in other countries and other languages. Shining in a Latin American one, for instance, would be the obvious examples of Vallejo, Huidobro, Neruda, Paz, and their immediate successors —a few of whom are here present.

There is nothing new, of course, in the claim that one of the arts, or all of them, are dying: witness, for instance, Lévi-Strauss's ability to foresee the possibility of a world without art. Or there is Arthur Danto's persuasive argument in his *The Delegitimization of Art* that art has, as it were, entered a post-historical era and disappeared up its own philosophy. *Para acabar*, it is merely that, after a great deal of life creeping toward death there is, finally, death. As Lorca said, "también se muere el mar."

So where, or out of what or whom, does the future arise? Where is the creative energy of the first part of the next millennium to come from? An idea out of Octavio's *The Other Voice* has always struck me as valuable. It is that we must look for the survival of true poetry not in the horizontal deployment of an ever-shrinking population of readers at any given historical moment, but in a vertical time-depth: poetry surviving as a diachronic passage of culture from one generation of readers to another. For me, this time-depth is without limit: it reaches back to whatever we can envisage as the beginning of all and any time, encompassing the poetry voiced by any human from that beginning onward, not to mention the immense population of the dead. For me, however, there would be a horizontal dimension too, this one stressing not the verticality of any one culture, but the horizontal passage of the torch from one culture to another or one set of cultures to another.

My sense then is that the future of poetry will probably arise, for the English language, out of the indigenous Anglophone so-called "Third World," which is still closer to the foundations I spoke of at the start than most of us are. From there and also from the so-called "Minorities" in this and other Anglophone First World countries who, it may be argued, are or can be in many ways, whether deliberately or not, closer to indigenous thought than we are. These "Minorities" in this country have produced many of the poetries I have called "Liberation Poetries," stemming in large part from the Civil Rights Movements of the 1960s —but they are still far from completely integrated into what we label as American Poetry.

Two problems here. The first is that the more indigenous of our worlds are rapidly being homogenized by such forces as economic imperialism and globalization so that the environments that poetry prizes may well be shorter-lived than we might hope. They may yet be defeated by corporate greed; the manipulations of the financial markets; consumerism; the stripping of environmental assets; the atrocities of genetic engineering; AIDS and other such horrors; the massive digital divide. The second problem is that many, perhaps most, of the poets and writers from there that we value, from an Anglo perspective, have made their names by using the same methods and poetics as the Anglo Elite Poetries. Here and there, one can pick out a few names that differ. Kamau Brathwaite, for instance, who, not forgetting Aimé Césaire, was the true candidate for the Caribbean Nobel Award some years ago, is an experimenter and bridger of gaps who may represent the future of poetry as I see it here.

To end on a slightly more upbeat note, let me propose a couple more points about our art. I have wondered for years what makes so many young people hunger for the poetic career when the latter offers, except for a very, presumably happy, few, no rewards of any kind: no money, no lovers, no status, no fame, above all no Mercedes-Benzes, in short none of the goodies our consumerdom hankers for. I used to think that a poet was a god, later that the average poet was a dog, now I believe our average poet, if it can survive, is lucky to be a liver fluke progressing through the guts of a sheep. I have finally concluded that the drug of choice here may be the *Prinzip Hoffnung*, that famous particle of Hope without which no human being can live or be creative for very long. But Hope by itself is not enough. It needs to be conjugated with Will —the wayward possibility of any new, unexpected and unexpectable, desire arising and manifesting— so well argued for in Dostoevsky's *Notes from Underground*. In other words, that which, by

propelling Hope into action, finally manages to abut upon the unacknowledged legislatordom of the world.

I recently found the following in Eliot Weinberger's magnificent
edition of Jorge Luis Borges's *Selected Non-Fictions*:

> But the best immortalities —those in the domain of passion— are still vacant.
> There is no poet who is the total voice of love, hate or despair. That is: the
> greatest verses of humanity may still not have been written. This imperfec-
> tion should raise our hopes.[2]

When it seems to me that the treasures of diversification are being
hopelessly polluted by the satanic mills of homogenization and when, at
the end of this abyssal century, I conclude that the human race is a calami-
ty waiting to be extinguished, it is to such hopes that I turn for the energy needed to get beyond our so-called "Millennium" the *famoso* year 2000.

A final word. As I'm sure we'll hear directly, Octavio Paz was able and
willing many times to uphold his membership in the international
avant-garde. He was above all, however, a deeply traditional poet conscious of the whole vast historical range of his craft. I remember here
that fifty years ago, walking back together from one of the meetings of
André Breton's Surrealist Group in Paris, Octavio told me, in the course
of a particularly vehement conversation, that he foresaw a difficult fate
for poetry in the postwar world. Solidly anchored in his native country, perhaps the greatest Mexican of this century, Octavio Paz was also
a man of international scope, one who took the whole world as his
province. Doubtless there is something symbolic in the fact that, in this
Library of the Congress of the United States, we are celebrating not a
United States poet but a citizen of the whole of America from Tierra
del Fuego to the Arctic shores. Through a long life of writing, editing,
and endless promoting of poetry's cause, Paz worked to defend the arts
he lived for against the kinds of dangers outlined here. His was a heroic
life in a far-from-heroic time. His own generosity will be greatly missed,
but his defense will stand. I hope too that his message will continue
spreading against murderous tides.

[2] Jorge Luis Borges, "Literary Pleasure," *Selected Non-Fictions*, ed. Eliot Weinberger, Viking Press, 31.

PAZ AND VANGUARDISM
(CIRCULATIONS OF THE SONG)

MICHAEL PALMER

By way of a brief preface, I am reminded of a moment many years ago at the house of a friend. On her wall was a Diego Rivera from his so-called Cubist period. Rivera had indeed taken on the compositional means, the simultaneism of the Cubists. Yet there were already signs of a formal transformation, an overcoming. The palette itself was less restricted than early Cubism, hinting at a nascent new style. More important, in the place of the newspapers, carafes and ashtrays of the Cubist still-life was a sky bristling with the guns of the Revolution. And it occurred to me that these guns were also pointing back toward Cubism itself, that they were saluting a new pictorial language even while paying homage to the old. (It's an ironic recollection, no doubt, given Paz's multiple reservations, over time, regarding the Mexican muralists other than Orozco.) Roughly cognate with this is a trip to São Paulo some years later, where I was to introduce an anthology of contemporary Brazilian poetry I had helped to edit and translate. The other editors and I discussed the arrival of Blaise Cendrars there in the 1920's and how his presence had been a key to Brazil's entry into the field of both modernism and vanguardism. The immediate result was Mario de Andrade's *Hallucinated City*, Brazil's first vanguardist work, and one that still speaks to that self-devouring entity, São Paulo. It is no imitation of Cendrars, but a response, and a call to arms. Later in the same visit, Haroldo de Campos presented me, from his astonishing library, with the liberated cosmopolitanism, the wild literary collaging, of Sousândrade, a proto-vanguardist of the most exemplary order. We could multiply without effort a thousand-fold instances of the complex back-and-forth, call and response, that constitute the cultural flows of our century and that explain the spread of vanguardism beyond the small urban coteries where they are initiated. They are transactions that are at once personal and artistic, as much a matter of chance, a chance encounter, as of any abiding cultural logic or necessity.

It is perhaps the agony and joy of the poem itself, as Paz and others have conceived it: we write not from but toward an emerging subject and a reconfigured subjectivity. We wonder, continually, how the pronouns, how the I and the we, the you and the they, the he and she, are spoken, invoked, and meant. Here we ask, What is it? and wait anxiously for some response from the other side of the page. The ostensible is something of a cloak, beneath which is found the body, or a snow-layer, beneath which is to be found... whatever is to be found. So, in Paz's writings, beneath the question of vanguardism, its origins and the narratives of its practice, are to be found irony and analogy, passion, negation, the lineaments of desire, alienation, conversation, history and time, the political and the atemporal, revolution and reaction, hermeticism, reason and dream, identity and difference, rupture and recurrence, the aesthetic and the anti-aesthetic, the present, the social, the Great Wheel, the movement ("revolution" once again) of the spheres.

What is beneath, but equally what precedes and what follows. Have we finally witnessed the last "last avant-garde"? Are not all avant-gardes, in their self-imagining, the last, the beyond, beyond which no other beyond is conceivable? And also the first, the origin? And is there a before to these eruptions, a presaging? Or does such thought in linear, historicized time betray the active imagination itself, the movement of words and forms among the communicating vessels, the circulations of the song, to borrow a phrase from Robert Duncan in his homage to Rumi?

A disclaimer is perhaps needed here. I will not pretend to engage directly in this brief talk with various theories of modernism and vanguardism, such as those of Peter Bürger, Renato Poggioli and Andreas Huyssen, Habermas and Jameson, or Adorno's theory of modernity, relevant as they may be (or, indeed, may not be) to an examination of Paz's critical and poetic practice, and to his place among the various movements of recent times, and to difficult questions of social and political agency. I am more interested in exploring (or at least establishing a few initial terms for exploring) the poetic conversation he establishes, asystematically, across time and the vision of discordant community it implies. I will also pretend neither to objectivity nor to comprehensiveness, but rather to a continuance of the conversation, as best as I'm able, leaving it open and fluid, subject to its own inconsistencies and paradoxes, as Paz himself might have preferred. From Baudelaire, Paz borrowed the term "partial criticism" as his own mode of critical thought, and now I will borrow it from Paz, with its paronomasia intact.

Both modernity, as Baudelaire understands it in *L'art romantique*, and vanguardism as it later developed, belong for Paz to a "tradition against itself," a paradoxical tradition of discontinuity, rupture, and change. A tradition, that is, with paradox at its heart, far from the fantasy of "tradition" invoked by Eliot as reactionary cultural critic but rather closer to the actual vision of textual circulation, citation and human circumstance envisioned by Eliot, the modernist poet of *Prufrock* and *The Waste Land*. The modernity of modernism and the vanguards, is, then, never self-identical, but always its own other, taking difference as identity. From this central paradox, vanguardist theory (whether Russian or Italian Futurism, Dada, Surrealism, Expressionism, Negritude, Ultraism, *et al.*) will generate a host of other paradoxes and internal contradictions and inconsistencies. Far from disqualifying them as generative movements, as more than one critic has claimed, Paz will plead that their particular energies arose from the irresolvable tension between reason and dream, the personal and the political, the spontaneous and the formal, the negation and the invocation of the past, the critique and celebration of the present, the yearning for, and sometimes dread of, the future. In a broken age, broken time: exaltation of a utopian future of social emancipation and of the liberated imagination, a future of the never-to-become, or appositely, a revenant, a Golden Age that never was. At the same time, these movements, in their various ways, sought to vitalize the present, to strip it of the habitual, the given, and replace that with the actual, the act. The poem as act, displacing the institutions of art. To anneal by rupture and displacement. To enter the social by assaulting it. To cure time of itself by means of time itself, rhythm, recurrence, and difference within language, the fashioner of consciousness. Extension of the Romantic paradigm of the poetic imagination, yet also an echo of the most ancient magical and incantatory practices in language. Breton as magus, Khlebnikov as shaman, Lorca as medium for the *duende*, Artaud as ritual sacrifice.

A further paradox might include the historical moment of Paz and this aftertime of the (pseudo-millennial) present. Paz himself came into his first maturity as a poet at a time when historical vanguardism was either in its waning stages as a movement, as with Surrealism, or had been annihilated by the forces of history, as was the case with Russian Futurism. Perhaps, Paz notes, only Brazilian Concretism can be seen as a genuine extension of historical vanguardism into that now recent past. In addition, we should at least mention a host of neo-vanguardist movements, such as Xul in Argentina, the Vienna Circle, Fluxus, the Situationists, the Novissimi in Italy, Language Poetry in the United States, all of which share certain characteristics regarding the place of theory, and political and aesthetic (or anti-aesthetic) practice, with the historical avant-gardes. Yet there is the essential difference: that they arrive with a precedent, a model; they are not self-fashioned. For the present writer and his generation in the United States, it may well have been, again paradoxically, the historical amnesia of the Anglo-American critical tradition in the fifties and early sixties that kept the earlier movements vital. The critical histories and classrooms of the time not only erased or simply ignored the fact of artistic vanguardism, but in their Cold War fervor, they tended to ignore as well the recent history of all radically resistant movements within the culture. Thus, a generation was able to rediscover them, in the turmoil of the Vietnam years, with the "shock of the new" still affixed. The particular ways in which the principles of Surrealism, among other movements, remained vital for Paz, we will discuss below.

Vanguardism is a historical fact, of course, a phenomenon of our century, its wars and political upheavals, its bourgeois hegemony, its tyrannies, its anti-colonial movements. Yet it is also a contended, discursive site, defined and historicized in multiple, conflictual ways according to the agendas and attitudes of the artists, cultural theorists, literary and social historians fashioning the narratives. Paz's own view is inseparable from his poetics. In fact, this alone may make his perspective, his poet's perspective, of special interest, since his sense of the Romantic origins of vanguardism, even of its occasional anti-romanticism, is, as Paz himself admits, widely if not unanimously shared. However, as a practicing poet of world acclaim, and, it must certainly be emphasized, a Mexican poet, he brings a singular point of view not only to vanguardism, toward which his own relationship is complicated, but to its place in relation to the poetry of past, present, and future. Paz's method is at once subjective in outlook and universalist in range. His thoughts tend to overflow, beyond any neatly bounded limit of the subject, in all senses of that word. In that regard, his approach mirrors his sense of the poem itself, and ultimately Paz is always, one way or another, writing poetics, writing it into the social, into the imaginary and into history, whether the history of our multiple futures or multiple pasts. And always, one need hardly add, in search of the present. The governing figure for such work is analogy, which is to say, similarity among things otherwise dissimilar. That in turn means that his work is by nature expansive, almost endlessly so. And that in another turn means that in a paper of such brevity as this, we can do little more than examine a few key figures and key moments and hope to illuminate a few distinctive features.

The first stirrings of vanguardism in the nineteenth century can be glimpsed here and there, at least retrospectively. They can be found in the theoretical matrices of German and English romantic theory, with its revolution of forms, its conflating of genres, its collapsing of life into art and art into life. They can be found in the circle of literary eccentrics around Nerval (*les bousingots,* "the rowdies"), walking their lobsters on the boulevards, eating ice-cream out of human skulls, holding literary seminars in the nude, while attempting to subvert the new, official aesthetic of "realism," as decreed by Louis Bonaparte's *apparatchiki,* soon after the Eighteenth Brumaire, history as farce. Two decades later, at the time of the Commune, Rimbaud and his circle would create the *Album Zutique,* mocking both authorship and high literary values, to say nothing of conventional morality. Perhaps the comic-nihilistic side can even be glimpsed in prototype among the "incohérents" of Montmartre, the Paris pranksters of ca. 1875-1905, with their empty canvasses, Eugène Bataille's "Mona Lisa with a Pipe," their cabarets, their shadow theaters and mock exhibitions. Difficult to imagine Pataphysics without such a precedent. Difficult to imagine Oulipo without Pataphysics. Yet the ground of an altered subjectivity and consciousness are to be found less, for Paz, in such epiphenomena than in Rimbaud's *alchimie du verbe;* in Nerval's oneiric defiance; in Baudelaire's double vision and his envisioning of the poem as the universe's double, a new cipher for the first code (the poet in Baudelaire's view becomes the translator of an unknown language into an unknowable one). One must add to the list Fourier's society of desire and Mallarmé's void, his dice-cast, and the silent explosion of the arrival in Paris, from Montevideo, of Isidore Ducasse, le Comte de Lautréamont. (He would die at 24 during the Siege.) These, to cite only a selection, will form the system of communicating vessels that in turn will enter and alter the dreams of certain twentieth-century writers and activists. In turn, their own preceding works will be forever altered. Hölderlin, Kleist, Novalis, Schiller, Shelley, Coleridge, and others will never again be the same.

Paul Celan, a poet to whom, within my very restricted knowledge, Paz nowhere refers,[1] has spoken of the poem as "a conversation... along the way." Paz, too, speaks often of the same thing, stressing the poem's dialogic nature, its completion not as an object but as a thing always in process. The poem converses first with its first reader, the poet him- or herself, as Other, then others in the world, the present world, and the world of the future, should the poem survive for a time. The conversation, of course, is also with figures from the past, such as poets who may be said by their works to read and modify and make place for the poem, even as the poem reconfigures the space of reception for their work and our sense of temporality. Returning now to Romantic theory, I hear it differently through the work of Paz.

Novalis, in his *Aphorisms and Fragments*: "Ordinary experience of the present connects past and future through contraction and limitation. This results in contiguity, a kind of crystallization brought about through reflection. But there is a kind of spiritual sense of the present that identifies the two by means of dissolution, and this mixture is the element, the atmosphere of the poet."[2]

---

[1] *Author's note*: Eliot Weinberger has found what he considers the only published reference by Paz to Paul Celan, in a 1973 memoir of the Mexican poet José Carlos Becerra. Paz recalls a dinner with Becerra in a Chinese restaurant on King's Road. Unexpectedly, they ran into Michael Hamburger, who joined them. "The conversation turned to Paul Celan and German poetry, from there to Hölderlin, and from Hölderlin to the relationships between madness and poetry" (*Obras completas (OC* from now on) 4:339).

[2] Novalis, "Aphorisms and Fragments," trans. Alexander Gelley, *German Romantic Literary Criticism*, ed. A. Leslie Willson (New York: Continuum, 1982), 67.

We sometimes forget the central place of wit, humor, irony in the theoretical writings of the Romantics. Paz reminds us that irony, ironic subversion, is the crucial antipode to analogy both for the Romantics and their inheritors. It is these two functions, in play, that lead to the totalizing claims for life as art and art as life, and for the endlessly dialectical becoming of the work. Friedrich Schlegel, in his *Dialogue on Poetry*, writes:

> Romantic poetry is a progressive universal poetry. Its mission is not merely to reunite all separate genres of poetry and to put poetry in touch with philosophy and rhetorics. It will, and should, now mingle and now amalgamate poetry and prose, genius and criticism, the poetry of art and the poetry of nature, render poetry living and social, and life and society poetic, poetize wit, fill and saturate the forms of art with solid cultural material of every kind, and inspire them with vibrations of humor. It embraces everything poetic, from the greatest system of art, which, in turn, includes many systems, down to the sigh, the kiss, which the musing child breathes forth in artless song... The romantic type of poetry is still becoming; indeed its peculiar essence is that it is always becoming and that it can never be completed. It cannot be exhausted by any theory, and only a divinatory criticism might dare to characterize its ideal. It alone is infinite, as it alone is free; and as its first law it recognizes that the arbitrariness of the poet endures no law above him. The romantic genre of poetry is the only one which is more than a genre, and which is, as it were, poetry itself; for in a certain sense all poetry is or should be romantic.[3]

We see in that final claim a characteristic that would be foregrounded by the Surrealists, that in a sense all true poetry "is or should be" surreal. By implication then, the movement, in essence, claims timelessness. Late in life, when Breton was asked whether Surrealism had waned, the question quite literally had no meaning to him, for Surrealism was the key that unlocked the limitless field of desire. In an essay on Breton, Paz writes, "I have no idea what the future of the Surrealist

---

[3] Friedrich Schlegel, "Selected Aphorisms from the Athenaeum (1798)," *German Romantic Literary Criticism*, ed. A. Leslie Willson (New York: Continuum, 1982), 126-127.

group will be; I am certain, however, that the current that has flowed from German Romanticism and Blake to Surrealism will not disappear. It will live a life apart; it will be the *other* voice."[4]

As Novalis and Paz may be said to read and thereby modify each other, in the same way the poem moves at once forward and backward, both as a form in time where a last word may propel us back to a first, and as form in the other time of poetry, that future-past where it oscillates. We are brought back to the notion of conversation, the open exchange, which is also the mutual acknowledgement, invention and imagining of the other. If Baudelaire offers to Walter Benjamin the definitive figure of the *flâneur*, and eventually thereby a new understanding of the Surrealists in the crowd, Benjamin at the same time creates Baudelaire anew for his time. The Baudelaire we have, has passed through Benjamin's hands. Nerval is the presiding figure of Breton's *Les Vases communicants*, the exemplar of the intertwining of day and night, reason and dream, thought and sensation, reason and madness, life and death. Yet he is also a vessel into which the time-traveller Breton will pour the stuff of his own oneiric projections. It is not a matter of influence in a given direction, or one and the other, but the alchemy itself, the mutual transfiguration which, for Paz, lifts the core of the vanguardist intervention out of time and literary fashion and into an other company. It is not of course uniquely a company of poets and visionaries. Rather it is the company of all who would willingly be so translated out of the self-same, the fixed, and into the open. It implies also the courage of losing one's self, of coming to nothing. So Keats, "The Sun, the Moon, the Sea and Men and Women who are creatures of impulse are poetical and have about them an unchangeable attribute —the poet has none; no identity..."[5] It is interesting to speculate that even a poet of such famously abiding ego as Breton, and one so fixed on realization of the resonant core of self, might agree.

Breton is, for Paz, the paradigmatic figure of vanguardism, as Surrealism can be said to offer the model against which other vanguards will inevi-

---

[4] *Alternating Current*, trans. Helen R. Lane (New York: Viking, 1973), 55.

[5] *Letters of John Keats*, ed. Robert Gittings (Oxford: Oxford University Press, 1975). Letter to Richard Woodhouse, October 27, 1818.

tably, justifiably or not, be compared. The cause of the latter must be found in the unprecedented international reach of the movement, whether through the nations of Western Europe, or east into what is now the Czech Republic and Romania, and west of course to the Caribbean and the states of the Spanish —and Portuguese-speaking Americas. In the case of Breton himself, Paz will state that it is above all Breton's commitment to "the language of passion— the passion of language," that attracted him. "To him", Paz writes, "the powers of the word were no different from the powers of passion, and passion, in its highest and most intense form, was nothing less than language in its wildest, purest form: poetry."[6]

Paz first kept company with Breton at what must have been a curious and troubling moment in the history of Surrealism. In adolescence, he recounts that at a moment of "isolation and great elation," he had come across what he would later learn was Chapter 5 of Breton's *L'Amour fou,* and that this, along with Blake's *The Marriage of Heaven and Hell,* had "opened the doors of modern poetry to me."[7] During the war, some years later, he had "met Benjamin Péret, Leonora Carrington, Wolfgang Paalen, Remedios Varo, and other Surrealists who had sought refuge in Mexico."[8] In Paris in 1946, he met Péret again, who took him to the Café de la Place Blanche where Breton often held court.

Arriving in Paris at that moment, Paz encountered a Surrealist group much altered from its earlier years. Aragon and Eluard had long since defected to the Stalinist camp. Soupault, Desnos, and many others had wearied of Breton's iron-fisted control of the movement and departed, or else had been excommunicated for various heresies. Breton himself was under attack from Tzara and others for having the temerity to judge the Occupation from exile, "from high atop the Statue of Liberty," as Tzara phrased it, with striking mean-spiritedness. Replacing earlier generations in the Surrealist camp, as Mark Polizzotti relates in his biography of Breton,[9] were now such younger figures as "Alain Jouffroy; philosopher and sociologist Nora Mitrani; Stanislav Rodanski, a scholar

---

[6] *Alternating Current, op. cit.,* 47.
[7] *Ibid.,* 53.
[8] *Ibid.,* 54.
[9] Mark Polizzotti, *Revolution of the Mind* (New York: Farrar, Straus and Giroux, 1995), 544.

of Hegel and Tibetan yoga; poets Yves Bonnefoy and Claude Tarnaud; and Henri and No Seigle, painters who worked in collaboration." It has usually been assumed that this was an unfortunate moment to associate with Surrealism, for evident reasons. Yet I would suggest that for Paz it was a most useful time. The principles of Surrealism were in flux and undergoing adjustment to post-war political, social, and artistic conditions. Breton's control was certainly weakening, to the advantage, I think, of the younger members. Most of all, however, he was under increasing, often virulent attack. Had Paz associated himself with Breton at a moment of acceptance and adulation, the gesture would have been less meaningful. Instead, he was able to witness Surrealism under assault, as it had been in its earlier years. I would also imagine he was never to forget the rhetoric of the Stalinists and the Sartreans as it filled the air with accusations and admonitions during that time.

Breton is celebrated by Paz less in terms of historical vanguardism itself or the technical elements of the Surrealist program. For Paz, Breton is a quest figure, free of the morality of Christendom, in search of the "originary word," when language and thought were one. Automatic writing is downgraded by Paz as a "method" for writing poems (the trap into which so many aspiring Surrealists fell), and is instead praised as representing "the belief that speaking and thinking are the same thing. Man does not speak because he thinks; he thinks because he speaks." Once again, we confront both the Romantic paradigm and *l'alchimie du verbe*. The poem overcomes time, even as we die into time. In the face of instrumental reason, the poet steeps him- or herself (invariably "him" among the Surrealist poets) in a magical practice that will dream of restoring a lost unity. We must not forget Breton's sincere, if somewhat exoticist, reverence for Mexico as itself a magic site, a hieroglyph of the lost Book. Breton, then, represents analogy in its transhistorical power. That Paz chooses to disregard or deny Breton's arrogance and occasional self-caricature, his replication of some of the worst aspects of the discourse of power, and his hand in the often farcical political machinations within the movement, is understandable and perhaps necessary. Breton is meant to exemplify the tragi-comic artistic figure caught in the double bind of magic and revolution, two faces of death. With *Les Vases communicants*, Breton offers Paz one of his central metaphors, one he will expand well beyond Breton's initial meanings. He also offers a text where an oddly resistant critical prose is set beside the narratives of dreams and objective chance. It is a text where dream and action, night and day, are not opposed, but interpenetrate to create an active world of poetry. As always, Breton is interrogating the poet's domain of liberty. At the end, truth appears at the dark window, "its hair streaming with light." It is a vision of the vessels united. Breton, for Paz, is Mount Analogue.

If Breton is the Master of Analogy, then Duchamp is the Metaironic Master of Irony. He responds to Breton's fire with coolness and distance, to Breton's interventionism with inactivity. He is Rimbaud's refusal of labor, as well as Bartleby. To Breton's judgments, Duchamp responds by suspending judgment, sometimes by a wire from the ceiling, sometimes between panes of glass. By means of the eye and the word, he annihilates the ocular and the verb. By means of the gaze, he opens the gaze to itself. Passing through the great Arensberg collection at the Philadelphia Museum of Art, we confront a sequence of stoppages, at once termini, endings, and measurements or ratios with no basis other than chance, and no necessary end in sight. Stoppages without end. If he is a Surrealist at all, he is one without portfolio, without papers, the singular in the face of Breton's many, the exception. If Breton spent a lifetime denying he was making art, then Duchamp spent a lifetime cultivating an art of denial itself, denial of the hand and eye and object, while often secretly constructing, by hand, his objects of denial. The aesthetic is displaced from matter onto thought, onto speculation itself, if I may be permitted an obvious pun (and Duchamp was a great fan of the obvious pun). Each of his works enfolds and embraces contradiction. To Paz, Duchamp mirrors Mallarmé, in the use of silence, of course, but also in the way both "turned criticism into myth and negation into [a provisional] affirmation."[10] "Duchamp, critic of the subject who looks and of the object looked at..."[11] For Paz, he is the necessary Other to Breton, on "the axis of erotic affirmation and ironic negation." He is the final point of Romantic irony, the moment of closure that we now

---

[10] *Marcel Duchamp or The Castle of Purity*, unpaginated.

[11] *Children of the Mire: Poetry from Romanticism to the Avant-Garde*, trans. Rachel Phillips (Cambridge, Mass.: Harvard UP 1974). 112.

can see also as (perhaps an ultimate Duchampian irony) the opening of a path in artistic exploration for the final years of the century.

Two other essential, vanguardist precursors must be mentioned here, one a poet of sky, the other, as Paz says, a poet of earth. Vicente Huidobro was born into a wealthy family in Santiago, Chile, in January of 1893. His early work was profoundly influenced by the Modernismo of Darío, but by his second book he was (apparently) already experimenting with the calligram. (There is significant scholarly controversy over the provenance of that first edition.) After four more youthful books, tired of "the senseless mockeries, the unbreathable air," he left for Buenos Aires. As he writes, "It was there that they baptized me a Creationist for having said in my lecture that the first condition of the poet is to create, the second to create, and the third to create." There he published his first book of Creationist poems, *El espejo de agua* (*The Mirror of Water*). From there he sailed for Paris, where he arrived toward the end of 1916, and where he immediately fell in with Apollinaire and various of the Cubists. In 1916 and 1917, with Apollinaire and Reverdy, he published the influential review *Nord-Sud*, before moving on once again, to Madrid, where he established a salon. In Madrid, he published two books, *Ecuatorial* and *Poemas árticos*. As Paz notes, "With them the Spanish avant-garde commenced." His presence in Madrid, along with Borges (stopping over on his way home to Argentina from Switzerland), was at least in part responsible for the birth of Ultraism. The books and statements of this time, including the various Paris periods, are strongly marked by the influence of Reverdy and Apollinaire. The work of this stage is remarkable for its precocity and its skilled assimilation of an advanced idiom, its casting off of provincialism. At the same time, it is a body of work clearly inflected by Europe, whereas *Altazor* (1919-1931) is unmistakeably a flight and a parachute descent into the New World. From the beginning of Canto V:

> Here begins the unexplored territory
> Round on account of the eyes that behold it
> Profound on account of my heart
> Filled with probable sapphires
> Sleepwalkers' hands

And aerial burials
Eerie as the dreams of dwarfs
Or the branch snapped off in the infinite
The seagull carries to its young

(trans. Eliot Weinberger)

Writes Paz, "Not a language of earth but of aerial space…Words lose their meaningful weight and become not signs but traces of an astral catastrophe."[12] The debt with Europe has been settled.

Huidobro's dark twin, his Other, is surely César Vallejo, born in 1892 in Santiago de Chuco, an Andean town in north-central Peru. In his introduction to *The Complete Posthumous Poetry*, Clayton Eshleman informs us that Vallejo's grandmothers were both Chimu Indians, his grandfathers Spanish Catholic priests. His first book, *Los heraldos negros* (1919), is very much within the tradition of *Modernismo*, yet his second, *Trilce*, published in Lima in 1922, is like nothing that had come before. Its stammerings, wrenched syntax, neologisms, and sheer viscerality remain emblematic of the singularity and estrangement that would mark Vallejo's entire poetic life. Each poem in *Trilce* feels like a fevered, incomplete reassemblage of scattered limbs. His work as a whole is a desperate act of internalization. It seems to sum up the agony of a fractured post-colonial consciousness (with its ancient echoes), where the body itself has always already been sacrificed, yet where desire continues to survive as a consuming force.

In 1923, under threat of imprisonment for reasons that remain somewhat obscure, Vallejo would depart from Lima for Paris. There he would meet Juan Gris and Juan Larrea, and Huidobro. Yet, often desperately poor, his experience there could not have been more unlike that of Huidobro. He maintained an acute mistrust of vanguardist circles and the "pseudo-new," though his own work seems to almost magically internalize and, as Paz says, "transmute" the "international forms of the avant-garde." Late in the decade, he took up the study of Marxism and began to teach in workers' cells. Yet his poetry, unlike Neruda's at points,

---

[12] *Ibid.*, 153.

never becomes a conduit for doctrine or ideology. It is too resistant, too ungovernable, and too internal. Its passionate negation is the necessary counterpoint to Huidobro's "miraculous fountain," his "ecstatic bird," and his "dawn with the hope of aeroplanes." Though Vallejo would never return to Peru, dying in Paris in 1938, it could also be said that he never left. Like Huidobro (whom he is so unlike), he assimilated European forms in order to escape both provincialism and assimilation. The two might be said to have imagined the sky and the ground of the coming poetry. The parallels as well as the differences with the experience of Paz and European vanguardism are too striking to ignore and almost too obvious to need much elaboration.

The founding significance and influence of such figures on the poetics of Paz, and what we might call the project of Paz, is unquestionable. From Breton he learned the primacy of desire, the dynamic of reason and non-reason, and a particular relationship to rhetorical figures and the image without which the following, for example, would not be possible:

> The downpour comes into your dreams
> green hands and black feet
> wheeling around the stone
> throat of the night
> tying your body
> a sleeping mountain
> The downpour raves
> between your thighs
> soliloquy of stones and water[13]

Through Duchamp, Paz reasserted the contemporary, critically subversive force of irony. Breton's nearness; Duchamp's distance. Breton's heat; Duchamp's cool. The example of Huidobro and Vallejo is less one of strict poetic influence (though that could use discussion), and more one of example: of how the forms and discoveries of international vanguardism can be profitably ingested without loss of cultural particularity.

---

[12] Fragment of *Storm*, from *Salamander: The Collected Poems of Octavio Paz, 1957-1987*, ed. Eliot Weinberger (New York; New Directions, 1991), 119.

(Parallels in the United States might include the influence of Apollinaire on William Carlos Williams and Louis Zukofsky, and of the Surrealists on Frank O'Hara and John Ashbery —many more could be cited.)

Yet Paz's relationship to vanguardism, both as poet and critic, is anything but a simple one. It makes no sense, first of all, to think of Paz as a pure vanguardist himself, if the term is to retain any meaning at all. He is not a poet of coteries (this is not to me necessarily a derogatory term), despite his lifetime's multiple cultural and political interventions and controversies. He became, in his lifetime, a nation's representative poetic voice. For a vanguardist, such a position seems to me unthinkable and self-cancelling. And finally, of course, his own poetic and cultural perspective stretched well beyond any given program, indeed, beyond any one historical moment. He freely critiqued both vanguardist left utopianism and the fascist sympathies of certain Anglo-American modernists. He says the following of the post-war period in Spanish-American poetry, the time when he published *Libertad bajo palabra* (1949) and *¿Águila o Sol?* (1951), the time that would soon be followed by publications from Nicanor Parra, Jaime Sabines, Roberto Juarroz and many others:

> The beginning: a clandestine, almost invisible action. At first almost nobody paid attention to it. In a certain sense it marked the return of the avant-garde. But a silent, secretive, disillusioned avant-garde. Another avant-garde, self-critical and engaged in solitary rebellion against the academy which the first avant-garde had become. It was not a question of inventing, as in 1920, but of exploring. The territory which attracted these poets was neither outside nor inside. It was the zone where external and internal merge: the zone of language. Theirs was not an aesthetic preoccupation; for these young men language was, simultaneously and contradictorily, their destiny and their choice. Something given and something we make —and which makes us.[14]

It is a territory, then, of a very real ambiguity and uncertainty, a moment after, after both the war and the time of the historical avant-gardes, and also a beginning. "A silent, secretive avant-garde," is in one real sense, of course, an absolute contradiction in terms, as Paz is well

---

[14] *Children of the Mire...*, op. cit., 160.

aware. Yet it is perhaps only contradiction and paradox which make sense, as evidence of the Holocaust and of Stalinist depravities become public knowledge, and the atomic bomb prefigures apocalypse.

As a critic, a "partial critic," Paz performs what seems to me a two-fold operation on the historical vanguards. He places them within an eternal tradition of innovation and renewal. The affirmation of Surrealist desire and magical-alchemical practice is seen as part of a continuum of change and invention stretching back beyond the Romantics, to the Renaissance, to the poets of *trobar*, and beyond to the sources of magical speech in prehistory. Granting the historically particular nature of vanguardist formations, he at the same time denies them the poetic singularity, the never before and the never after, that was their initiatory impetus. They are recovered within the circulations of the song. This two-fold evaluation in turn frees him to inherit without having to join, and to inherit selectively. He jettisons, for example, not the political agency of the poet, but the particular illusions of both utopian and nihilistic worldviews. The historical dilemma of the double bind, magic or revolution, imagination or action, is displaced by the vision of the "other voice," whose time is the time of the poem, yet whose world is that of the present. The time of the poem, its play of difference and recurrence, is in itself a projection of community, and perhaps of utopia. Paz builds that vision of the poem in time and poetic time on a characteristic set of paradoxes. He writes, "The time of the poem is inside history, not outside it." He continues,

> Text and readings are inseparable, and in them history and ahistory, change and identity, are united without being dissolved. It is not a transcendence but a convergence. It is time which repeats itself and is unrepeatable, which flows without flowing: a time which turns back upon itself. The time of the reading is here-and-now: a now which happens any moment, and a here which exists anywhere. The poem is history and it is that something which rejects history in the very instant of affirming it.[15]

The poem, Paz seems to say, must have it both ways —or not at all.

---

[15] *Ibid,* 177.

THE LABERYNTH
OF THE ELEVEN SYLLABLES*

DAVID HUERTA

The formal selection of hendecasyllabic verse to channel the greatest poem of his so-called "early years" was, perhaps paradoxically, a question of fate for Octavio Paz. In his case, choosing and acquiescing to that fate were both acts —or both sides— of the poetic coin: a Mexican coin like those in circulation some years ago, with the eagle from the national seal on one side and the sun over a pre-Hispanic pyramid on the other. His use of this type of verse could be attributed to both historical and formative motives: a choice explained by Paz's admiring passion for the stoic sonnets of Francisco de Quevedo and the eight-line stanzas of Gongora's "Polifemo."[1] On the other hand, halfway through his life, just as he was about to end his youth in order to usher in "the violent season" —in other words, the solid yet ardent summer of his maturity— classical meter seemed to impose itself with all the vigor of a Dantean recapitulation. The same verse that distinguishes the great poems of the Golden Age of Spain was to him, at that juncture in his poetic work, the ideal vessel in which to pour the images of profound reflection on his life's experience.

Now we know —sadly, for that knowledge is inferred from the facts surrounding his death— that the poem *Sunstone*[2] was written and published at mid-life: nothing less than the Dantesque *nel mezzo del cammin*. The greatest poet of medieval Christendom was bearing in mind the canonical sum of the age of a man (the 70 years a life should last, according to the Scriptures) when he told us allegorically, in the *Divine Comedy*, of what befell him at age 35; Octavio Paz, who was 84 years old when he died in April 1998, wrote *Sunstone* and brought it to light

---

* All footnotes are by the translators and do not appear in David Huerta's original Spanish text.
  [1] Luis de Góngora y Argote, *The Fable of Polyphemus and Galatea*, trans. Miroslav John Hanak (New York: P. Lang, 1988).
  [2] *The Collected Poems of Octavio Paz, 1957-1987*, ed. Eliot Weinberger (New York: New Directions, 1991) 13-35.

around 1957, that is to say, around the age of 42. This is the first and last similarity between Dante's work and the Mexican poem of 1957. Octavio Paz's is a fully modern poem, written, curiously enough, in classical form. It is a lengthy poem, not unlike other verse written in Spanish during the 20th century: *Muerte sin fin* by José Gorostiza,[3] *Altazor* by Vicente Huidobro,[4] *Catedral salvaje* by César Dávila Andrade,[5] and *Canto General* by Pablo Neruda[6] come to mind.

The hendecasyllabic tercets of the *Comedy* consecrated what was known in 16th-century Spain as "el modo itálico."[7] The lesson of Francesco Petrarch, and to a lesser degree that of works idealizing the classic Greco-Latin past, such as Jacopo Sannazzaro's *Arcadia*, determined the formal choices that, in a short time, and thanks to a few men of genius (Garcilaso de la Vega, Fernando de Herrera, San Juan de la Cruz, Fray Luis de León), would develop great expressive possibilities as well. The golden circle of Spanish poetry would reach its pinnacle in the first half of the 17th century through the works of Francisco de Quevedo, Lope de Vega, and Luis de Góngora y Argote. During the second half of the 1600s, the work of Pedro Calderón de la Barca would close the circle on two literary centuries.

The work of Francisco de Quevedo (1580-1645) —impregnated with Senecan stoicism in his sonnets on the brevity of life, veined with a popular flavor in his poems of lesser meters, always lively and of extraordinary intelligence— would constitute for the Mexican Octavio Paz a permanent lesson in poetic fidelity. Three centuries later, in a country on the other side of the Atlantic Ocean, the Quevedian vein of golden poetry would find its radiant prolongation in Mexico, a prolongation that implied, of course, expansion and embellishment.

The labyrinth of eleven syllables —hendecasyllabic verse— has a history and a series of peculiarities that are well worth noting. The pace of octosyllabic verses that predominate in volumes of romance poetry contrasted with the heavy frame of the solemn and monotonous dodecasyllable of Juan de Mena, "poet of the Spanish pre-Renaissance," as

---

3 *Death Without End* (Austin: University of Texas Press, 1961).
4 *Altazor, or A Voyage in Parachute*, trans. by Eliot Weinberger (St. Paul, MN: Graywolf Press, 1988).
5 There is no available translation into English of *Catedral salvaje*.
6 Trans. Jack Schmitt (Berkeley: University of California Press, 1993).
7 *El modo itálico*: Italian lyric meters and strophe forms.

he is described by María Rosa Lida de Malkiel in her monumental work
on the subject. During the emperor's wedding feast in 1526, Venetian
ambassador Andrea Navaggiero suggested to a friend of his, the Catalan
courtier Juan Boscán, that Spanish poets adopt the Italian model: prin-
cipally, the tercet, the sonnet, and the eight-line stanza in the strophe;
eleven syllables with an ambulatory accent in the verse —a verse liberated from what Fernando Lázaro Carreter called "the coercion of the ictus," that is to say, the obligatory nature of accents in a fixed position—
a flexible, fluid, vigorous verse that was ductile yet solid. This gave
them a leeway inconceivable with the "arte mayor"[8] verse inherited
from the poets of the court of John the Second. Juan Boscán adopted
"el modo itálico" and did something even better: he invited his friend
Garcilaso de la Vega to accompany him on this literary adventure. De
la Vega brought extraordinary nobility to Spanish poetry, elevating it to
new heights with a dazzling yet small body of work. His example was
followed by, among others, the mystic San Juan de la Cruz, who
rewrote some of the most moving Garcilasian passages "in divine fashion." All of this ultimately signified the naturalization in Spain of
eleven-syllable Italian verse in its wide array of forms. From the initial
15th century efforts of the Marquis of Santillana to the Baroque splendor of Gongora's *Fábula de Polifemo y Galatea*, the Spanish hendecasyllable acquired its definitive shape. One of the heights it reached was
accounted for by a great deal of the poetry written by a nun from the
Order of Saint Jerome in New Spain, Sor Juana Inés de la Cruz, during the second half of the 17th century. It is well known that Sor Juana's greatest poem, *Primero Sueño*,[9] is an explicit imitation of the poetry
of Góngora and particularly of the *Soledades*,[10] the culmination of the
poetic art of the so-called "Andalusian swan."

  In Spanish poetry —in the very practice of writing verse— the adop-
tion of the *modo itálico* would mean respite or liberation from the struggle between the iron-clad predominance of the accent, on one hand, and

---

[8] *De arte mayor*: a meter of obscure, probably Galician origin, rhythmic rather than syllabic, each
line has four beats and ten, eleven, or twelve syllables.

[9] *Poems, Protests and a Dream*, trans. Margaret Sayers Peden (New York: Penguin, 1997).

[10] Trans. Gilbert F. Cunninghem (Baltimore: Johns Hopkins UP, 1968).

syllabic accommodation within each enunciation, on the other. Unlike the dodecasyllables of Juan de Mena (for example, the first of his *Labyrinth of Fortune*: "To the most prepotent Don Juan the Second"),[11] the hendecasyllable is an uneven verse; because of this, the accents in the verse of eleven syllables can be distributed much more freely, with the only obligatory accent (ictus) falling on the next to last syllable, i.e., the tenth.

Of course, not all lines with eleven syllables are hendecasyllables; the forms depend on the best —the most euphonious— placement of the accents. But this permits the modification of accentuation from one line to the next, without losing the prosodic and rhythmic values —preserved in the unchanging count: always eleven syllables— of this form and its diverse strophic combinations. The struggle between accent and syllable as a decisive element in the rhythm of Spanish verse was thus abolished or resolved: within the syllabic count of the "*modo itálico*," accents changed their position, thereby permitting an expressive force laden with possibilities.

The origins of the hendecasyllable can be traced back to the acatalectic line —in technical terms, acatalectic iambic trimeter— found in Horace's *Beatus ille*. Beyond a doubt, the prosodic and poetic revolution in Italy not only revived a classic form by shifting our focus towards the past; turning its gaze towards the future, it also opened a thousand doors in terms of the instrumental dexterity available to poets. The hendecasyllable made the golden works of Spanish poetry shine: from the melancholic gallantry of Garcilaso de la Vega to the noble effusion of Francisco de Quevedo. In other words, it was a stupendous formal instrument of unique literary abundance, unsurpassed in the history of the Spanish language.

In a poem from the book *Sombra del paraíso*, published in 1944 by the Sevillian Vicente Aleixandre, lies the phrase that gave its title to Paz's poem:

> Stone of boundless sun: a world entire,
> and at its rim the frailest nightingale bewitches it…[12]

<hr />

[11] There is no English translation available.
[12] Trans. Hugh A. Harter (Los Angeles: University of California Press, 1987), 173. The first verse reads in the original: "Piedra de sol inmensa: entero mundo".

The poem is entitled "Farewell to the Fields" and has little or nothing to do with the pre-Hispanic, calendrical, cosmic connotations that the same phrase holds in the poem by Octavio Paz; but there it is —a coincidence, but a significant one nonetheless. In the same year of 1944, at age thirty, the Guanajuatan poet Efraín Huerta, a contemporary of Paz in the strictest sense, having like him been born in 1914— his companion, likewise, in the schoolyard quarrels of the National Preparatory School and in his first steps towards leftist political militancy —would publish one of the vital books of modern Mexican poetry: *Los hombres del alba (The Men of Dawn).*[13] In that same year, Dámaso Alonso, the most important Gongorian exegete of the first half of our century, would present in Madrid his heartrending book of poetry entitled *Hijos de la ira (Children of Wrath),* so similar to that of Efraín Huerta in its accent as well as, in turn, its tone of desperate imprecation, desolation, and strange nobility, so evocative of the Old Testament. The times apparently demanded extreme poetic testimonies. Vicente Aleixandre and Dámaso Alonso belonged to the so-called Generation of 1927, built around the 300th anniversary celebrations of the death of Don Luis de Góngora. This Spanish generation corresponds, give or take a few years, to the Mexican generation of the *Contemporáneos,* in many ways the masters of poets like Paz and Huerta who were born during the second decade of the century. They are generations that fully experienced the cutting edge of modernity: in Spain, beyond the Generation of '98; and in Latin America, after the modernism that spread following the final third of the 19th century, as a result of Nicaraguan poet Rubén Darío's work.

The determination to write a modern poem in a classical meter, like the hendecasyllable, reveals an accomplished and demanding will to form. The verse of *Sunstone* is scattered verse, without rhyme; however, it is not free but rather blank verse, thus named for its lack of consonance; each line is carefully measured, and the variety of accentuation is also closely guarded. It is important to point out that the same care a poet takes in seeking out and adjusting the rhyme of an entirely classical poem must be taken by the poet who writes in blank verse in order to avoid the rhymes.

---

[13] There is no available English translation.

Octavio Paz tells us that during the composition of this poem he lived moments similar to those of a "trance": he felt the lines of the poem were "dictated" to him while he walked in the street or sat in his office. This can or must have a reasonable explanation: once the modulation of eleven-syllable lines was acquired and internalized, so to speak, any one of them would "call" to the rest in such a way that the series of lines would go on building themselves, or writing themselves —mentally at times. Still, we cannot help but be impressed by the emotional testimony of an author habitually so reserved in regards to his literary working methods: *Sunstone* was, from the very moment of its conception, an exceptional piece, and it was appreciated as such by the poet Paz as he advanced in its composition.

The poem has 584 lines, all of them written in lower-case; some split more or less at the caesura, in such a way that the second hemistich is left "dangling" typographically, on the right-hand side of the page. The poem is scrupulously punctuated. The first six lines are repeated identically at the end of the text: thus, an allusion is made to the possibility of rereading the poem and of seeing or understanding *Sunstone* as a ring of sorts. They might indicate, according to Paz, "the end of one cycle and the beginning of another," not unlike the calculation of time used among the ancient Mexicans, for whom the conjunction of the planet Venus and the Sun signaled a moment of regeneration —nothing less than the regeneration or resurrection of time itself. The number of verses is equal to that of the days in the orbit (or "synodic revolution") of Venus, the star of dawn and dusk, and from that occurrence evolves all its meaningful density on several levels of imagery. In the first, 1957 edition of *Piedra de sol* (Tezontle Collection, Fondo de Cultura Económica), there was a note —which disappeared in later editions or appeared incomplete— in which Paz offered the reader curious facts about the poem.

Sunstone is not, evidently, a "circular poem," despite the allusions to cycle in which it abounds. Many years would pass before Octavio Paz would compose a poem which really can be said to be circular: the so-called *Poema circulatorio*,[14] written on the interior walls of the Museum

---

[14] There is no available English translation.

of Modern Art in Mexico City, making a full turn inside that round building. Many readers and critics are tempted to describe, however inaccurately, this Pazian composition then as "a circular poem." It is true, nevertheless, that *Sunstone* is a poem comprised largely of allusions to the symbolic, astronomical, and vital realities of cycles that constitute both cosmic and individual existence. A fundamental role is played in all this by the epigraph taken from the French poet Gérard de Nerval's (1808-1855) poem *Arthémis* belonging to the cycle of the *Chimères* which appeared one year before his death. Paz translated this poem twice. Here are the two versions of this passage:

> First version:
> Vuelve otra vez la Trece —¡y es aún la Primera!
> Y es la única siempre —¿o es el solo momento?
> ¡Díme, Reina, tú eres la primera o la última?
> ¿Tú eres, Rey, el último?, ¿eres el solo amante?

> Second version:
> Vuelve otra vez la Trece —¡y es aún la Primera!
> Y es la única siempre —¿o es el único instante?
> ¿Díme, Reina, tú eres la inicial o postrera?
> ¿Tú eres, Rey, el último? ¿eres el solo amante?[15]

---

[15] Translator Eliot Weinberger chose to leave the epigraph from "Arthémis" in its original French:

> La treizième revient... c'est encor la première;
> et c'est toujours la seule—ou c'est le seul moment;
> car es-tu reine, ô toi, la première ou dernière?
> es-tu roi, toi le seul ou le dernier amant?

The following version was found in English:

> The Thirteenth comes back... is again the first,
> And always the only one—or the only time:
> Are you then queen, O you! the first or last?
> You, the one or last lover, are you king?...

Gerard Nerval, *The Chimeras*, Trans. Peter Jay (Redding Ridge, Connecticut: Black Swan Books, 1984) 25.

In each of the first lines of this initial quatrain of the Nervalian sonnet, an hour is spoken of: an experiential dimension of time. The remaining two lines speak of persons who are both royal and real: the lovers. The double theme of *Sunstone* is concentrated in this epigraph: love within time, its fundamental role in direct experience. Naturally, this generalization does not exhaust the multitudinous themes undertaken by the poem; but at the very least it is indicative of a denser, more noteworthy nucleus of meaning.

Some of those who read Nerval disagree with the speculation that the thirteenth hour (one in the morning or one in the afternoon) is the first hour: wouldn't twelve midnight or noon be a better candidate for first hour? No: twelve is a nullified hour, a kind of suspended time, a non-time. The first or thirteenth hour is therefore the first, within this system of imagery or symbolism. All this has to do as well with the demise of love —the real or symbolic death of one's lover— and is fully present in the Nervalian spirit of *Arthémis*. Jeanine Moulin, one of the major exegetes of the French poet, notes that Nerval, during his famous voyage to the Orient, read an inscription in Latin on a Syrian tomb where a great lord was buried alongside his three lovers, whom he loved equally; according to what can be gleaned from the triple epitaph, he was unable to determine which of them should be positioned foremost or given preeminence. The theme can most definitely be traced back —Moulin indicates— to the Apocalypse of Saint John: God, the Almighty, says he is the Alpha and the Omega, the beginning and the end of all things. At any rate, the dimension of time presents itself here as an eternal or incessant return to the beginning. The main theme of *Sunstone* is underlined thus: love in time, lovers submerged in the chance occurrences of the past and the passage of time.

The poem opens with a long, impersonal presentation of the poetic treatment of natural realities:

> a crystal willow, a poplar of water,
> a tall fountain the wind arches over,
> a tree deep-rooted yet dancing still,
> a course of a river that turns, moves on,

doubles back, and comes full circle,
forever arriving {...}[16]

    As far as I know, no one has indicated the similarity between the beginning of *Sunstone* and a passage from the *Soledades*, in the version reproduced by Dámaso Alonso in his 1927 edition. "Góngora," explains Robert Jammes, the great Gongorist of our time, in his monumental edition of the *Soledades* (1994), "reduced these thirteen lines to six in order to satisfy the objections of Pedro de Valencia..."[17] In Dámaso Alonso's 1927 edition of the *Soledades*, however, these lines appear to be reproduced in keeping with Góngora's first version, before the corrections of the severe humanist Valencia were made. This curious description of the precarious course of a river, taken from the manuscript that belonged to Antonio Rodríguez-Moñino, is reproduced below:

> ...Orladas sus orillas de frutales,
> si de flores, tomadas no a la roca,
> derecho corre mientras no revoca
> los mismos autos el de sus cristales;
> huye un trecho de sí, alcánzase luego;
> desvíase y, buscando sus desvíos,
> errores dulces, dulces desvaríos
> hacen sus aguas con lascivo juego;
> engazando edificios en su plata,
> de quintas coronado, se dilata
> majestüosamente
> —en brazos divididos, caudalosos
> de islas, que paréntesis frondosos
> al periodo son de su corriente—
> de la alta gruta donde se desata...

---

[16] *The Collected Poems of Octavio Paz, 1957-1987*, ed. Eliot Weinberger (New York: New Directions, 1991), 3.

[17] There is no available translation into English of Jammes' prologue.

Jammes itemizes the objections of Pedro de Valencia, a keen and erudite reader who doubtless merited Góngora's respect, inasmuch as the poet incorporated nearly all of his corrections into the poem: Valencia "criticized two metaphors: that of the *autos*, which encloses an implicit comparison with a process (one that runs straight, i.e., following its normal course, while a court decision or *auto* does not revoke previous *autos*), and that of the islands that are included in the course of the river as parentheses of an oratory period." Joseph de Pellicer, another Gongorist critic, adopted the early version that Alonso reproduced in 1927 with two exceptions: *provoca* in place of *revoca* and *altos* in place of *autos*. Edward M. Wilson, admirable translator of the *Soledades* into English, rendered it as follows —with some blunders due to the muddled transferral of the text— having judged that the early Gongorist version was aesthetically superior to the one corrected at the behest of Pedro de Valencia:

Its borders lined with many an orchard lawn,
if not with flowers stolen from the Dawn,
the stream flows straight while it does not aspire the heights with its own
crystals to attain; flies from itself to find itself again, is lost, and searching
for its wanderings, both errors sweet and sweet meanderings the waters
make with their lascivious fire; and linking buildings in its silver force, with
bowers crowned, majestically flows into abundant branches—there to wind
amid isles than green parentheses provide
in the main period of the current's course;
from the high cavern where it first arose...

Thanks to Edward M. Wilson, iambic pentameter, the canonical verse in English, interprets here the spirit of the Gongorist silva with its resonant alternating hendecasyllables and heptasyllables, always rhymed; a model followed by Sor Juana Inés de la Cruz in *Primero sueño*, although in her poem there are a few unrhymed lines. The *silva* —an alternation of heptasyllables and hendecasyllables— was the closest approximation to free verse in the Golden Age that, for so many reasons, concludes with Calderón de la Barca and with Sor Juana Inés de la Cruz on either side of the Atlantic, on the European and American shores, respectively.

The similarity between this Gongorist passage and the beginning of *Sunstone* seems self-evident to me; by which I do not mean to say that the *Soledades* should necessarily be considered as one of the "sources" for the Mexican poem. Despite Paz's objections to the *Soledades* —he preferred the octaves of *Polifemo*— it seems to me that this is the trail that leads to his reading of the 1927 Dámaso Alonso edition of Góngora's great poem. They are comparable rivers that advance, are diverted, then continue to follow their course. The beginning of *Sunstone* seems clearly Gongorist to me: a salient concordance, many centuries later and on the other side of the Atlantic Ocean, between Quevedo —so admired by Paz— and Góngora, accomplished through a Mexican poem.

The naturalist impersonality of this principle concludes in line 32 ("the world is visible through your body"), where the second person, or perhaps the first, emerges and is reinforced with the appearance of an "I" in line 34: "I travel my way through galleries of sound." The drama of the poem —understood as poetic action— then begins to unfold over the course of more than five hundred lines.

Sunstone gradually becomes, at the pace of the lines and the hypnotic rhythm they create, a literally seductive rhythm (that is to say, one that takes us somewhere else: an authentic vision). All that the poet sees and puts into words is transfigured, as Paz himself said brilliantly in line 334: "all is transformed, all is sacred," having pronounced with singular gravity and only two rhythmic accents, on the sixth and on the tenth syllables, a euphonic deed well worth noting for its sensory richness. The experience of love shows its lunar and solar facets: blood, pain, oblivion, memory, light, shadow: the world, ultimately, its objects and phenomena, becomes an extraordinary and palpitating diorama.

Before the poetic vision of nature, personal —or individual— dramas are set alongside historic tragedies: the death of Socrates, the assassination of Francisco I. Madero, the visions of Brutus preceding the Battle of Philippi, evocations of the *Oresteia*, Churruca's wounds at Trafalgar, and the ideological horrors of the 20th century. Everything, all human experience lived and thought, is placed beneath an intense beam of light and projected onto the poetic mind of the "violent season" in its summer of vital and artistic maturity. *Sunstone* is the poem that concludes *La estación violenta (The Violent Season)*[18] of 1958, a book named, to be sure, after a line of Guillaume Apollinaire's. Traditionally, criticism has considered this long poem as a kind of hinge that separated while at the same time uniting the "first" and "second" stages of Octavio Paz's poetry. Now we know that *Sunstone* remains at the center of his life and his literary work, like the center of a labyrinth that continues to illuminate us in the midst of the "nightmare of History."

Translated by Tanya Huntington and Alvaro Enrigue

---

[18] There is no full translation available of *La estación violenta.*

THE WORK OF OCTAVIO PAZ, FACING THE NEW MILLENIUM

VERÓNICA VOLKOW

Poetry, Paz writes in *The Other Voice*, is "time in its purest form," and he describes a verbal stream that ascends and disappears into the air, at times sculpted by rhythms, accents or unchanging syllables, at times simply impelled by a breath or an emotional melody. It is not even a river, the poem, as the river is dressed by two banks, while poetic discourse stands naked, alone, erect in the moment of time before it is gone. It is like a monument to that moment, the chiseled flow that remains.

Nothing is more nothingness than time, nothing could be more vacant while at the same time containing everything. The category of time might in fact compete with any of the *arkés* of the ancient Pre-Socratics, water, air, fire, or the undetermined *apeiron*, held to be the originating substances from which the cosmos was derived. It is like a blank page, time, where history is unraveled, the same page on which the course of the poem is inscribed. Time, as a shared substrate, approaches the act of living and writing in an equation which is not one of equality but rather of constant unfolding. There is no unity in time; there is dichotomy, transit, transformation, otherness, reader and poem, encounter and disencounter, solitude and eroticism. There is no god and his creature, there is only creation, perpetual creation manifested in a transfer of metaphors and rhythm, a play on the analogies that secretly arrange everything.

And it is time, more than the space of the physicist or geometrician, which shows us human reality in all its complexity. There are not just three, but four, five, six; the dimensions captured by the antennae of the poem are infinite. More so than architecture, poetry is constructed within the true dimensions of human occupation of the cosmos. Some of these dimensions are forms of time.

Poetry is a privileged time machine; it is a glass filled by the present, a perpetual present impregnated with all times, with the here and past, with the here and future, with the here and memory of all mankind, the street and the mythical *illo tempore*.

In the Bible, creation was the act of a verb which was manifested as it was pronounced: God is language. For Paz, before the verb there is time, and in order to understand the verb, the poem, the world, and being in the world, one must first understand time. Both his poetry and his poetic and political thought are shot through with vast reflections on time.

Paz is a thinker radically committed to modernity, while at the same time having completely assumed his role as a poet. Committed to the modern poetic tradition, he established his own: one of free —in a manner of speaking— criticism with regards to any tradition. This consubstantial critical dimension implies a break from the fidelity of a founding text, or the concept of an authorized model —be it divine or human— that dictates the final configuration of that which already exists. Modernity is open to a new liberty: the creation of man, starting with himself. That is why Paz seeks time, the nothingness that is time, behind his poetic work. Writing and the verb are a foundation, yes, but only because behind them, we fly through time. There is no cancellation of nothingness. Behind any construction whatsoever, there is liberty, there is nothingness. The beginning on which our time is founded, Paz writes, is not eternal truth, but rather the truth of change.

For the ancient Mexicans, time was the dimension that sustained everything in existence, and the *tlacuilos* were great wise men, knowledgeable about time. A contemporary Mexican poet, Paz also inherited this tradition from ancient Mexico. It is no accident that *Sunstone*, wheel of Mexica time, serves as the title of one of his most important poems. Here, the poet secretly begins what was once the journey taken by Quetzalcoatl through the circles of the underworld until the climactic moment of his resurrection. It is a very modern poem, but one which, for all its great freedom, repeats a mythic Pre-Hispanic cycle.

Also, the very wide, critical, Pazian vision of Western culture and history attentively experiences different forms relative to time. Primitive societies are sustained by a circular concept of time, the desire to return to an archetypal past. This return to a germinal, original moment vivifies the passage of time and of all creation.

Christianity introduces a linear concept of time —history does not repeat itself— and breaks with the imperative of returning to a chimerical Golden Age. A new category of time is inaugurated, Eternity, in which passage is abolished and opposites are reconciled. This new idea of time carries with it a new way of life, elevated to eternity.

Modernity emerges as a criticism of Christianity, and criticism will be its distinctive trait, its birthmark: "Everything the Modern Age represents," writes Paz, "has been the work of criticism, in the sense of a method of investigation, creation, and action. The key concepts of the Modern Age —progress, evolution, revolution, freedom, democracy, science, technology— had their origin in criticism."[1]

Modernity will exchange Christian eternity for an idealization of the future, which in turn becomes the most important tense. One must live, not for eternity but for the promise of tomorrow. The idea of time perfecting as it advances seems guaranteed by the indisputable tenets of evolution and progress.

The contradiction of the modern age consisted, he indicated, "in the attempts to build systems based not on an atemporal principle but on the principle of change."[2] In the political sphere, the positive manifestation of change was incarnated in the concept of Revolution, born out of myth as well as history. Revolution seeks the restoration of an original, Eden-like time in which there are no inequalities. However, it seeks the restoration of that Eden-like time not by magic or ceremony, but rather by the incorporation and imposition of rationality onto history.

In the domain of art, the exaltation of progress was manifested through the avant-garde, which continually celebrated its rupture with the immediate past. But, after the Second World War, we are left with a profusion of stereotypes both in literature and the other arts. There is an artistic eclecticism to which the name of postmodernity has been given. The ancient exchange of literature and art has been substituted with the modern world of finance, and this has affected both painters

[1] *The Other Voice: Essays on Modern Poetry*, trans. Helen Lane (New York, San Diego, London: Harcourt Brace Jovanovich, 1991), 33.
[2] *Children of the Mire: Poetry from Romanticism to the Avant-Garde*, trans. Rachel Phillips (Cambridge, MA: Harvard University Press, 1974), 26.

and writers, who find themselves compelled to fill the unifying standards of a prefabricated market.

Indeed, Paz was clairvoyant with regards to his diagnosis of the essential problematic of our time. We witnessed the breakdown of the essential concept of modernity, he observed, the vision of time as a linear succession oriented towards a better future, and the notion of change as a privileged form of succession through time. We live in the bankruptcy of progress.

And as for the critical intelligence that constitutes us, it has devoured itself in the end. Modernity founded itself on criticism, but criticism led to a permanent schism. Hegel exacerbated negation, and through dialectics attempted to find a cure for this schism that was once our cornerstone. But dialectics only resolves contradictions in order for them to emerge again. The last great Western philosophical system, Hegel's, "is a thought which sets itself up as a system only to split in two."[3] The spirit of opposition that provided the basis for our era will also one day become the cause of its demise, the poet predicted.

Modern poetry, born out of Romanticism, was a passionate and rebellious response to the dictatorship of Enlightenment reason in the 18th century. Romanticism was more than a change of style and language; it implied a revolution in our system of beliefs. It involved breaking with Greek and Latin tradition and seeking diverse roots in turn. It rejected the standard of classic beauty by exalting singular, bizarre beauty. With Romanticism begins the Western tradition of critical poetry.

It is within this Western, critical, poetic tradition that Paz's major essays and works of poetry are to be found. Poetry is our heritage, the Memory of humanity, while modern poetry is likewise the spearhead of modern critical thought:

> Only the moderns could be as wholly and heartrendingly antimodern as all our great poets have been. A modernity founded on criticism naturally secretes criticism of itself. Poetry has been one of the most energetic and vivacious manifestations of this criticism. However, its criticism has not been rational or philosophical, but rather passionate and in the name of realities

---

[3] *Ibid.*, 27.

ignored or denied by the Modern Age. Poetry has resisted modernity and by denying it, has revived it. Poetry has been its reply and its antidote.[4]

As a modern, critical poet Paz is radical, even belligerent. In *The Bow and the Lyre* he writes: "it is not possible to disassociate the poem from its pretensions of changing man without the risk of turning the poem into an inoffensive form of literature."[5] The author of *Libertad bajo palabra* took this transforming, critical role of poetry very seriously, to the degree of carrying it to what we might call monumental dimensions, in a symphonic dialogue that engages the main currents of Western thought. There is a revision in his work of the main voices that make up our tradition, a revision in which agile lucidity and the finest penetration are united by a great sensibility, where nuance does not elude the vast multitude of gazes. Although his intelligence quite often challenges us in the acrobatics of its unexpected twists and is capable of immersion in the most hermetic themes, it also surprises us in the virility of its commitment to clarity. It is an intelligence committed to a community of free individuals sustained by the logos. The logos creates community and works to build community as a reader is built, an "other" who is increasingly free and in charge of his options. Every real poem manufactures its reader, transforms him into another. And the work of Paz, never content with being merely read, is dedicated to transforming us.

As for our time, which is deteriorating and yet has scarcely begun, Paz enumerates the main problems liberalism and democracy have not been able to provide an answer to: for example, an important link has yet to be established between liberty and fraternity. Although liberal democracy is our most civilized form of society, liberalism exalted individuality and personal freedom while failing to provide a solution for the great isolation and solitude in which contemporary man lives. This translates both into the social sphere and our relationship with nature: we are incapable of healthy coexistence with nature.

Paz tells us that a generation of new ethics, new erotics, and new aesthetics for this new era is imperative. We will have to learn to live, not cen-

[4] Translator's note: The translation is mine. Helen Lane's English version of *The Other Voice* omits the paragraph where this quote was found in the original Spanish text.
[5] *The Bow and the Lyre*, trans. Ruth L.C. Simms (Austin: University of Texas Press, 1991), 102.

tered on future time —which, as it turns out, does not exist— but rather in the present. We must take into account that the *now* postulated by Paz is the privileged instant of poetic experience, that perpetual present in which all times coexist, a time impregnated with all our memory and possibilities. Faced by the tradition of rupture that was the avant-garde, Paz gave the name of "art" to the convergence between art and this new era and wrote:

> The poets of the modern age sought the principles of change; we poets of the age that is beginning seek the inalterable principle that is the root of all change… The poetry that is beginning now, without beginning, is seeking the intersection of times, the point of convergence. It asserts that between the cluttered past and the uninhabited future, poetry is the present… The present is manifest in presence, and presence is the reconciliation of the three times.[6]

Another great contemporary problem is that of the spiritual vacuum that manifests itself as a thinly disguised nostalgia of the sacred. A ubiquitous rationalism has attempted to abolish the experience of the sacred. However, the return of that which was repressed has encountered a dangerous symptom in the systematization of absolutist wisdom aspiring to control history and human behavior through the authority of old religious institutions. Poetry has felt both attracted and repelled by these constructions of critical thought, and together with the great revolutions it has set forth a history of love affairs and divorces, conversions and apostasies, fascinations and suicides that began during the last century. Confronted by a rationalism that takes pride in its conquests and efficacy, poetry has always presented the irrational side of man, the force of his darkest impulses, of archetypes and myths, of the unquenchable thirst for the sacred. Poetry continues to be seduced by the idea of revolution, but for reasons analogous to those that made the religious phenomenon attractive to it in the first place. "Neither philosophers nor revolutionaries can patiently tolerate the ambivalence of poets who see in magic and revolution two parallel but not mutually exclusive methods of changing the world."[7] This inclination towards the mythical and the religious has always been repudiated by those practical men, the revolutionaries.

---

[6] *Children of the Mire, op. cit.,* 57-58.
[7] *Ibid.,* 107.

On the other hand, poetry is not content with this solution to religion; it is faced by dogmas; it seeks to create new forms of the sacred. Many poets have not rejected Christianity, but rather situated it within a wider tradition in which different esoteric beliefs —alchemy, Kabbalah, gnosticism, theosophy— have played an essential role. If there is a religious belief among poets, it is that of analogy, wherein nature is conceived of as a "magical book" and objects become signs. God did not construct the world; rather, he pronounced it. The world is not a set of objects, but a set of signs; objects are in reality words. "Nature is a temple of living columns / that utter, at times, confusing words," as Baudelaire wrote.

Poetry has attempted to provide answers to the three great problems —lucidly analyzed by Paz— of the modern age: the exaltation of the future and a blind faith in progress; the difficulty in reconciling liberty with fraternity; and the spiritual vacuum with which critical reason has left us.

Poets never bought into the promise of future and progress, because poetry privileges an experience other than time: poetic time is analogous to mythical time. Mythical time is sustained by the personal experience of the return to a generating origin of the cosmos; that turning back towards the origin, that reviving return, is what permits the experience of creation, always the recreation of this original condition. The original time of creation, which can always be experienced again as the present, sustains the cosmos and provides its breath of life.

One of the most illuminating concepts found in the poetics of Paz is that of the perpetual present. The perpetual present is an extraordinary possibility offered to us by poetry. If rhythm is time with direction and intent, poetry is, above all things, the creation of a new time. On the one hand, the poem is time. It is a historical product, and its body of words unravels in an evanescent flow; but on the other hand, the poem creates the existence of another kind of time within time: the perpetual present. Through the poem, a fantastic time machine, we gain access to the perpetual present. It is a universe that lives always in the present, and when it is presented, it re-presents itself, in the sense that it makes itself present again. It not only makes itself present; it is present. The perpetual present is a dimension other than that of simple linear passage, condemned to disappear like the moment which proceeds towards the future and disappears in the past. The perpetual present is a time that encases all other times: it is the future, but a future which will be projected as the present; and it is also the past, because once the poem is written, it is the representation of a past, a past that has become present. Wherever the poem exists, it exists in the present. The poem transforms all time into the present.

As to this great problem of how to reconcile fraternity and liberty, which liberalism has left unanswered, poetry offers us the response of Rimbaud: *I is another*. Poetry is the journey of the "I", an experience that permanently questions one's own identity. In order to exist, the images of the poem reincarnate in us, in the others that are we, the readers. In turn, the experience of writing confronts us with the enigma of who is writing, of who is the other that speaks within me. The I is another. The I is not a substance, a substantive, the I is a transit, a going towards the other, a finding myself again in the other. It is through others that we may truly acquire our existence: "door of being, dawn and wake me, / allow me to see the face of this day, / allow me to see the face of this night, / all communicates, all is transformed, / arch of blood, bridge of the pulse, / take me to the other side of this night, / where I am you, we are us, / the kingdom where pronouns are intertwined."[8]

In Paz's work, liberty is very closely linked to the problem of identity. If there is a freedom that concerns Paz above that of moral or political freedom, it is the freedom to be, to go on being, transforming and finding ourselves in the other and in others. Both in poetic and erotic experience, as well as in the personal experience of the sacred, we throw ourselves into the arms of otherness and the other, seeking to find ourselves again, desiring to come across our lost identity. It is this great liberty that concerns Paz insofar as the mutations, encounters, and discoveries of being. That is why there is no divorce between liberty and fraternity. True liberty is that which gives us access to the other through love or the transfer of the poetic metaphor, in an encounter which shows us that we are also others: we are also the others. Otherness is not opposed to identity, otherness constitutes us as human beings.

Man is launched towards the other like an arrow, never static, never identical, always in motion. He transforms that other into himself, and

---

[8] *Sunstone*, trans. Eliot Weinberger, *The Collected Poems of Octavio Paz, 1957-1987*, ed. Eliot Weinberger (New York: New Directions, 1991), 44-45.

thus conjugates the opposites of his search. The union of that which is contrary does not take place in eternal life, Paz writes; it is given here, it is called time. We might add: it is called poetry, it is called love, it is called community.

Another response that poetry can provide to the problem of the spiritual vacuum of the Modern Age is the possibility of full, daring contact with otherness. The author of *The Bow and the Lyre* picks up the concept of otherness from Machado, in the sense of "the essential heterogeneity of being." Otherness is an experience that precedes the sacred and generates the sacred nature of the poetic as well as the erotic.

Incomplete and limited, man essentially needs the unknown otherness that transforms and prolongs him. Like Proteus, in search of himself, he throws himself at the images of the poem in order to adopt a different reincarnation in each verse; he becomes the word in order to find himself. Finding ourselves is one way of becoming others, of advancing as we discover ourselves.

Both the poetic and the sacred are manifested in revelation, but the poetic implies the revelation of otherness, not as the emergence, like a palimpsest, of something previous or given, but of something created or invented. The sacred revelation looks towards a previous or hidden order that is manifested by signs or poetry in exchange for revealing nothing aside from its own tasks. The sacred also presupposes that there is a supernatural potency that nurtures writing; the poet, on the other hand, must withstand the gale of nothingness. Thus, nothingness becomes creative in the way proposed by Heidegger. Thrown towards nothingness, mankind is created in its presence. Given that death is what constitutes us, our being consists of the mere possibility of being. The being has no other choice but to be itself. In nothing can the being find support, given that nothingness is its foundation, yet this conditional nothingness hurls him into the search for his own nature, which will, in the end, define him. Man is a being opened by nothingness. The revelation of that nothingness as poetry leads him to the creation of himself. The poet, Paz writes, "reveals man by creating him."[9]

Translated by Tanya Huntington and Álvaro Enrigue

[9] *The Bow and the Lyre, op. cit.*, 138.

ART CRITICISM
IN THE WORK OF OCTAVIO PAZ

NEVER TO ABOLISH CHANCE:
OCTAVIO PAZ AND THE VISUAL ARTS

DORE ASHTON

He said it himself: Octavio Paz was a "simple aficionado" when it came to the visual arts. Carlos Fuentes called him a pilgrim of civilization, and it appears that Paz, in his wanderings in the world, quite fortuitously came upon paintings and sculptures that in some way corresponded to his deepest feelings. In them he found ideas that conformed to his own powerful pulse; his own passions, that drove him —and that he drove artistically— into *hechos*, or made things. He understood very well that he, like his art-critical mentor Baudelaire, saw painting from the point of view of poetry, and agreed with the great French poet that there was no point in trying to develop a system of appraisal. It was better to be available to the chance encounter and preserve one's naïveté.

But of course, it was Baudelaire's very special definition of naïveté that attracted Paz: "a complete knowledge of technique combined with the *know thyself* of the Greeks, but with knowledge modestly surrendering the leading role to temperament." It follows that Paz, by temperament, agreed with Baudelaire that criticism "should be partial, passionate, and political" and from a point of view that "opens up the widest horizons." Starting from such generous principles, Paz was free. But he, with his specialized knowledge of technique —poetic technique —was nonetheless driven to think and not just surrender to sensuous experiences. He noticed in his close reading of Baudelaire's writings on the visual arts that "all the critical work of Baudelaire is inhabited by a contradictory tension."[1] I would say that Paz himself in his response to works of visual art was driven by a fruitful contradictory tension.

The tension I see is between Paz's responses to two important figures in his life: André Breton and Marcel Duchamp. It may seem strange to see these two pillars of the surrealist pantheon as aesthetic antagonists,

---

[1] "Presencia y presente: Baudelaire, crítico de arte," *Obras Completas (OC)* 6: 46.

but beneath their life's work lay vastly different passions. Surrealism, Paz wrote, thinking of Breton, sought meaning in the magnetic excitement of the instant: love, inspiration. The key word, he said, was *encounter*. He remembers a stroll with Breton in Paris in the summer of 1964: "To me, it was an *encounter*, in Breton's meaning of the word: predestination and election."[2] And to this we must add Breton's preoccupation with the meaning of what he called the *fortuitous* encounter, for Paz himself pondered the origins of "poetic instants" and wondered, as did Breton, how much the fortuitous guided his own hand.

In Duchamp, Paz found a goad to his own deep intelligence that spoke less to his sensibilities than to his mind. What interested him in the work of Duchamp, as he said in 1985, "was the creative operation of negation." Or, as he wrote several times, Duchamp's adventure in "annulling art."[3] He understood better than any other critic that Duchamp's philosophy of indifference was an intellectual rather than an aesthetic challenge, and although he found marvelous ways to discuss Duchamp's towering presence in 20th-century art, I believe he understood that it was Breton's celebration of love that lay closest to his heart. When he expressed his doubts, he used strong language, such as "to suppress subjectivity is to tear out the heart of art," or "It is hard to resign oneself to the corruption of the word no..."

It is apparent to me that in his response as an aficionado, Paz was akin to Breton and not Duchamp. In fact, Breton's deeply graven thoughts recur in Paz's own writings, as when he takes that wonderful Breton metaphor, the communicating vessel, as his own: The first sentence in an essay in *Alternating Current* (1967) reads: "A civilization is a system of communicating vessels."[4] More than twenty years later, Paz wrote to Pere Gimferrer: "poetry and philosophy form, for me, an invisible but very real system of communicating vessels." But it was not only the images Breton made available to a highly receptive younger poet and art aficionado. It was Breton's capacity to be *disponible* that served as Paz's model, and his desire to be astounded, dazzled. I don't need to remind his readers that Paz often used the word "deslumbrar", or "dazzle," to

[2] *Alternating Current*, "André Breton and the Quest for the Beginning," trans. Helen R. Lane (New York: Penguin Books, 1970), 54.

[3] See, for instance, his essay on Breton, *ibid.*

[4] *Ibid.*, 192.

describe his immediate responses to certain works of art, and that Breton was committed to the word "éblouir".

It was natural enough for Paz to play out his own contradictions in his long meditation on the poet Mallarmé, which culminated in his great homage *Blanco*. Paz had always been aware of the importance of space —the very means and meaning of the visual arts— in the poetic forms, and it was Mallarmé, who gambled both with space and chance, that was the master. In a way, I think Paz identified with the master of that storm-lashed ship in *Un Coup de Dès*, and who, doomed to failure, nonetheless hoped that in art, chance could be overcome (overcome, that is, by form). Paz's understanding of Mallarmé's supreme struggle against linear reading, and his peculiar affinity for space as he perceived it in the works of artists he liked, enriched his commentaries. There is no more acute description of sculptural space, or indeed the idea of space itself, than we find in his discussion of the sculpture of Chillida. In that essay, Paz says space is "anterior to the 'I' ":

> The apprehension of space is instinctive, a corporeal experience: before thinking it or defining it, we feel it. Space is not outside us, nor is it a mere extension: it is that in which we are. Space is a *where*... We are the space in which we are...our where follows us, it is more faithful than a dog and more faithful than our shadow itself which abandons us each night.[5]

It was that instinctive apprehension of space that Paz, taking his inspiration from Tibetan mandalas, made in *Blanco* a spatial division of the faculties —sensation, perception, imagination, and understanding. "To write *Blanco*," he said, "was for me to try to return to space. It is our forgotten homeland." Paz would not forget the forgotten homeland, and when he and Charles Tomlinson published their *Airborn* —shared sonnets on the themes of day and house, exchanged by mail, and based on the experience of Japanese renga poets— Paz cited in his introduction a poem by his beloved Sor Juana. In it she speaks of the god of air, Aeolus, "whose office is the government / of the Birds' imperium where / through transparencies of space / ...[they] people and adorn its sway..."

[5] "Chillida: del hierro al reflejo," *OC* 6:101.

The spaces into which Paz threw himself in the world of visual arts are immensely varied, and often speak of his awareness of contradictions in himself. In 1980 he saw contemporary art as two extremes: either radical conceptualism or strict formalism. "The first negates, that is to say, the substance itself of art, its sensible dimension; the work of art is nothing if it is not something we see, hear, touch: a form. The second is a negation of idea and emotion." Since Paz craved the substance of the senses, but honored the works of the mind, he was always thrusting himself from one to the other. Anyone who conversed with Paz knew that his most frequent compliment was to say that someone was intelligent. Intelligence he valued in a special way when it appeared in works of visual art. Naturally, he was attracted to artists who could talk, and in some cases write well. One of his few weaknesses as an art critic was to suspect that Duchamp was right when he excoriated French painters for being *bête comme un peintre*. As he wrote to me in 1995, the painter Motherwell "had the arrogance (*orgullo*) of all artists, especially painters; nevertheless, unlike the majority of painters, he was intelligent. And to be intelligent demands autocriticism, irony, and a certain modesty." So it is not surprising that an artist such as Valerio Adami, who is both a wonderful talker and writer, and an outstanding visual artist, attracted Paz. In his essay on Adami, Paz recognized the unique character of Adami's draftsmanship and discussed his use of color: "In his paintings space doesn't appear as an abstract extension but as a chromatic vibration" laid on in flat masses, and limited by his precise lines. In this, Paz says, Adami, "beyond being a very intelligent painter, his painting is intelligent —I mean, it doesn't seduce only our sensibility but also our thought… It is a painting that questions, something rare these days."[6]

There were other visual artists with whom Paz could converse, and whose intelligence he honored. I think of Tàpies, with whom Paz was eager to undertake projects, and who he thought would be a good reader of his poetry. One of Tàpies' characteristics that attracted Paz was "his passionate curiosity about the great non-occidental civilizations." In Tàpies' laden surfaces, with their enigmatic imprints of time, Paz could find again what he had so much admired in Breton:

[6] "La línea narrativa: Valerio Adami," *OC* 6:278.

the other voice, the other time, the *más allá* that he felt belonged to the long vistas of human history. (He stated this with great simplicity in his introduction to his collected works: *Todas las obras de arte pertenecen a un suelo y un momento, pero todas ellas tienden a transcender a ese suelo y a ese momento: son de aquí y son de allá.*)[7] Tàpies, like Adami, could be assimilated to the writing impulse, as could Cy Twombly, whom Paz also admired.

But Paz's most engaging art criticism occurs when he has a true encounter in Breton's sense. He never abandoned his quest for encounters, and the importance he placed on their apparition in his life can be gauged when we read the first lines of one of his last lectures in Madrid: *Nuestras vidas son un tejido de encuentros y desencuentros: físicos, mentales, afectivos.*[8] Paz's account of his sojourn in the small apartment of Paul Eluard's widow where he discovers, almost hidden, a small black-and-white print by the 19th-century draftsman and lithographer Rodolphe Bresdin, is of an authentic encounter which inspires him to think about almost all his principal interests as a poet-philosopher. Paz admires and enters Bresdin's teeming universe, compares it to encounters he had in India, cites Baudelaire's admiration for the eccentric and impoverished artist, and speculates about the human gaze, in perpetual search of signification. Baudelaire had tried to get Théophile Gautier, another poet-critic, interested in Bresdin as "an old friend," since "that is what I think you will feel when you see his works." This idea of the old friend, or as Paz would have it, a contemporary, is dear to Paz's heart. He often called up figures from the past, such as Quevedo, as "contemporaries," and when he wished to honor an older artist who seemed a little out of fashion, he would always declare him or her "our contemporary." The universe of related temperaments, not bound by time or space, was Paz's territory, and he traversed it with immense enthusiasm. The print Paz discusses, *The Good Samaritan,* he says "is an example of the essential poetic operation: in this see that."[9] And it was

7 "All works of art belong to one land and one moment, but all of them tend to go beyond that land and that moment: they are from here and from there."

8 "Our lives are a web of encounters and misencounters: physical, mental, emotional."

9 Paz, "Arte de penumbra: Rodolphe Bresdin", *OC* 6: 261-264.

usually the kind of visual art in which Paz could see both this and that, that most engaged him.

He had his hesitancies and doubts. Like a good amateur, he revisited the works of artists with whom he had no basic affinity, and in whom he tried to find meaning despite his natural repulsion. His basic dislike of one of our greatest 20th-century masters, Picasso, can be read throughout his work again and again, and yet he caught certain of Picasso's traits with great accuracy, as when he said "sometimes the mask devours the countenance of the artist," or "for him, reality was never real enough: he always asked for more." In an essay about another artist, he calls Picasso's verbal statements "puerile provocations" —a totally unjust evaluation— but nonetheless invokes the figure of another great artist, Lope de Vega, to discuss Picasso's enormous scope and intensity. But Paz's most critical remark reflects his deepest commitments as a poet to the fabled *más allá*: Picasso, he says, "was a painter without a beyond, without another world, except for the world of the body, which in truth is *this world*."[10]

Another modern master who attracted Paz, but who also bestirred doubts, was Miró. Paz vacillated for years about the meaning of Miró's work, often deferring to Breton, who admired it without reservations. At times, Paz stressed the childlike quality of Miró's paintings, and at times, its profound poetic reverberation. Miró was not a talker, and this alone impeded Paz's access to the work. Yet for years he had pondered its meaning. We can read in Paz's correspondence with Gimferrer his desire over years to know Miró's work and to collaborate with him on a renga-like project, together with Vieira da Silva, Wifredo Lam, Tàpies, and Gunther Gerszo. Sometimes he doubts, and calls Miró a man of another generation. Sometimes he is enthusiastic and calls Miró "our youngest contemporary." But finally, inspired by a letter from the artist himself, Paz responded with all his heart in a long poem. His own letter to Miró speaks of his pleasure ("I trembled with happiness") and of his "fear," and of how "During years and years the text had matured within me, under the sun and rain of your painting" and how, with a

---

[10] "Picasso: Hand-to-Hand Combat with Painting," *Convergences: Essays on Art and Literature*, trans. Helen Lane (San Diego/New York: Harcourt Brace Jovanovich, 1987), 182.

spontaneity that astounded him, the "Fábula de Joán Miró" had sprung up in just a few days. The poem, which calls Miró a "mirage with seven hands" (one can't help seeing an Indian deity there), is very much in the genre Breton called "illustration," when he spoke of his own Miró poems, and does not forget to mention one of Miró's own written comments, "I work like a gardener." But Paz transforms Miró's repertory of forms into all his favorite analogies: to wind, to earth, to women, to stars, to "living alphabets that send out roots, shoot up, bud, flower, fly off, scatter, fall."[11] And he manages, finally, to see and express the artist's splendor. After Miró died in 1983, Paz wrote about his wartime paintings, *Constellations*, and likened his life's work to a long poem, ruled by a logic "irreducible to concepts." In his homage, he unabashedly states his loyalty to the old lessons of Breton and writes:

> The mission of art —of modern art, at least— is not to reflect history me-chanically or to make itself the spokesman of a given ideology, but to voice, in opposition to systems, their functionaries and executioners, the invinci-ble Yes of life.[12]

It is clear that what Paz valued in an artist was his single-minded-ness, his passion. "It is impossible," he wrote in the first sentence of an essay on Breton, "to talk about Breton in any other language than that of passion."[13] If Paz faulted a visual artist, it was usually for a de-ficiency of passion. He wrote of Rivera, for instance, "In Rivera there is skill, great skill, sometimes even mastery, indubitable talent, but never, or almost never, passion."[14] He knew that passions drew with them exaggerations and sometimes distortions, but he always pre-ferred them to the calculated. He well knew, as he once wrote to me, quoting the poet Wallace Stevens, that "we are not at the center of a diamond." Yet, in his peregrinations in time and space, and in his pe-rusal of the visual art that he encountered, often accidentally, there is

[11] From the poem *A Fable of Joan Miró*. See *The Collected Poems of Octavio Paz, 1957-1987*, ed. Eliot Weinberger (New York: New Directions, 1991), 571.

[12] "Constellations: Breton and Miró," *Convergences*, 284.

[13] *Alternating Current, op. cit.*, 47.

[14] "Re/visiones: la pintura mural," from *Los Privilegios de la Vista II (arte mexicano) OC* 7:190-191.

a scaffolding, if not a theory, of grand dimensions that finally can be seen to have coherence. If I had to sum up what I believe about Paz as a commentator, not only of the visual arts, but of any art, since they all spring, as he well knew, from the same source —imagination —I would borrow what he said about his older contemporary, Pablo Neruda. We all know that Paz had his differences, deep differences, with Neruda, but in the end, with his great intelligence, Paz bowed to the truth of Neruda's greatness. In a letter to Gimferrer written in 1990, Paz says he has re-read Neruda and that perhaps he is the great poet of his generation in America and Spain. *La voz más amplia, la que viene de más lejos y la que va mas allá. La palabra océano le conviene* —as it does for Paz himself.

---

[15] "The voice with the widest range, that comes from the farthest point and goes beyond any other. The word ocean suits it."

OCTAVIO PAZ AND MEXICAN MURALISM

LINDA DOWNS

As a poet, essayist, and critic, Octavio Paz was intimately involved in the visual arts. His poetry honored work by artists such as Rufino Tamayo, Joseph Cornell, Robert Motherwell and Tàpies. He so thoroughly understood their work that he was able to reconstruct the formal characteristics of their paintings in words on the page. His books on Marcel Duchamp and André Breton celebrate those elements of surrealist art that are also found in Paz's poetry —unusual juxtapositions that surprise or shock; the implied rather than the stated; and concern with revealing structure and process. His essays on artists such as Edward Munch, Valerio Adami, and Joan Miró created a genre that combined poetic descriptions within carefully analyzed aesthetic contexts. Paz also collaborated with artists who illustrated his books of poems such as Cy Twombly, Juan Soriano, Tamayo, and his wife Marie-José Paz.

Paz was a great advocate of Mexican art. He wrote about the elements of continuity between ancient and popular art of Mexico. He admired its architecture from ancient pyramids to fantastic Baroque churches and the colorful minimalist designs of the modern architect Luis Barragán. Most of his essays on Mexican art are positive explorations. He normally remained silent about artists whose work he did not like, except for the Mexican muralists. His antagonism toward the Mexican muralists was articulately expressed on many occasions. As Paz stated in the 1960s, "Mexican mural painting has provoked my criticism rather than my praise."[1]

My first encounter with Octavio Paz as an art critic was in 1986, when he attacked the work of Diego Rivera, then on view in a major retrospective exhibition at the Museo de Bellas Artes, Mexico City. In organizing that exhibition I had come to understand Rivera as an important modern artist. His murals visualized an indigenous history of Mexico in

---

[1] *Pasión crítica*, Introduction, selection and notes by Hugo T. Verani (Barcelona: Seix Barral, 1985), 86.

the public medium of fresco, which promoted the new cultural nationalism of post-revolutionary Mexico. Paz saw little value in the work and accused Rivera of lacking passion, a cardinal sin in Mexico:

> It is odd, but Rivera, a great connoisseur of modern styles and a great admirer of pre-Columbian art, reveals in his forms a quite academic and European vision of the indigenous world. [...] His Cubism came from outside, and the same can be said of his other manners and styles. His art does not spring from within himself. In Rivera there is ability, great ability, at times mastery, unquestionable talent, but never, or almost never, passion.[2]

Of all the Mexican muralists, Paz was most critical of Diego Rivera and David Alfaro Siqueiros. He was less critical of José Clemente Orozco. Orozco was never a member of the Communist Party and held a nihilistic attitude toward war and revolution, which was far from the nationalistic fervor of Rivera's murals. And his painting style reflected a more modernist approach, which Paz characterized as expressionistic.

Three factors emerge as basic to Octavio Paz's critique of the work and politics of Rivera and Siqueiros. First, Paz was a generation younger than the muralists. He had a second-generation perspective on post-revolutionary Mexican art. Second, Paz analyzed the muralists through the lens of post-World War II modern art. And third, his view of the role of the artist sharply contrasted with that professed by Rivera and Siqueiros.

Paz was born in 1914 in the midst of the revolution in Mexico. However, he was not of the revolution. Nor was he a part of the cultural revolution of the generation of the muralists. His interest in Mexican modern art began in 1937 when he returned to Mexico from Spain at the age of twenty-three. The Mexican Mural Movement had started fifteen years earlier in a tremendously optimistic period of post-revolutionary Mexico. In the early 1920s, José Vasconcelos, the Secretary of Education, instituted vast educational and cultural reforms to heal the social schism in the country. He hired painters, writers, musicians, and teachers to celebrate the indigenous arts of Mexico. His aims were threefold: to throw off centuries of colonial cultural domination, to el-

---

[2] *Essays on Mexican Art*, trans. Helen R. Lane (New York: Harcourt Brace, 1993), 116, 118.

evate the peasant and Indian in the eyes of the upper classes by showing the value of their culture, and to integrate peasants and Indians into
society through education. The muralists created a new history of Mexico on the walls of public buildings that linked ancient traditions to the
present through Indian culture. With the exception of Orozco, the muralists identified themselves with the workers by demanding plasterer's
wages, donning overalls, and creating a union. The painters were at
once idealistic, nationalistic, communistic, and optimistic about putting their art in service of social change.

Paz later captured the post-revolutionary optimism when he wrote
about the muralists in the 1970's:

> The Revolution revealed Mexico to us... It made us look back so as to see
> it. And it made painters, poets, and novelists above all look back: Azuela,
> Rivera, Martín Luis Guzmán, López Velarde, Vasconcelos. The Revolution
> was a return to the source, but it was also a beginning, or more precisely, a
> re-beginning. Mexico turned back to its tradition not in order to repeat it-
> self but in order to initiate another history. This was the idea, a more or less
> confused one that inspired the new regime and particularly the Minister of
> Public Education of those years, José Vasconcelos. Vasconcelos believed in
> the mission of art. He also believed in freedom and therefore forced no aes-
> thetic or ideological dogma on the artists. In his artistic policy he was in-
> spired not only by the example of the great religious painting of the Middle
> Ages and of the Renaissance, but also by that of New Spain.[3]

When Paz first wrote about Mexican muralism in the late 1930s and
early 1940s, he saw it as an anachronism. Fifteen years after the muralists first began to paint and formed their union; they were still receiving government commissions to paint public walls, still espoused
Communist ideology, and still employed a realist style. The post-revolutionary fervor had begun to die out in Mexico. In its wake was a
strong national state that, although it did not contain all the ideals of
the revolution or the reforms of Vasconcelos, stabilized the economy
and social classes, and introduced new technologies. Many writers, in-

[3] "On Criticism," *Alternating Current*, trans. Helen R. Lane (New York: Viking, 1973), 115.

cluding Martín Luis Guzmán, became disenchanted with the new revolutionary government as early as the late 1920s, when presidential can-
didates were dead before election day. But the government and
muralists clung to each other in order to maintain the dreams of the
revolution. The muralists, particularly Rivera, needed the government
for their livelihood and their public identities. Not only did the government change but the visual arts changed as well. The next generation of Mexican artists shared an international focus on formal aspects
of art and on the artistic process itself. This new interest left socially
useful art behind.

When Paz took up an interest in muralism in the late 1930s, his perspective on the muralists was shaped by the new international vision of
art. Reflecting on his return to Mexico from Spain in 1937, he recalled:

My admiration for the muralists turned to impatience first of all and then,
later, to reproval. With the honorable exception of Orozco, some of them
were apologists, and others were fronts, for Stalin's bureaucratic dictatorship. Moreover, they had become the new academy, more intolerable than
the preceding one... My reservations about the Muralists were political,
moral, and aesthetic, but above all, they were legitimate and necessary: the
Muralists' rhetoric was suffocating young artists. I wanted to breathe the
world's free air.[4]

Paz later elaborated on this position:

The Mexican muralists have been turned into saints. People looking at their
paintings are like devotees of sacred images... Mural painting belongs to
what might be called the wax museum of Mexican nationalism.... These
works that call themselves revolutionary and that, in the cases of Rivera and
Siqueiros, expound a simplistic and Manichean Marxism, were commis-
sioned, sponsored, and paid for by a government that was never Marxist
and had ceased being revolutionary.[5]

---

[4] *Essays on Mexican Art, op. cit.,* 11.
[5] "Social Realism in Mexico: The Murals of Rivera, Orozco and Siqueiros," *Arts Canada,* December 1979/January 1980, 59.

Paz revealed his generational perspective when he labeled the muralists as academics. He represented the new wave opposed to the old guard. He needed to breathe the "free air" of new aesthetic directions.

His antipathy to Rivera and Siqueiros was also based on political ideology. Rivera and Siqueiros both supported Joseph Stalin well after his political and genocidal purges became public. Leon Trotsky's exile in Mexico and his assassination in 1940 were dramatic evidence of Stalin's terror reaching far beyond the borders of the U.S.S.R. Rivera initially helped Trotsky find a safe haven in Mexico through a special appeal to the President. He also invited the exiled revolutionary to live in the Casa Azul, the house in Coyoacán that Frida Kahlo inherited from her family. Rivera later had a falling out with Trotsky and was implicated in his assassination. Tolerance of leftists ended when Mexico joined the Allied effort against the Nazis. Mexico entered World War II in 1941 after Japan bombed Pearl Harbor and the Nazis torpedoed a Mexican tanker. After 1941, Mexico had greater interaction with the United States, which began "red-baiting" during the war. The nationalistic mood among the Allies for the war effort, together with the shock of Stalin's purges, created an anti-leftist atmosphere.

Paz, along with many other artists, writers, and intellectuals, could not tolerate Rivera's and Siqueiros' support of Stalin, and saw it not only as a political stance but also as traitorous. The public personae of Rivera and Siqueiros were intricately intertwined with the hopes of Communism. Stalin was the symbolic figurehead of their idealistic beliefs. Denouncing Stalin, from the muralists' perspective, would have meant denial of their own political identities.

From 1943 to 1945, Octavio Paz lived in New York, where he often visited the Museum of Modern Art and studied the work of Pablo Picasso, Georges Braque, and Juan Gris. It was a period in the development of modern art when the issues of abstraction and art criticism of formalism were emerging. Many critics such as Meyer Schapiro made a dramatic shift from the philosophical support of socially relevant art to the supremacy of abstraction. While Paz did not embrace total abstraction *per se*, he did believe that modern art should address formal concerns. Paz recalled that time in New York:

My learning was also an unlearning… Little by little I threw off my beliefs and artistic dogmas out of the window. I realized that modernity is not novelty and that being truly modern meant returning to the beginning of the beginning. A turning point was meeting Rufino Tamayo and his wife Olga.[6]

What Paz described was his introduction to formalism. Tamayo had studied in Paris and had come under the influence of Cubism. While he addressed social issues in his work, his paintings are first and foremost aesthetic statements. Tamayo's art was abstracted from nature but addressed both painterly and mythological issues in the subtle and nuanced form that Paz's poetry shared. Paz learned about the formal concerns of color, form, and composition from his understanding of Tamayo's work.

With the shift away from socially relevant art, the Mexican muralists were soon seen as anti-modern, since they deliberately chose realism to convey didactic themes in their work. Their importance in post-revolutionary Mexico faded with the advent of formalism and abstraction.

Of *Los Tres Grandes*, only Orozco was spared total condemnation, since his work was seen as being closely aligned with Expressionism and thus more acceptable as a modern representation. As Paz wrote, "painting is not an ideology but the forms and colors which the painter, many times involuntarily, discovers himself and makes us discover his world."[7]

Paz described the role of the artist and compared it to the revolutionary:

The artist is the man misunderstood, the eccentric; he lives in a closed group and even the section of town he lives in with his fellow artists is a dubious sort of place; the bourgeois, the proletarian, the professor look upon him with suspicion. The revolutionary is the man hounded by the police of every country, the man with no passport and a thousand names, denounced by the press, and sought by the examining magistrate: any step taken to neutralize him is considered legitimate. Another surprising contradiction: once the artist is recognized, he returns to the world, he is a mil-

<hr>

[6] *Essays on Mexican Art, op. cit.*, 19.
[7] *In/mediaciones* (Barcelona: Seix Barral, 1979), 68.

lionaire of a national glory, and if he is Mexican, he is buried in the Pantheon of Illustrious Men when he dies [...] The artist seeks to realize himself or realize a work, rescue beauty or change the language, dynamite men's consciousness or free their passions, do battle with death, communicate with men if only the better to spit on them. The revolutionary seeks to abolish injustice, force us to be free, make us happy or virtuous, increase production and consumption, cast our passions in the perfect mold of geometry. Changing the world/changing life: these two formulas of Marx and Rimbaud, which affected Breton so deeply, sum up the modern wisdom of the West.[8]

On face value, Paz's description of the artist and the revolutionary was what the muralists publicly aspired to. But to Paz, these artists had become the complacent bourgeoisie. What he recognized as revolutionary art had little to do with its social function and political leanings. For Paz, revolutionary art was a new way of seeing. Its new expression focused on formal aspects, deciphering its structure, self-awareness, divulging its process and skeletal organization. What Paz sought in modern art was aesthetic purity without social contamination.

Paz's criticism of the Mexican muralists was based on a different moment than that of the early 1920s, when Rivera, Orozco, and Siqueiros were swept from relative obscurity to international fame. Paz was twenty-three when he had his first mature encounter with the Muralist Movement. This was fifteen years after the heat of its inception. By 1937-1938 profound changes had created new paths in the government, the arts, and the role of the artist. Paz's perspective as part of the next generation made him see the muralists as the old guard that must be overthrown. The art of the muralists was seen through the lens of a new formalist understanding of modern art. Paz rejected political ideology in art and the use of art as a medium for social change. He condemned Rivera's and Siqueiros' support of Stalin particularly after the atrocities were known. And finally, he saw the role of the artist as an aesthetic revolutionary, not a social revolutionary. Late in life, Paz attempted to look at the work of the Mexican muralists in purely aesthetic terms and

---

[8] *Alternating Current*, "On Criticism," *op. cit.*, 133-134.

to delimit the political aspect of their work. But his age, aesthetic, and political beliefs prevented a full re-evaluation of their work.

A great part of the work of these painters is an artistic commentary of our history and especially of the Mexican revolution; its importance does not lie in their opinions or political attitudes. The work itself in all three cases [Rivera, Orozco, and Siqueiros], despite the enormous differences among them, is remarkable for its energy and diversity.[9]

---

[10] *In/mediaciones, op. cit.*, 65.

Octavio Paz: His Labyrinths and Solitudes

SYLLABLES IN LOVE

JESÚS SILVA-HERZOG MÁRQUEZ

Parmenides' Knife and Mixcoac's Tablecloth

Thought is founded in an uprooting. "To lay siege to words", says Octavio Paz, "is to carry out an uprooting of being from the primordial
chaos."[1] In the knife of a poet born in Elea over twenty-five centuries
ago, we discover the origins of this scission of the West. Parmenides
tells of his journey to the light in a fantastic chariot escorted by
damsels of the Sun. After opening the portals of day and night with
honeyed words, he encountered a nameless goddess who graciously
welcomed the poet and revealed to him the "beautifully circular" entrails of truth.

Take heed:
I will be the one who speaks
As for you, pay attention to the tale I tell:
These are the only paths of thought to be explored

It is this:
Being comes from the Entity; non-being cannot come from the Entity
It is a path to be trusted
since Truth follows it.

There is Parmenides' sharp knife, the blade of the disjunction that
continues to divide us. Man is not dust; water does not burn; that which
is light is not heavy. Reality is one, imperturbable and infinite: "that
which is now a single continuous whole *was* not, nor *shall it be*." Many
of Parmenides' contemporaries thought he was an idiot: whoever opens

---

[1] *The Bow and the Lyre*, trans. Ruth L.C. Simms (Austin: University of Texas, 1991), 87.

his eyes observes the exuberance, the incessant change in corporeal entities. Reality, answers Parmenides, is not seen with the naked eye, but
with the shut eyelids of intelligence. Imagination is thus proscribed: that
which is nothing has nothingness within it.

If for Rousseau, property spelt the fall of our civilization, for Octavio
Paz, our helplesness began with definition. Our misfortunes were not
born the moment somebody said "this is mine," but when somebody
said, "this is this and cannot be that." Two human sins: to take possession of nature, which belongs to all; and to imprison the ever-changing
meaning of things. That boundary of being, that wall dividing the world
in two, that logical prison that our thought cannot penetrate, is the house
of the West. Uprooting comes from this: the word was torn to shreds.

> Todo era de todos
>> Todo era todo
> Sólo había una palabra inmersa y sin revés
> Palabra como un sol
> Un día se rompió en fragmentos diminutos
> Son las palabras del lenguaje que hablamos
> Fragmentos que nunca se unirán
> Espejos rotos donde el mundo se mira destrozado[2]

Words tear asunder, but they also bind. The poet's task is to recreate
the originary fraternity of meanings. The poetic image scales the wall
and speaks the unspeakable: feathers are stones. "The universe ceases to
be a vast storehouse of heterogeneous things. Stars, shoes, tears, loco-
motives, willow trees, women, dictionaries, all is an immense family, all
is in mutual communication and is unceasingly transformed, the same
blood flows through all the forms and man can at last be his desire: he
himself."[3] The root of poetry is the communion between the world and
man, plants and volcanoes. In Stockholm, while receiving the Nobel

---

[2] *Fábula, OC* 11:123. [Everything was everyone's / Everyone was everything / There was only one
word, immense, with no reverse / A word like a sun / It broke one day into tiny fragments / These
are the words of the language we speak / Fragments that will never join / Broken mirrors where the
world see⌐ itself destroyed].

[3] *Ibid.*, 97-98.

Prize, Paz reminisced of a night in the forest when he perceived the correspondence between the stars and the insects:

> The sky's big.
> Up there, worlds scatter.
> Persistent,
> unfazed by so much night
> a cricket: brace and bit.[4]

The poem is the field of conciliations. As an instant pact between enemies, the poem encounters the occult affinity between distant realities: the cricket and the universe. To write is to recreate this cosmic fraternity that logic has mutilated. The awareness of contradiction and the longing for reconciliation blossom in Paz very early in his life, since his childhood in Mixcoac. He tells Julio Scherer that his house was "the stage of the struggle between generations."

> My grandfather —a journalist and liberal writer— had fought against French intervention and afterwards believed in Porfirio Díaz. A belief that he regretted at the end of his life. My father used to say that my grandfather didn't understand the Mexican Revolution, and my grandfather used to reply that the Revolution had substituted a dictatorship of one, the caudillo Díaz, with the anarchical dictatorship of many: the leaders and mini-leaders who used to kill each other over power in those days.

> My grandfather, taking his coffee,
> would talk to me about Juárez and Porfirio,
> the Zouaves and the Silver Band.
> And the tablecloth smelled of gunpowder.

> My father, taking his drink,
> would talk to me about Zapata and Villa,
> Soto y Gama and the brothers Flores Magón.
> And the tablecloth smelled of gunpowder.

---

[4] *Stars and Cricket [On the wing (1)]*, trans. Eliot Weinberger *The Collected Poems of Octavio Paz, 1957-1987, op. cit.*, (New York: New Directions, 1991), 491.

I kept quiet:
who was there for me to talk about?[5]

The grandfather's coffee confronted the father's alcohol. Both liquids confront each other: they collide, they entwine with and strangle each other. Afterwards, they become one in the palate of Octavio Paz Lozano. There was no need for liberalism to kill the ancestral community; the attachment to land did not require the annihilation of legality. From that point onward, Paz rejects the choice: it is not this *or* that, but this *and* that. "My grandfather was right but what my father said was also true."[6] Ever since those fiery discussions, we can see the trademark of Paz's literature: the reconciliation of opposites. Paz knew that even in the most distant of voices there was a profound kinship. His work extends these breakfast conversations: dialogue with John Donne and Apollinaire, dialogue with the serpents of the goddess Coatlicue and the dancing colors of Miró; dialogue with Pessoa and his heteronyms; dialogue from the three points of Surrealism; dialogue with Quevedo, Machado and Ortega; dialogue with Sor Juana, Jorge Cuesta, Alfonso Reyes; dialogue with the smells and tastes of India, its myths and shapes; dialogue with Chinese poetry; dialogue with the dissidents of the century's end and the colonial inquisitors; dialogue about eroticism and democracy. Dialogues that enlighten a civilization: the civilization of Octavio Paz.

Conversations that transcend contradiction. Mixcoac's tablecloth slices Parmenides' knife. The tablecloth is the bridge that banishes classifications and disjunctions. As Manuel Ulacia has rigorously analyzed, the prose and poetry of Octavio Paz repeatedly enact the weddings of contraries.[7] The rhythmic drops of water that underpin his thought are fraternally antagonistic columns: solitude and communion; union and separation; arrow and target; rupture and conciliation; modernity and tradition; junctions and divergence; immobility and dance. The key lay outside the West. The

[5] *Interruptions from the West (2): (Mexican Song), Ibid.*, 223.
[6] "Suma y sigue (Conversación con Julio Scherer)", *OC* 8:366.
[7] See "La conciliacion de los contrarios," (The conciliation of opposites) in Adolfo Castañón, Ramón Xirau et al., *Octavio Paz en sus obras completas* (México: Consejo Nacional para la Cultura y las Artes y Fondo de Cultura Económica, 1994), and *El árbol milenario. Un recorrido por la obra de Octavio Paz* (Barcelona: Círculo de Lectores, 1999).

Taoist philosopher Chuang-Tzu said: "If there is no other that is not I, there is no longer myself either. (…) Truth comes through the other: it is understood beginning with oneself. (…) The other knows about himself but he himself also depends on the other… To adopt affirmation is to adopt negation."[8] In *Blanco*, a multiple-voiced poem that travels through the territories of love, word, knowledge, and which Paz considered one of his most complex and ambitious works, we find the following lines that synthesize the effort to find the lost, denied half of man.

No and Yes

together

two syllables in love.[9]

An invisible being enchants lovers: imagination. In Paz's work, imagination is not the "madwoman of the house," as Santa Teresa nicknamed it, but the supreme exercise of intelligence. The ability to bring together apparently distinct entities is to penetrate into truth. "Poetry is the entrance into being," he wrote in *The Bow and the Lyre*. It is neither the being of appearance nor the being of logic: it is the being of what is most human, the word.

The operative mode of poetic thought is imagining, and imagination consists, essentially, of the ability to place contrary or divergent realities in relationship. All poetic forms and all linguistic figures have one thing in common: they seek, and often find, hidden resemblances. In the most extreme cases, they unite opposites. Comparisons, analogies, metaphors, metonymies, and the other devices of poetry —all tend to produce images in which this and that, the one and the other, the one and the many are joined.[10]

To write is to search. It is to pursue the center of an instant, to extract the world from its river, to rescue and petrify that which time dissolves.

---

[8] "Nosotros: los otros," ("We: the others"), *OC* 10:33.

[9] *Blanco, The Collected Poems…, op. cit.*, 329.

[10] *The Other Voice: Essays on Modern Poetry*, trans. Helen R. Lane (New York: Harcourt brace Jovanovich, 1991), 158.

"Writing is the endless interrogation that signs make to a sign: man; and also the interrogation this sign makes to signs: language." The passion for language is nothing else than passion for knowledge, which, in turn, is nothing else than love for words. Pere Gimferrer calls Octavio Paz "a poet of thought."[11] Gimferrer knows the rigors of Paz's poetic imagination. A letter written by the Mexican poet to his Catalonian friend, on a day like any other in 1967, can be taken as a sign of his demanding nature.

> Dear Gimferrer: you may question words or trust them but do not attempt to guide or subdue them. Struggle with language. Go ahead with the exploration and explosion you began in *Arde el mar*. Today, as I read a story in the newspaper about some movie or other, I stumbled upon this phrase: man is not a bird. I thought: to say that a man is not a bird is to say something too obvious for words. But to say that a man is a bird is commonplace. Then... then the poet must find the *other* word, the unspoken word indicated as a silence by the ellipses following the word "then." Thus, struggle with silence.

In another letter, the reading of his friend's work continues:

> I think you should continue on the path you have undertaken and take experience to its conclusion. I would make so bold as to advise you to carry it out rigorously, otherwise it will not be an experience but rather a false step. I like the new poems you sent me more than the previous ones even though they don't substantially modify my first impression. I repeat: it is not a matter of theme, but of rigor. In the first place: vocabulary. I would delete many obvious or predictable adjectives. One example: the *subtle* step of the ghost, the *floral* whispering of the sargasso, etc. I would also delete explicative phrases: the voice of the sirens that seems to come from our own breast. Isn't there a more "economical" way to say this? You wish, I imagine, to *show* more than to *evoke*, but often your poems are not so much instantaneous as they are evocations: you don't allow things to speak and you intervene.[11]

The rigors of imagination.

---

[11] "Poesía del pensamiento," (Poetry of thought), *Vuelta*, May, 1998.

[12] *Memorias y palabras. Cartas a Pere Gimferrer. 1966-1997* ("Memories and Words. Letters to Pere Gimferrer"), (Barcelona: Seix Barral, 1999).

The Forbidden Orange and the Shared Bread

Paz's work is a prolonged and convincing argument in favor of poetry's rights.[13] As Enrico Mario Santí has argued, poetry is the trademark of all his work: not only to create poetry and think about poetry, but also to think *from* poetry.

> Between seeing and making
> contemplation or action,
> I chose the act of words:
> to make them, inhabit them,
> give language eyes.

A clear declaration of a vocation: to make, to inhabit words. The inhabitant of language listens poetically to the world; that is how he names it. Poetry in Paz is not fantasy: it is a contemplation navigating between philosophy and history. Without being one or the other, it is, like philosophy, contemplation; and like history, concrete. The poetic statement goes towards the rendezvous with man, art, letters, customs, and power. Paz's critical passion embraces political passion. In his speech upon receiveing the Alexis de Tocqueville Prize in 1989, Paz said:

> Since my adolescence I have written poems, and have never ceased writing them. My ambition was to be a poet and nothing but a poet. In my books in prose it was my intention to serve poetry, to justify and defend it, to explain it to others and to myself. I soon discovered that the defense of poetry, scorned in our century, was inseparable from the defense of freedom. That is the source of my interest in the political and social questions that have convulsed our time.[14]

Poetry meddling with matters of sovereignity. There has been no more severe condemnation of this intrusion than that of Plato, a poet.

---

[13] "Los derechos de la poesía,"in Adolfo Castañón, Ramón Xirau *et al.*, *Octavio Paz en sus Obras Completas*, México, (Consejo Nacional para la Cultura y las Artes and Fondo de Cultura Económica, 1994).
[14] *The Other Voice...*, *op. cit.*, 61.

Plato expels poetry from the perfect city frozen by reason. Poetry as the rival of reason and order. To invent worlds for the word, to remember that which has lost its name, to designate the nonexistent, is to hack Utopia's impenetrable sculpture to bits. Heretical, drunken, subversive, melancholic, poetry cannot claim jurisdiction over serious matters of State. The poet may cheer up the banquet but can never judge Parliament. The struggle between the two modes of speech —philosophical and poetic— is resolved in Plato with the condemnation of poetry. Then, as María Zambrano says, the hazardous and illegal life of poetry —its curse— has begun.[15]

Paz did not want to disguise himself in the vocabulary of the specialist to speak of history or politics. "I'd rather talk about Marcel Duchamp or Juan Ramón Jiménez than about Locke or Montesquieu. Political philosophy has always interested me but I have never attempted nor shall attempt to write a book on justice, liberty or the art of governing."[16] With no theoretical ambitions, his political reflections are the lucid and profound writings of a witness of his times. The strength of his words comes from his impotence, he says. "The word of the writer has strength because it emanates from a situation of non-strength. He does not speak from the National Palace, the popular tribune, or the Central Committee's offices: he speaks from his room."[17] In this century, intoxicated by ideologies —enclosed, satisfied beliefs— Paz grasps the nettle of criticism. Criticism, he writes, "is our only defense against the Caudillo's monologue and the Mob's yelling, those two twinned deformations that extirpate the *other*."

To write, to defend poetry, demanded the confrontation with politics, that is, the defense of freedom. But what is freedom for Octavio Paz? Again and again in his essays he struggles against facile definitions. To specify the meaning of the word "freedom" would be to enslave it. This is why Paz says it is not an idea, but an act —better yet, a wager. The

---

[15] María Zambrano, *Filosofía y poesía* (México: Fondo de Cultura Económica, 1993), 13-14.

[16] "La democracia: lo absoluto y lo relativo," *OC* 9:473.

[17] "El escritor y el poder" *OC* 8:549. "From where do you speak, from the center, from the left, from where?"asks Braulio Peralta. Paz answers: "From my room, from my solitude, from myself. Never from others." Braulio Peralta, *El poeta en su tierra. Diálogos con Octavio Paz* (México: Raya en el agua, 1999).

man who says no is free, the one who refuses to follow the path and turns his back on it. Freedom is invented when it is practiced. Like Camus, Paz says: to be is to rebel. That is why the poet does not follow the trail of the technicians who wish to reduce freedom to the shield that protects us from the State. Benjamin Constant's freedom of the moderns or Isaiah Berlin's negative freedom are shelters that lock us within ourselves. Contrary to engineers, Octavio Paz wants a freedom of awakened walls. What is dangerous is a complacent freedom, imprisoned in its solitude; wretched is the man who cannot become detached from himself: "a rotten idol." Freedom is the prowess of imagination.

> La libertad es alas,
> es el viento entre hojas, detenido
> por una simple flor, y el sueño
> en el que somos nuestro sueño;
> es morder la naranja prohibida,
> abrir la vieja puerta condenada
> y desatar al prisionero:
> esa piedra ya es pan,
> esos papeles blancos son gaviotas,
> son pájaros las hojas
> y pájaros tus dedos: todo vuela...[18]

At the age of twenty-one, Paz wrote that "to be is to limit oneself, to acquire an outline."[19] Freedom, the very existence of man, demands the other. The other is the heart of oneself. That is the key to *The Labyrinth of Solitude*, and the conclusion to *The Other Mexico*: otherness constitutes us. "In looking for ourselves we found others." He says it very clearly when speaking of Luis Cernuda's verses: to be is to desire the other. "Every time we love, we lose ourselves: we are others. Love does not realize the individual ego: it opens up a possibility for the ego to change and transform

---

[18] *Vigilias: diario de un soñador*, *OC* 13:147. [Freedom is wings, / it is the wind amidst leaves, held / by a simple flower; and the dream / in which we are our dream; / it is biting the forbidden orange, / opening the old sealed up door / and untying the prisoner: / that stone is already bread, / those white papers seagulls, / birds are the leaves / and birds your fingers: everything flies...].

[19] *Conscriptos USA: Razones para morir*, *OC* 11:76.

itself. In love, it is not the ego that is fulfilled but the person: the desire to be another. The desire to be."[20] To be is to overflow.

Liberalism can be the most hospitable vision of the social world, but it leaves all questions about the origin and meaning of life unanswered. In Paz, we find a moderate, that is, Tocquevillian, love for liberal democracy. He loves the civility of its coexistence, its hospitable atmosphere, and the oxygen-giving acid of criticism. Nevertheless, he is also aware that democracies lack the other and have a tendency towards conformity, towards the "smiles of idiotic satisfaction." Liberalism "based freedom on the only foundation that was able to sustain it: the autonomy of conscience, and the recognition of the autonomy of consciousness in others. Admirable, but terrifying, too, because it locked us inside a solipsism, it broke the bridge that connected *I* to *thou* and both to the third person: the other, others. Between liberty and fraternity there is no contradiction, only a distance —one that liberalism has been unable to do away with."[21] It has been unable to end the distance because it has not completed its immersion in the other. His is a liberalism that wants to be detached from itself. In *Sunstone*, Octavio Paz writes:

> ...in order to be I must be another,
> leave myself, search for myself
> in the others, the others that don't exist
> if I don't exist, the others that give me
> total existence, I am not,
> there is no I, we are always us,
> life is other, always there,
> further off, beyond you and
> beyond me, always on the horizon,
> life which unlives us and makes us strangers,
> that invents our face and wears it away...[22]

More than by liberalism, Paz is moved by an idea that is still nameless. In the future, it could be called fraternism. A politics that has at

---

[20] "Luis Cernuda," *OC* 3:253.
[21] *The Other Voice...*, *op. cit.*, 69.
[22] *Collected Poems...*, *op. cit.*, 29, 31.

its center fraternity, the forgotten word of the French triangle that in-carnates Paz's poetic project. A poem, let us recall, captures cosmic fra-ternity: the brotherhood of the cricket and the stars. That is the other voice that the new political philosophy needs to hear. "The word fra-ternity is no less precious than the word freedom: it is man's bread, shared bread."

> In my viewpoint, the central word of the triad (liberty, equality, fraternity) is fraternity. In it the others are bound. Liberty can exist without equality and also the other way around. The former, isolated, deepens inequalities and gives way to tyranny; the latter oppresses liberty until it annihilates it. Fraternity is the link that communicates the two, the virtue that humanizes and harmonizes them. Its other name is solidarity, live inheritance of Chris-tianity, modern version of ancient charity. A virtue unknown to Greeks and Romans, enamored with freedom but ignorant of true compassion. Given the natural differences between men, equality is an ethical aspiration that cannot be accomplished without the use of despotism or the action of fra-ternity. Furthermore, my freedom confronts the other's liberty fatally and tries to abolish it. The only bond that can reconcile these two sisterly ene-mies —a bridge made with arms that are tied together— is fraternity. A new political philosophy can be founded on this humble and simple evidence in the days to come. Only fraternity can dissipate the circular nightmare of the market. I warn that I do nothing more than imagine or, more precisely, fore-see that thought. I see it as the heir of modernity's double tradition: liberal and socialist. I don't believe it should repeat them, but transcend them. It would be a true renewal.[23]

His politics is, thus, a politics of freedom, a politics of communion. If poetic imagination is capable of making the syllables of affirmation and negation fall in love, this same power ought to reconcile hostile doctrines. It is not strange, then, that he would find in Cornelius Cas-toriadis the road to a profound philosophical renewal, because in his work imagination acquires a constitutive character. "Soul —he quotes Aristotle— never thinks without ghosts." The crisis of our civilization

---

[23] *The Other Voice...*, *op. cit.*, 148-149.

is thus the exhaustion of our ghosts, emptiness of meaning, desiccated imagination. It is the poet's duty to reanimate it in order to find a new world of meanings where ideas lose their worn-out trappings. To imagine the future is to bind hostile strands, as Leszek Kolakowski has done in his guide for conservatives-liberals-socialists that fights that old philosophy of excluding philosophies.[24]

It is up to the imagination to find the bridge of reconciliations, the point of convergence between the two great modern traditions: liberalism and socialism. It is true: Octavio Paz says little about how this pact may be achieved. The poet names, illuminates, shows; he does not draw up blueprints. He seeks the other shore.

Translated by Lorena Becerra

---

[24] Leszek Kolakowski, *Modernity on Endless Trial* (Chicago: University of Chicago Press, 1990). A Spanish translation has been published by Editorial Vuelta.

LIBERTY, EQUALITY, FRATERNITY, POETRY: REFLECTIONS ON OCTAVIO PAZ[1]

YVON GRENIER

Octavio Paz was arguably the last great intellectual of our time. There are many reasons why Paz was great, but the one I want to examine today is this. Paz is one of the very few twentieth-century intellectuals who wrote extensively about politics and for many turbulent decades, without ever exposing himself as an irresponsible fool. This, in and of itself, is a remarkable achievement, one that contributes to restoring the tarnished reputation of the intellectual as the moral and critical conscience of this century.

Definitions of the intellectual are many. Yet they are always self-definitions. Not surprisingly, they are usually quite flattering. They tell the story of the "unacknowledged legislators of the world," the voices of the voiceless who alone hold the keys to La Realidad, the discoverers of buried truths, and the genuine aristocracy of the word that, miraculously, radiates in the midst of mass alienation and collective brain damage.

But facts are stubborn. Indeed, intellectuals have so often succumbed to the siren song of dictatorship in their quest to invent or discover "the lost village" (Leszek Kolakowski) or the new *Gemeinschaft* of Warriors and Producers, that someone like Paz, who defended democratic freedoms unflinchingly, is more an exception than a rule in this century. In fact, the defense of guardianship comes so naturally to intellectuals that one would be forgiven for concluding that the intellectual's elective affinity is not with freedom —though intellectuals are the ones who benefit the most from it— but with dictatorship, for the latter is nothing but the arrogant and unequivocal triumph of One Idea.[2] The bottom line is: how many intellectuals have defended pluralist democracy in this century? How many of the ones who defend it today would con-

---

[1] My warmest thanks to David Huerta and Carlos Monsiváis for their comments on this paper.

[2] On this theme, see Carlos Pereda, *Crítica de la razon arrogante* (México: Taurus, 1997).

tinue doing so if tomorrow we were to face a period of hyper-inflation and political instability? My guess is: not many.

The proper response to this problem is not to become "anti-intellectual." In fact, the case could be made that so many intellectuals erred precisely because they suspended their critical faculty, ceasing to be intellectuals. What we need to do is to defend freedom with solid and rational arguments, do it loud and clear and whenever we can. Hence, the most useful and constructive critique of the intellectual has to be made by the intellectual.

As Paz said countless times, we should criticize reason, but with the instruments of reason. Reason is not a deity: it is simply a method that empowers the main engine of modernity: criticism. Reason and liberty are coextensive. They are the pillars of liberalism (and romanticism) provided they never transform themselves into systems, "cárceles de conceptos," *ends* rather than *means*. As Paz states clearly:

> The key concepts of the Modern Age —progress, evolution, revolution, freedom, democracy, science, technology— had their origins in criticism. In the eighteenth century, reason turned to the criticism of the world and of itself, thereby radically transforming classical rationalism and its timeless geometries. A criticism of itself: reason renounced the grandiose constructions that made it synonymous with Being, Good, or Truth; it ceased to be the Mansion of the Idea and became instead a path, a means of exploration. A criticism of metaphysics, and of its truths impermeable to change: Hume and Kant. A criticism of the world, of the past and present; a crticism of certainties and traditional values; a criticism of institutions and beliefs, of the Throne and the Altar; a criticism of mores, passions, sensibility, and sexuality: Rousseau, Diderot, Choderlos de Laclos, Sade. And the historical criticism of Gibbon and Montesquieu: the discovery of the *other* in the Chinese, the Persian, the American Indian. The changes of perspective in astronomy, geography, physics, biology. In the end, a criticism embodied in historical events: the American Revolution, the French Revolution, the independence movement of the Spanish and Portuguese colonies.[3]

---

[3] *The Other Voice: Essays on Modern Poetry*, trans. Helen Lane (New York/San Diego/ London: Harcourt Brace Jovanovich, 1990), 33-34.

Reason helps us understand that what we fail to do in this century is to consider freedom as a bloc, a bloc that requires a certain routinization of power (institutions, rules), but also an enticing "content," a bloc that is made of both stability and predictability on one hand, and a vigilant, even (when necessary) a rebellious citizenry, on the other hand. To see freedom as a bloc is easier for someone who has the intellectual and cultural background to make all the necessary linkages between politics and culture, that is to say, between the social arrangements and the "real life" of "real people."

Paz was not a political scientist, a philosopher, or a professional of ideas (professor). With whom can we compare him today? Not many examples come to mind. As a matter of fact, it is easier to compare the thinker of "the present" with luminaries of the past.[4] One thinks of Emile Zola, the first artist to be labeled an "intellectual." Zola was, however, a man of one big idea, whereas Paz was a man of many ideas in one big century. To use Isaiah Berlin's analogy: Zola was a hedgehog, Paz, a fox.[5] More comparisons come to mind. Voltaire: indeed, I like to think that Paz was a Mexican Voltaire.[6] Both were champions of tolerance, reason, freedom of speech; both loved to overturn stereotypes, to go against the current. In a remarkable and bittersweet essay on Voltaire, Roland Barthes calls him "the last happy writer" and speculates that Voltaire's hatred for any "system of thought" would have made him, in our days, an opponent of Marxists, progressives, existentialists, and left-wing intellectuals in general —"Voltaire would have hated them" the way "he hated the Jesuits in his time."[7] There are important differences too. Paz never believed that men were much the same in most ages, that the same causes produce the same effects, and so on. This shouldn't matter as much, however, for neither man was *candide* about the world, and

---

[4] On the key concept of "the presence," see his Nobel Lecture, "In Search of the Present," 8 December 1990, translated by Anthony Stanton, *The Georgia Review*, vol.49, no.1 (Spring 1995), 255-64.

[5] Berlin took the idea from the seventh century B.C. Greek poet Archilochus who said that the fox knows many things but the hedgehog knows one big thing. See Berlin, *The Hedgehog and the Fox* (London, 1953).

[6] Gabriel Zaid too would qualify as a Mexican Voltaire, minus the love of social recognition and publicity.

[7] "Postface" by Roland Barthes in Voltaire, *Candide et autres contes* (Paris: Gallimard, 1992).

Paz's romanticism never deterred him from playing the role of intellectual with the maximum reason possible.

Contemporary comparisons could be made with Raymond Aron, who like Paz proved to be right about the left. Unlike Aron, however, Paz made his critique both from the left and from outside the left-right divide. A more complex and rich comparison could be made with the philosopher and historian of ideas Isaiah Berlin (1909-1997). Both Paz and Berlin are what I call Romantic Liberals. Berlin was a liberal who wrote rather favorably about the Romantics. Paz was a romantic who wrote rather favorably about Liberals. Berlin wrote as an historian of ideas; Paz wrote as an artist who constantly sought to go beyond ideas. From their different vantage points, both provide a criticism of liberalism and of the Enlightenment that gives ammunition to the critics of modernity, but without giving up on the essentials: that is to say, freedom, pluralism, and anti-utopia in its twentieth-century form (anti-totalitarianism).

Of course, it is also possible to compare Paz with great Mexican thinkers. It is fascinating to compare him to Jorge Cuesta, for instance, or with the likes of Daniel Cossío Villegas, José Revueltas, or Carlos Fuentes. Nevertheless, I think that in Mexico, the most interesting comparisons, or shall I say the most stimulating dialogue with Paz is yet to come. Most of the great debates opposing Paz to his contemporaries in Mexico belong more to the history of passions than to the history of ideas. For example, the debate between Paz and Carlos Monsiváis in 1977, a benchmark in post-World War II intellectual life in Mexico, seems completely lopsided today.[8] Conversely, Paz's romantic criticism of progress and mass society, conjugated with a strong defense of political liberalism, has arguably more resonance at the end of this century, when the triumph of liberal democratic institutions is conjugated with a crisis of the values upon which these institutions supposedly rest.

---

[8] In the 1990s, nobody would endorse Monsiváis position that left-wing dictatorships could only be criticized with credibility from the "inside" —least of all Monsiváis himself. For a discussion on this debate, see Xavier Rodríguez Ledesma, *El pensamiento político de Octavio Paz: Las trampas de la ideología* (México: UNAM/Plaza y Valdés Editores, 1996).

In Mexico today, the public political debate is no longer between democracy and guardianship: it takes place within the democratic family. I think Paz saw this coming for at least twenty years, urging his fellow Mexicans to keep pushing for more democracy but without falling into the trap of "everything or nothing." Be principled, keep your eyes on the ball, but also be patient. As French sociologist Michel Crozier said: *On ne change pas la société par décret.* In the decades to come, there will be democrats of the right and the left, participationists and Schumpeter-like institutionalists, top-down reformers and grassroots activists, and so on. But for what concerns meta-politics (the fundamental rules of the game), the general and dominant passion of the time will be inescapably democratic.

Paz's conception of democracy, it seems to me, is not so different from the French Romantic tradition, in which liberty is an absolute, a pre-political right for "man and citizen." It is not indifferent to the Anglo-Saxon Revolutionary or Whig tradition either, for Paz obviously appreciated the necessity for a firm political order corrected horizontally by checks and balances and vertically by mechanisms of accountability. But more than anything else, Paz's vision of democracy for his own country is firmly rooted in the Mexican Revolution, which he always presented as both a romantic upsurge from below and a Jacobin (or even Girondin) process of state-building from above.

The ingredients of Paz's political thought are many: loyalty to the Mexican revolution, one that invites and endures criticism; a unique *sense of the polis*, as Gabriel Zaid once wrote; and from this republicanism derives his defense of democracy, understood as an age of reason.

Paz's politics begins with the state, but all the rest in Paz —the essential— begins with the unique individual. From the tensions between these two perspectives derive the important questions raised by our political modernity: who are we? How shall we live together? How shall we construct a free society with a material called the free individual? Does society need a transcendental or metaphysical foundation to prosper? What should be the roles of art, religion, and love in modern society? And so on.

As a political scientist, Paz's romantic liberalism is what interests me the most. As we all know, liberalism is the child of the Enlightenment.

It advocates liberty, equality, progress, and universalism. Romanticism is a much vaguer concept than liberalism. Indeed, it seems to mean everything and its contrary.[9] Romanticism is a romantic notion. And yet an intellectual truce can probably be reached around the proposition that Romanticism is a reaction to the Enlightenment; that its individualism is potentially anti-social; and that it rejects the notions of equality, progress, and universalism. Liberalism comes from the minds of statesmen and philosophers; Romanticism is the product of the artist's passage from the condition of being to the predicament of nothingness. Enlightenment and Romanticism are the two faces of modernity —political modernity is no exception. By offering a Romantic criticism of universalism and progress (particularly "utilitarianism" and "materialism") while championing liberty and liberal democracy, Paz shows that it is possible, perhaps even necessary, to criticize modernity without losing the essential. He shows that skepticism and criticism are not only possible from within modernity: skepticism and criticism *are* modernity. He also reminds us that Liberals, Romantics, and Socialists are "cousins" who share a faith in the individual, an individual who is critical, active, assertive, not the slave of authority and tradition. From a liberal and democratic point of view, Paz is "our man" in romantic territory. From an illiberal or anti-liberal perspective, Paz is a rare bridge to liberal democracy.

Why is this important? Going back to my first point: intellectuals erred, and our century was, until very recently, a political disaster, largely because the men and women who were willing to preserve the essential —liberty, democracy— could not communicate effectively with people who were not. As Nancy Rosenblum says, "The problem with orthodox liberal thought is that some men and women cannot recognize themselves in it."[10] Nowadays, we witness the triumph of democratic institutions in the world. In 1900, only six countries out of the 43 then recognized as nation-states had something that began to deserve the

---

[9] See Isaiah Berlin in *The Roots of Romanticism,* A.W. Mellon Lectures in the Fine Arts (1965) (Princeton, NJ: Princeton University Press, 1999).

[10] Nancy L. Rosenblum, *Another Liberalism: Romanticism and the Reconstruction of Liberal Thought* (Cambridge, MA.: Harvard University Press, 1987), 3.

name "democracy". In 1980, of the world's 121 countries, only 37 were democracies, and these accounted for a mere 35% of the world's population. By 1998, 117 of 193 countries were broadly democratic, accounting for 54% of the world's population.[11]

This is good news, but while "clones" of democratic institutions are reproduced all over the world, we witness growing skepticism, even cynicism, toward the democratic values upon which they are supposed to rest. I don't see democratic culture and democratic values as particularly strong nowadays. This is interesting for a political scientist because it reverses an intuition that the great Alexis de Tocqueville had a century and a half ago. Tocqueville saw democracy (understood as equality) as an inescapable social revolution, with institutions painfully adjusting to this new reality (one finds the same in Ortega y Gasset's *Revolt of the Masses*). Today, we have the contrary: democratic governments floating in the air. Paz once said: there is no underground in art because there is no ground any more. This reflection applies equally well to politics. How democratic can a country be without strong democratic principles?

The main challenges for democracy in the twenty-first century will be to build impersonal and impartial laws while engaging people, to build stronger horizontal and vertical linkages in our societies, based not only on respect for, but on *celebration* of everybody's uniqueness. Paz once said: "there is no common man." This will be even truer tomorrow. Hopefully, liberal democracy will continue to provide us with a general framework of conviviality, but for the original impulse, the vitality, we will need something like *la otra voz (the other voice)*. The other voice could be found in poetry, which is, as I understand it, whatever is timeless and unique to the human experience. Intellectuals and artists, we now know, are not much better equipped to defend freedom than are any other citizens. In fact, their unique gifts —reason, sensibility, passion— are instrumental for both right and wrong, *Eros* and *Thanatos*. This being said, art may well be one of the few bridges to our "souls" (to use Paz's term) as human beings, which is to say a precious key to (re)discovering a form of humanism. Paz may well be right: without poetry, with-

[11] In *The Economist*, Sept. 11, 1999, 20th Century Survey, 7.

out the poetry that life contains, we may lose sight of the religion of humanity altogether, and this certainly with the most dismaying consequences. Remember the slogan of the French Revolution: *Liberté, égalité, fraternité.* Paz often commented that what is missing in the Western experience is fraternity. There is no liberty without equality, and no genuine civilization of liberty without fraternity. Thanks to Paz, we can now renovate our politico-philosophical arsenal for the next century: Liberty, Equality, Fraternity, and Poetry.

THE MEXICAN AND OTHER EXTREMES

CARLOS MONSIVÁIS

The Word, "freedom that invents itself and invents me every day…"[1]
In Octavio Paz's work, the Word —an expression we may interpret to
mean the assimilation and verbal creation of the world or as the reality
constructed by language— is the way in which literature is embodied by
unique beings capable of understanding and projecting their cause, their
sound, their enlightenment of mystery and their revelation of the invisible and visible. From *Raíz del hombre* (1937) and *Libertad bajo palabra*
(1949) to *A Draft of Shadows* (1974) and *A Tree Within* (1987), the poetry
of Paz, ranging from displays of eroticism to reflections on language, is
classic and renovating, having assimilated the lessons of both Surrealism
and Quevedo. In his prose, the process of integrating opposites is different. In his essays or articles, Paz favors a classical perspective, engaging
a variety of themes with harmonious, limpid language, buttressed by
poetic images to which complex ideas and allegations are bound.

In the thirties, when Paz made his dazzling appearance, there were two
archetypes predominant in the intellectual circles of Latin America: the
enlightened man (as the French would describe him, a writer who represents the scope of his culture through the practice of all literary genres,
while at the same time staging his commitment to the Spirit), and the
Teacher of Youth (or National Consciousness), a typical Latin American
paradigm, with the writer as equivalent to the collective Gaze over his
readers' moral structure. It was the time of Spain's Miguel de Unamuno,
Antonio Machado and José Ortega y Gasset, Mexico's Alfonso Reyes and
José Vasconcelos, and Peru's José Carlos Mariátegui. In certain parts of
his work, Paz accepts the fundamental traits of this heritage and almost
from the start, proposes to take intellectual action as the equivalent of a

---

[1] *Early Poems, 1935-1955*, trans. Muriel Rukeyser *et al.* (New York: New Directions, 1973), 5.

combination of the projects associated with the Enlightened Man and the Moral Consciousness. That is why he provides as unifying a version as possible of the resonance of poetry, the correspondences between poetry and society, of tradition and of the international avant-garde, of the literary canon in Mexico, and of the significance of modernity.

When Paz first published his poems and articles, the foremost group in Mexico was the *Contemporáneos* (named after the magazine published by them from 1928 to 1930). The *Contemporáneos* were fundamentally poets and, pretty much for the same reason, they expressed formal preferences and challenges in their essays. Paz carefully studied the precision of their criticism and their literary visions, which would flourish decades later. He was especially enthusiastic about the essays of Jorge Cuesta and the essays and poems of Xavier Villaurrutia, which were very good at specifying notions pertaining to the literary ambiance of the time, such as, for example, the certainty that French culture was the best available synopsis of Western culture, and also that the study of national traditions was necessary in order to continue raising the level of quality attained thus far by anti-intellectual societies resistant to art and the humanities. Paz concentrated on French culture, and from there, he opened himself to very different civilizations. Throughout his various stages, he attended to the Mexican tradition that concerned him, through his precise and polemical readings of its poetry, visual arts and great cultural figures.

The revelation of that which is personal, nontransferable and precise

In 1949, Paz published *The Labyrinth of Solitude*, the critical work that introduced him to a vast audience. Shortly thereafter, *The Labyrinth* became a classic within the trend of investigating the specifics of Mexicanness, inaugurated at the turn of the century by authors such as Julio Guerrero (*La génesis del crimen en México*) and diffused on an almost massive scale through the work of philosopher Samuel Ramos (*Profile of Man and Culture in Mexico* [1934]).[2] This tendency was ingrained

---

[2] Samuel Ramos, *Profile of Man and Culture in Mexico*, trans. Peter G. Earle (Austin: University of Texas Press, 1962).

with Paz's book and the "ontological search for the Mexican being" carried out by the philosophical group Hyperion. Why so much interest in Mexicanness? When *The Labyrinth* appeared on the scene, Mexico was experiencing an intense optimism as a result of the forced march towards industrialization, a selective and highly fragmented modernity, faith in Progress, and the reduction of the Mexican Revolution to institutions that monopolized all political power while forming a devoted alliance with economic power. "What does it mean to be Mexican?" had become by then an indispensable question. The answers tended to combine evocations of a heroic or sentimental past (nationalist romanticism), foreshadowing a future in which there would be no room for nationalism. It makes a lot of sense to use "The Mexican" as the starting point in a debate regarding history and the Other, given that, moreover, the notion of citizen did not prove very convincing to a weakened civic culture at the height of authoritarianism. In this sense, different words were used to express the same belief: as long as there is no democracy, let us concentrate on the Nation and capitalize on its myth. The Mexican is the inhabitant and synthesis of the country and also the emblem of a living culture, replete with indecipherable zones.

Something impedes us from being (O. P.)[3]

The solitude described in *The Labyrinth* is synonymous with the collective psychology that emerges from history, from language and, according to Paz, from the expression of hard facts: "We are truly different. And we are truly alone."[4] Different from whom? Above all, from North Americans, who are lost "in an abstract world of machines, fellow citizens and moral precepts."[5] And different from those who dwell in countries where development has guaranteed its inhabitants a planetary presence. The solitude of the Mexican, one might say today, is that of local isolation confronted with global arrogance. This is very difficult to pin down now

[3] *The Labyrinth of Solitude*, trans. Lysander Kemp (New York: Grove Press, 1961), 54.
[4] *Ibid.*, 19.
[5] *Ibid.*, 20.

that many of the theories of *The Labyrinth* have become commonplace and "The Mexican" has given way to a variety of Mexicans.

Beyond a doubt, *The Labyrinth* is the best version available of the manner in which a society visualized itself or verbalized its existence while at the crossroads between nationalism and modernity. The Mexico decoded and coded by *The Labyrinth* is a country of myths, rituals, and historical stages that are closed and adjourned; where differences with the Other are registered (e.g., the Anglo, "based on precision and efficiency"),[6] together with psychic characterizations and intellectual and moral history. It is a definitive book in terms of the analysis of these "national resources," which range from the sense of abandonment to Sor Juana Inés de la Cruz, from the Revolution to the sacred vision of death, from self-absorption to Alfonso Reyes. It is also, for Mexicans and foreigners, a means of gaining access to an entire spiritual repertory. Without doing justice to the richness of its writing, some of its central themes could very well be briefly outlined as follows:

—The country or the people are homogeneous entities ("The Mexican"). Their being is accessible and can be encompassed as such. Far from himself, the world and the rest, the Mexican dissolves in the end, becoming "shadow and phantom."

—The society examined in *The Labyrinth of Solitude* is a very restricted one. Paz states:

> My thoughts are not concerned with the total population of our country, but rather with a specific group made up of those who are conscious of themselves, for one reason or another, as Mexicans. Despite general opinion to the contrary, this group is quite small. Our territory is inhabited by a number of races speaking different languages and living on different historical levels [...] The minority of Mexicans who are aware of their own selves do not make up a closed or unchanging class. They are the only active group, in comparison with the Indian-Spanish inertia of the rest, and every day they are shaping the country more and more into their own image. And they are

---

[6] *Ibid.*, 13.

also increasing. They are conquering Mexico. We can all reach the point of knowing ourselves to be Mexicans.[7]

—Perhaps our traditionalism, which lends coherence and antiquity to our people, stems from the love we have for Form.

—Although the book addresses a representative minority, not of the nation but of what the nation will become, it also emphasizes that these same readers have a patrimony that cannot be renounced.

—The attitude of the Mexican "towards life is not conditioned by historical events..."[8]; "why search history for an answer that only we ourselves can give?"[9] Thus, Poetry and Myth are opposed to History, given that "we" (as a plurality) do not make history. Myth denies History or allows itself to be denied.

He who is born in disgrace starts from the crib

To nationalism, one of the great mobilizing and immobilizing elements of Mexico, one might add another angle, that of otherness. The nation interpreted by *The Labyrinth* ranges from rituals to the intellectual life that proceeds via great individuals and key phrases. None of them is as persuasive as *La Chingada*, the "obscene term" that in a mythological light loses its forbidden nuance and turns into Nothingness, the ultimate representation of original sin, the violated Mother, the atrocious incarnation of the Mexican condition, the word that is taken from the Conquest and the fate it dealt to Mexicans ("*¡Ya nos llevó la Chingada!*"), a cry that dramatizes, according to Paz, the technique used by Mexicans to shut out the rest of the world and, above all, the past: "*¡Viva México, hijos de la Chingada!*"[10]

—By repudiating La Malinche... "the Mexican breaks his ties with the past, renounces his origins, and lives in isolation and solitude."[11] As

[7] *Ibid.*, 11-12.
[8] *Ibid.*, 71.
[9] *Ibid.*, 21.
[10] *Ibid.*, 74.
[11] *Ibid.*, 87.

a result, he condemns his tradition altogether. This translates at times into "the embodiment of a will to eradicate all that has gone before": "It is astonishing that a country with such a vivid past —a country so profoundly traditional, so close to its roots, so rich in ancient legends even if poor in modern history— should conceive of itself only as a negation of its origins."[12]

A revolution is a revolution

Paz's book, and this is perhaps its most profound level, is an invitation to controversy. In the beginning, the success and influence of the book owed a great deal to its highly attractive explanation of both the country itself and the Mexican Revolution. In the deeply depoliticized years that fall (approximately) between 1940 and 1968, the middle classes and, above all, official culture accepted a mythical version of their historical processes that was much more persuasive than any bureaucratic justification, taking into account different interpretations of the Mexican Revolution from the perspective of the fifties: it was the destruction of a cruel dictatorship, the feat of arms that nourished the mythology and culture of violence, the war between factions later to be prolonged in politics without as much bloodshed, the creation of solid institutions and slight margins of tolerance, the construction of a strong State, the victory of secular spirit over clerical traditions, the concentration of power and privileges, the political "schizophrenia" that always does the opposite of what it says, and the highly uneven distribution of education. In *The Labyrinth*, Paz is especially concerned with the epic dimension of the Revolution, the emergence of the peasant armies of Villa and Zapata, the chain of battles and assassinations, the popular force of Emiliano Zapata and Lázaro Cárdenas:

> The Revolution was a sudden immersion of Mexico in her own being, from which she brought back up, almost blindly, the essentials of a new kind of state [...] [The Revolution] was a search for our own selves, and a return to

---

[12] *Ibid.*, 87.

the maternal womb. Therefore it was also a fiesta: "the fiesta of the bullets," to use the phrase by Martín Luis Guzmán. Like our popular fiestas, the Revolution was an excess and a squandering, a going to extremes, an explosion of joy and hopelessness, a shout of orphanhood and jubilation, of suicide and life, all of them mingled together… And with whom does Mexico commune in this bloody fiesta? With herself, with her own being. Mexico dares to exist, to be. The revolutionary explosion is a prodigious fiesta in which the Mexican, drunk with his own self, is aware at last, in a mortal embrace, of his fellow Mexican.[13]

The middle classes take this thesis far too literally; the Revolution is deprived in their eyes of its diverse and contradictory content, showing itself solely as a fiesta. Otherwise, the idea that Mexico is "buried but alive" is attractive. Sumptuously adorned as "a universe of images, desires and buried impulses," nationalism allowed itself to be expressed not only by the aesthetics of the exceptional (the Mexican School of Painting, the novel of the Mexican Revolution, the music of Carlos Chávez and Silvestre Revueltas, the Mexican School of Dance, etc.), but also through an extraordinary verbal codification that delves into the fatalistic theories of our History and transcends them with a method to be set by poetic illumination. On the verge of proving to be unacceptable due to its unwieldy nature, or of finding itself displaced by economic integration with North America, nationalism was concentrated and dispatched by *The Labyrinth of Solitude*, which gives the name "open solitude" to the demolition of internal walls. This was indeed the most laconic and expressive epitaph of nationalism: "For the first time in our history, we are contemporaries of all mankind."[14]

In 1950, it would mark the end of the isolation and isolationism of Mexican culture. Whether the nation's "solitude" is the product of the fatalistic psychology of Mexicans or the result of the *modus operandi* of history is debatable. What was evident in the fifties was the elimination of cultural nationalism (in the midst of what was still mystical nationalism) as well as an industrial, informational and artistic openness that,

---

[13] *Ibid.*, 148-149.
[14] *Ibid.*, 194.

in good time, would extend from the minority to the majorities. *The Labyrinth* announced the transition towards a modernity that would be assured with all its consequences. It is on this level (the least familiar, thanks to the touristic spirit that uses *The Labyrinth* in order to reach an understanding of the Mexico of cosmic signs and such festivities as the Day of the Dead) that the book has had its most far-reaching effect, amidst our slow and gradual immersion in democratic life.

Translated by Tanya Huntington and Álvaro Enrigue

OCTAVIO PAZ AND THE ENEMIES OF THE OPEN SOCIETY

CHRISTOPHER DOMÍNGUEZ MICHAEL

Octavio Paz is a classical contemporary. That dual status of traditionality-contemporaneity inhibits criticism. Not a few have backed away from the challenge presented by Paz; even fewer have been willing to undertake an honest and searching, generous but intransigent, critique of the thought of a poet who, from early in his career, developed through language a Politics of the Spirit.

Three Mexican political critics have addressed "Paz's politics" in works more or less exhaustive in intent: Jorge Aguilar Mora, Enrique González Rojo, Jr., and Fernando Vizcaíno. *La divina pareja: Historia y mito de Octavio Paz* [The Holy Couple. History and Myth in Octavio Paz] (1978) by Aguilar Mora, was a pioneering work that failed to arouse the discussion it deserved. Because of the indifference with which it was received, his provocative theses lapsed into desuetude. Twenty years later, *La divina pareja* has more to say on the theoretical radicalism of the seventies than it does about Paz. The criticism is at times Trotskyist, occasionally Nietzschean, and possibly Deleuzian, in which a heterodoxian, accusing Paz of a mistaken reading of history, calls on him to respond to the academic theoretical inquiry of those days. According to Aguilar Mora, the poet berates "Marxism" for being determinist but then blames Marx for the failure of his deterministic prophecies to come true. Aguilar Mora is an "ultrabolshevik" —the name Merleau-Ponty pinned on Sartre— who rejects the history/myth duality he finds in Paz. I believe that Aguilar Mora localized a basic association of Pazian thought but drew from it a partisan conclusion difficult to share when one is not lost in a dream of a nebulous "true Marxism." The marriage between history and myth is, paradoxically, one of the most eloquent virtues of Paz's Politics of the Spirit. What is for the critic a misreading becomes, for me, a poetic interpretation, not without grandeur, of history.

Curiously, that original and acerbic essayist, which Jorge Aguilar Mora is, finally turned into another mythographer. *Una muerte sencilla, justa, eterna* [A Simple, Just, Eternal Death] (1990), his great book on the Mexican Revolution, is a thanatography that exalts the romantic myth of revolutionary violence. Aguilar Mora's mythologies are as rhetorically dubious as those he attributes to Paz. But if Aguilar Mora is a loner, the poet González Rojo is a heresiarch. In the 70s, the poet organized a group called EIRA (*¡Espartaquismo Integral-Revolución Articulada!* [Integral Spartacism-Articulated Revolution!]) which, as its name indicates, seeks to articulate the old Revueltian Spartacism which had remained waiting for the celestial crown of Leninist theory to descend upon the brow of the headless proletariat. Following the Plekhanovist model of the study circle that plans the Revolution until the so-unpunctual historical conditions show up, González Rojo wrote *El rey va desnudo* [The Emperor Has No Clothes] (1989), in which the heresiarch and his catechumens analyze, in the style of Plato's *Symposium*, "the theoretical situation" created by Paz's ideas on "actually-existing socialism." Generously, the heretic explains to his initiates that Paz is not an agent of Yankee imperialism, but one of our first anti-Stalinists who strayed from the path of the Good Tidings for not having encountered the true gospels. But González's purpose is more human than divine. The professor needed an excuse for putting forward his heresies vis-à-vis a new mode of "intellectual" production that surfaced in the USSR and its satellites. Octavio Paz was his excuse. The fate of MIP (González Rojo, a sectarian to the core, loved acronyms) is not a subject for discussion in this article, since that stuff vanished from the face of the earth in a couple of years, an exceptional case in the history of modes of production which, like feudalism or capitalism, have lasted for centuries. González Rojo's doctrine, written in an abominably professorial prose style, is a concoction of the theses of Trotsky, Rizzi, Bettelheim, and Bahro. The matter remains in the domain of Mexican Marxist heresiology.

Cuando el rey se hace cortesano: Octavio Paz y el Salinismo [When the King Becomes Courtier: Octavio Paz and Salinism] (1990) is a pamphlet in which the heresiarch again seizes on Paz as a pretext for denouncing for the umpteenth time the intellectual mafias whose alliance with the state has shut off independent writers from the due recognition of the "proletariat"(?). Lacking the heretical drive of the previous book, González Rojo now expounds the program of the PRD (Democratic Revolutionary Party) inasmuch as this unusual professor of the meta-Leninist Left suddenly discovered that the articulated revolution was to be found perhaps in neo-Cardenist nationalism.

Xavier Rodríguez Ledesma shares the type of "ultrabolshevism" with Aguilar Mora and González Rojo that consists of forcing discourse whose conflict with "Marxism" is settled by taking the poet Octavio Paz to task in order to point out to him the sort of heresy that is compatible with history. Naturally, there are broad discrepancies between Aguilar Mora's fickle intelligence, González Rojo's sad professorial hermeneutics, and Rodríguez Ledesma's wavering academic neutrality. However, all three critics share the illusion that there is a true Marxism awaiting a second chance on earth. That is not so, to be sure, in the case of the *Bibliografía política de Octavio Paz o la razón ardiente* [Octavio Paz's Political Bibliography or Fiery Reason] (1993) by Fernando Vizcaíno, who was able to view the poet from a perspective unrelated to heresiology.

El pensamiento político de Octavio Paz [Paz's Political Thought] is the work of Rodríguez Ledesma, an author of my generation, born in 1960, and perhaps that explains why I am sympathetic to his dispute with Pazian criticism of Marxism, since I lived with it. Both of us entered public universities during the seesawing of that "crisis of Marxism" which seemed to sharpen between the 1973 coup in Chile and General Jaruzelski's repression of Polish workers in 1981. This crisis was one of those tertian fevers that seems to herald the patient's recovery when it is actually the healthy spasm that precedes death. It appeared, in those days, that the fecundity of the Marxist heresies —from Eurocommunism to Councilism, from Enrico Berlinguer to Rudolf Bahro, via Althusser— would replace decrepit Soviet orthodoxy. No sooner was *perestroika* initiated than the recurrent hopes in the West of USSR redemption, recently portrayed by François Furet, began to fade: on January 1, 1992, the Hammer and Sickle was lowered from the flagstaff of the Kremlin. But the swamping of the orthodoxy swept the heresies along, since without it their *raison d'être* was gone. The Trotskyist illusion of regeneration of the "workers state," based on the laughable idea that this system was, in principle, better than capitalism, went up in smoke.

Octavio Paz distanced himself from Marxism after a process conscientiously described by him and accurately documented by Rodríguez Ledesma. When the poet denounced the Soviet concentration camps in 1950, he cut himself off definitively from Stalinism. Later on, he no longer saw it as a dreadful pathology but rather a pathological process, when all is said and done, within the presumably sane communism of Marx, Lenin, and Trotsky. This second phase could end nowhere but in a reunion with the liberal tradition that Rodríguez Ledesma flatly rejects. That there is a heretical and fecund Marxism emblazoned on the patristic pages is an illusion to which the sociologist clings. Paz himself was assailed by the same doubts. From the utopian hopes cultivated with Victor Serge and André Breton, Paz shifted toward substantiation of Marx as a Janus-faced libertarian-totalitarian philosopher. The despotic potentialities of Marxist socialism were fiercely applied through Bolshevism, the concentration-camp character of which was prophesied by Proudhon —in a letter to Marx himself— dated as early as 1844.

In an effort to show up Paz's contradictions regarding Marx's thought vis-à-vis true socialism, Rodríguez Ledesma forgets the essential point. Paz is a critic of Bolshevism not as a historical aberration but rather in terms of the extent to which it is a closed society whose germ fatally passed from Marx to Lenin and from Stalin to the world Left, implanting a totalitarianism worse than Nazism, since Hitler never washed his hands in the waters of a humanist tradition. In preparing this piece, I came upon a page in Ernest Renan's *History of Israel*, a book I believe is pertinent to this case. "All human dreams are contradictory, since imagination turns in a narrow circle and the shapes it traces are like the rhomboid figures in oriental mosaics. The French Revolution defended liberty and brotherhood and had at its core an empire. The great idealistic Germanism of Herder and Goethe has changed into an ironfisted realism which recognizes nothing but action and power. What to say of modern socialism and the head-on changes it would carry out if it should come to power?" The great Renan wrote these lines in 1887.

When Paz says that liberalism and socialism should synthesize into a new type of utopia, I do not believe that he understands Marxism to be a synonym for socialism. But for Rodríguez Ledesma, Marx appears to be socialism's only theoretician, forgetting Babeuf, Fourier, Saint-Simon, and Louis Blanc, the "utopian" socialists whose discredit was one of the first missions of Mexican intolerance. That omission in *El pensamiento político de Octavio Paz* surprises me not at all.

Fifteen years ago in Mexico, "Marxist sociology" was the subject studied in the university classroom, occasionally illuminated by the deceptive fireflies of heresy. But the heretics —from General Trotsky to the martyred Rosa Luxemburg— would not have rendered different accounts than Stalin, Mao, and Castro, militants and unconditional enemies of the open society. The "social democratic" restorations in Russia and Central Europe will, in the worst scenarios, be a victory for belligerent nationalism —in the best scenario, the triumph of the Mensheviks. Lenin's enemies— also absent from our university culture —like Bernstein and Kautsky, imagined the fairest of Western democracies. The Mensheviks, as Edgar Morín said, await their Lamartine, who cleansed the honor of the Girondins, besmirched by the guillotine, the imperial eagle, and the Bourbon cockade.

Rodríguez Ledesma's well-documented and thorough effort, as useful for whoever rereads Paz as for those who approach him fresh, is a failure as far as theoretical interpretations go. Paz is no misled or closet Marxist. He is a man of his time who shared the Communist illusion and abandoned it to become a defender of the open society.

Octavio Paz's path as critic of public life in Mexico is effectively traced in this book. The poet's great polemics from the forties to his debate with Monsiváis in 1977 are recorded accurately and impartially. Rodríguez Ledesma confirms, with relevant documents, that Paz was a pioneer (and this was conceded by those who slandered him up till a decade ago) in describing Mexican despotism, having so masterfully dubbed it "the philanthropic ogre." I share Rodríguez Ledesma's impatience with a regime of the Mexican Revolution which, like the living dead of the Gothic *feuilleton*, wakens from slumber when the heroes are already celebrating their annihilation. Rodríguez Ledesma is annoyed with the parsimonious way in which Paz awaits the PRI's "Final Hour."

But the sociologist does not recognize that Paz's democratism is born of his abandonment, particularly in *Posdata [The Other Mexico]* (1969), of the cult of the goddess Revolution, the whore who deceived and infected the men of our century.

Paz's long-drawn-out battle against the Mexican left has finally dazed Rodríguez Ledesma. It was a solitary war on two fronts, in view of the statolatry of Mexican Revolution and against a Left whose democratizing concerns clashed with its dogmatic loyalties. And as Roger Bartra has said, it was the Left that benefited from Paz's aggressive interlocution.

The poet won ill-tempered abuse and was burned in effigy. On the other side of the coin, I knew many members of the Communist Party who were responsible democrats despite Leninist or Castroist waverings. Some of them belong to the PRD at the present time. I believe that Paz has been insensitive to the moral value of these democrats. However, I must say that in the days following January 1, 1994, when I saw so many "reformers" instantly reconvert to the Zapatista guerrilla cult, I realized that, once again, Paz's suspicion was well-founded. If the EZLN [Zapatista Army of National Liberation] would have extended the uprising beyond Las Cañadas, and the country were to have been plunged into civil war, I believe many of those who are now going on pilgrimages for peace in Chiapas would be singing the praises of the revolutionary army.

Regrettably, Rodríguez Ledesma ends his book in 1993, describing the 1988 election as the final episode in Paz's political life. The sociologist regrets that the poet did not take a more aggressive stance vis-à-vis the very controversial elections. I agree with Rodríguez Ledesma. I would have liked to see Paz join the demand for the cancellation and re-holding of the elections. But politics is the kingdom of the possible. Paz, like the PRI [Institutional Revolutionary Party] and PAN [National Action Party], was betting that President Salinas de Gortari would legitimize his status through a real democratic reform which would mitigate or settle the problem of the legality of his election. And upon taking their seats in the Chamber of Deputies and the Senate, the Cardenistas voted *de facto* support, against their will, for the transition agreement. Cuauhtemoc Cárdenas, on withdrawing and founding the PRD, doing what Vasconcelos did not do in 1929, saved the country from a bloody denouement. And

I do not believe that his party, despite its colossal inconsistencies, has been an obstacle to the country's democratization.

President Salinas de Gortari undertook economic reforms that received Paz's approval and that of a good part of public opinion. Then came 1994, the Zapatista uprising, the political assassinations, and economic collapse. The old PRI regime demonstrated its inability to change, yet that same year the cleanest presidential elections in our history were held, and the PRI won with 51% of the votes.

In the realm of Paz's political thought, the poet is criticized for his acceptance of the slow pace of democratic transition. Born in 1914, Paz is an intellectual whose biography runs concurrently with that of the Mexican Revolution. As a child, he lived through a civil war in which his father was involved with Zapatismo; he was an adolescent at the time of the Calles repression and, as a young poet, an enthusiastic supporter of General Cárdenas social reforms. In the diplomatic service of a regime internationally praised by the Left, Paz resigned his post as Ambassador to India in 1968 in protest of the October 2nd massacre, an event ignored by the Cubans and Soviets. Paz's biography is marked by a consistently responsible rejection of any violent break with the system. It is a deep-seated political choice that arouses impatience or anger, but whose intellectual integrity cannot be measured with the yardstick of the morality that so many critics demand of Paz. Rodríguez Ledesma regrets that Paz was not a revolutionary intellectual. He is not the first to do so.

I had a Bolshevist vision when Luis Donaldo Colosio was murdered: that, within a few hours, I would be witnessing the storming of the Winter Palace of the Mexican Revolution. I happened to be visiting Paz the next night and told him of my vision of hope and terror. He threw cold water on my epiphany. That the PRI should go out of existence suddenly would be not only improbable but undesirable. Paz's skepticism with regard to the Apocalypse —for my vision was simply that— surprised me. I understood his firm conviction that history, considered from the aspect of moral responsibility, could be freed of the effect of the vagaries of violence.

This anecdote is useful for communicating Rodríguez Ledesma's disappointment upon finishing his book. The poet does not share youth's haste to see the Father die, since the PRI is a binary power structure whose legitimacy has been affirmed by four generations of Mexicans. Vis-à-vis the Mexican state, Paz has operated like an intellectual reformer who seeks dialogue with the Prince. Not to overthrow him, since he already had that gloomy vision —the Revolution— in Mixcoac or Valencia, an illusion that clouded his eyes and shaped his critical reason.

Modernity in Paz resists the ways of the Marxist intellectuals, sometimes unsure, other times dogmatic, that Rodríguez Ledesma uses to round out his thesis. Dialectics —says Paz— is neither in history nor in nature. That is why Paz has been an intellectual enemy of that "betrayal of the intellectuals" denounced by Julien Benda, at a time when the enlightened were haranguing the masses justifying the means by dialectical eschatology in sanctioning the marriage of blood and hope.

Octavio Paz's politics of the spirit is a defense of the universal values of the Enlightenment, a project of an intellectual that does not yield to, or causes him to recoil in horror from, the temptation of selling his soul to the devil of the secular ideologies that seek to destroy the open society.

Translated by Asa Zatz

OCTAVIO PAZ: THE SMILE OF THE STATUES

GUILLERMO SHERIDAN

> Let us not forget that poetry is play
> and that one must learn to laugh with the poems.
> He who does not know how to laugh with the poem
> does not know what a poem is.
>
> OCTAVIO PAZ.[1]

Any pebble tossed into the lake of a great poet's work will produce unique reverberations. No matter how small it is, the expanding waves are carried by the water to the shore of his main interests or concerns. I will throw into the work of Paz a rather small question: what is the meaning of laughter, what is in a smile? It would seem a trivial issue. In our times, laughter is almost tantamount to silliness.

It is not unusual that upon recalling Octavio Paz, his friends remember him smiling during his last days. It is true. I also remember him that way, and that initial memory is what leads me to others. I remember Octavio smiling (maybe in order to protect myself from an intimidating though generous intellect). Once, like Aristotle, he wondered why exceptional men in philosophy, science, and the arts have a tendency towards melancholy.[2] I do not think he was one of them —though he certainly was exceptional. Regarding the melancholic character, maybe he was more interested in the sad and the pensive Heraclitus than the cordial and smiling Democritus.[3] Perhaps he adhered to the counsel of Epicte-

---

[1] "Una apuesta vital" (entrevista con Guillermo Sheridan) ["A Vital Bet", interview with Guillermo Sheridan], *Vuelta* 251 (October 1997), 7.

[2] In Manuel Ulacia, *Poesía, pintura, música, etc. Conversación con Octavio Paz* (Barcelona: Anthropos, 1990), 60.

[3] See his "Quevedo, Heraclitus, and a Handful of Sonnets," *Obras Completas (OC)* 3: 28; translation by Helen Lane in *Convergences: Essays on Art and Literature* (New York/San Diego: Harcourt Brace Jovanovich, 1987).

tus, who said that smiling should be neither frequent, nor ample, nor uncontrolled.[4] But one could read at once both the severity of his intelligence and the hospitality of his smile. Neither he nor his work stinted on smiles. Smiling came easily to him and to his thinking. It is unfair to deny him that virtue, as does a Mexican current of opinion adverse to him and intent on portraying him as intractable and pugnacious. His face, especially his eyes, were more wont to smile than his lips, and when he laughed, he did so with all of his face. He was smiling the last time I ever saw him, in spite of pain. Aside from my personal interest in laughter as a cultural issue, the joy of seeing him smile has led me to ask: at what did he laugh, at what did he smile?

There is a clear difference between laughter and smiling in the work of Paz. Laughter appears to be a cultural problem exclusive to his critical work, whereas the smile seems to be more of a lyrical, poetic sign, but both intrigue him as forms of expression. The fact that "the organs of laughter are the same as those of language: the tongue and the lips,"[5] seemed fascinating to him.

In his critical work, laughter could imply notions about the most varied issues: desire, joy, morality.[6] In his poetry, smiling is a gift and a cipher of the instant. Smiling is to the landscape of the face what the sun is to the morning, it is the accentuated syllable of what the face is saying. Sometimes it is an accent of eroticism, a celebration in miniature, a gap through which one enters or leaves a privileged instant. And still more: at times the poem itself is a translation to the "language" of smiling; not a laughable, amusing poem, but a poem in *smile*: a smile conveyed in writing. But —as happened to Baudelaire, Bergson, Freud, Nietzsche, and Lacan— the fact that humans laugh, how, why, and at what, led him to metaphysical, anthropological, and religious musings.

There are two crucial essays by Paz on the meaning of laughter. "Risa y penitencia" (Laughter and Penance), written in Paris in 1962,[7] deals

---

[4] *Encheiridion*, CLXV.

[5] *Conjunctions and Disjunctions*, trans. Helen Lane, (New York: Viking, 1974), 5.

[6] For example, in *A Draft of Shadows* [*The Collected Poems of Octavio Paz, 1957-1987*, ed. Eliot Weinberger (New York: New Directions, 1991), 451], while describing the teachings that he receives from every member of the family, he says "My grandfather, to smile at defeat, / and for disasters: *in affliction, conviction.*"

[7] *Los privilegios de la vista II, OC* 7:118 *et seq*; no English translation available.

with the ritual Meso-American human sacrifice, its relationship with art and the nature of labor, but also with the meaning of laughter within that context. In the other essay, *Conjunctions and Disjunctions*,[8] Paz studies laughter in another light: that of society, not myth. Let us comment on the latter, because therein lie elements that, to my understanding, we shall see come into play with poetry.

Conjunctions and Disjunctions analyzes the defensive nature of laughter in its confrontation with that which is unbearable, either because it is real or because it reveals a secret. In other words, laughter is a mitigating factor in knowledge, or to the force of revelation. Laughter, explains Paz, is a reconciliation between soul and body. Upon laughing, the soul speaks, without the customs duty of reason, of order, of rules of coexistence. However, that laugh, while "celebrat[ing] the reconciliation of the soul and the body...dissolves it and makes it laughable once again."[9] Much like Baudelaire, he proposes that

> smiles, and the comic in general, are the stigmata of original sin, or, to put the matter another way, they are the attributes of our humanity, the result of and the witness to our violent separation from the natural world. The smile is the sign of our duality: if at times we make fun of our own selves with the same acrimony with which we laugh at others every day, it is because we are in fact always two: the I and the other.[10]

The smile is also solution, the annulment of an insufferable intellectual responsibility, or a defense against the "psychic earthquake" of our "violen[t] sensations and mental images." Paz suggests: "Deeply disturbed by the violence of our sensations and mental images, we pass from seriousness to hearty laughter."[11] Uncontrollable laughter "is a (provisional) synthesis between the soul and body [...] It [laughter] is similar to the physical and psychological spasm: we burst out laughing. This explosion is the contrary of the smile..."[12] This uncontrolled laughter is also a

[8] *OC* 10:113 *et seq.*
[9] *Conjunctions and Disjunctions, op. cit.*, 5.
[10] *Loc. cit.*
[11] *Ibid.*, 6.
[12] *Ibid.*, 5-6.

metaphor of that very violence: upon breaking up with laughter, "the face becomes a phallus, a vulva, or an ass." Therefore, "a fit of laughter is not merely a response to the pleasure principle, nor its copy or reproduction (even though it is both these things): it is the metaphor of pleasure."[13] Crazy laughter is "a regression to a former state; we return to the world of our own childhood, either individual or collective, to myth and play. We return to the primordial unity —before there was a *you* and an *I*— in the form of a *we* that embraces every living being and every element."[14]

I am particularly interested in emphasizing two aspects of this argument, which will shed some light upon the subject. The first, which closes the preceding paragraph, addresses the idea that laughter, on the one hand, is the abolition of time and, on the other, a sign and a certification of the "primordial unity." This unity sustains that essential vector of his idea of things, i.e., the concept of a *we*, the abolition of individuality and contingency in poetry's "kingdom without a name." On the other hand, Paz's notion of laughter as "(provisional) synthesis between the soul and body" proves interesting to me, not only because it is on the mark, but because of the way such an identification will rule over the appearance, the presence, and the function of laughter in his poetic work.

The first essay to which I referred, "Risa y penitencia", is an anomalous piece of writing. Although it somewhat resembles an essay, there can be little doubt that it begins like a prose poem, not at all different in style from some of the poems in *Eagle or Sun?* It originates in a poetic circumstance: the poet gazes at the sun as it advances toward dawn, gradually illuminating his study. The sun seems to be looking for something: "...it brushes against the walls, makes its way through the red and green spots on the painting, ascends the ladder of the books." Suddenly, its rays touch a small pre-Hispanic statuette with a disturbing smile. Just as the sun strikes it, "it laughs" —writes Paz— "and holds the sun in its unblinking stare."

When their eyes meet, sun and smile recognize each other. The image of the tiny face staring at the sun, unblinking, makes the onlooker smile, and ultimately the reader. For Paz, the smile is always contagious,

---

[13] *Ibid.*, 6.
[14] *Loc. cit.*

a pact of mutual sympathy sealed by smiles that possess a certain musical quality, which join together, tune themselves, and blend in *harmony*. They are like the rhymes of the faces that write the text of what is shared. The instant in which the sun, the poet, and the statuette's face harmonize becomes a perfect poetic instant. That this harmony should occur between a solar, godlike face and a tiny Adamic piece of clay is amusing in the two Spanish meanings of the word *gracioso*, something amusing and touched by grace. In the act of smiling, the sun, the statuette and the poet, in a luminous instant, become equivalent. A complicity is established between them of a secret shared in the smile. In this complicity there is as well an extreme poetic joy: that of witnessing a correspondence between dissimilar beings and objects that reconcile.

> At whom or why is it laughing? It laughs with the sun. There is a complicity, whose nature I am unable to fathom, between its laughter and the light... It laughs to itself and just because... It ignores our existence; it's alive and laughs with all that is alive. It laughs to germinate and to make the morning germinate. Laughing is one way of being born (the other one, our own, is crying). If I could laugh as it does, without knowing why... Today, a day like any other, under the same sun of every day, I am alive and I laugh...[15]

The smile at the miracle is fleeting; it changes into the sad smile of someone who knows that he is condemned to think about the nature of his laughter, and who knows that every smile is fleeting. Every smile carries with it the sadness of its transitory nature.

This elementary recognition of "being alive and laughing" is frequent in Paz's poetry. Take *1930: Scenic Views*, where he exclaims: "to be alive, to crack open the pomegranate of the hour and eat it seed by seed!"[16] It usually occurs at dawn, as if laughter were a passport to cross the border of the beginning day and to be admitted to the land of the everyday. When the smile occurs at any other time of day, that hour is transformed into a sudden dawn. In the same poem, the young poet strolls around the city. Suddenly, "crossing the street for no particular reason, because it is,

[15] *OC* 7:118.
[16] *The Collected Poems of Octavio Paz, 1957-1987, op. cit.*, 523.

like a surge of the sea [...] like a sun breaking through a thick layer of cloud: happiness, fountain of instantaneous joy —to be alive [...]!"[17]

Laughter has two lips, two eyes, two edges: one turned towards the world, the other towards the inside. Laughter is also turned on oneself, against oneself. Paz writes: "Irony is a man who laughs at others and at himself; meta-irony goes beyond this dialogue with the I: meta-irony laughs at the I that laughs at the world. Irony is cruel, meta-irony dissolves cruelty"[18] into compassion and piety. Another reconciliation: if I laugh at myself, I acknowledge my weakness and at the same time appease it; if I laugh at myself, I am admitting that I like myself; and that I am the first object of my irony. And then, this self-love makes me feel sorry for myself and for all other things I laugh at. Laughter is sympathy and *compathia* with oneself. Between irreconcilable opposites —between life and death, between ignorance and knowledge— float the ribbons of laughter, ready to reconcile them.

Paz conjectures that what makes the tiny face smile is "the union of the two poles of existence," life and death, at the moment of human sacrifice. He proposes it to be the same kind of laughter that convulses the participants in the Bacchanalian and Saturnalian orgies of Mediterranean cultures. "Laughter shakes the universe, it puts it outside itself and reveals its entrails." Laughter makes us die laughing.

Laughter, as an expression of freedom, has a subversive strain as well. It is an expression peculiar to human beings and at the same time a parenthesis of reason. It means something, but we do not know what. It eludes reason, but defines its limits; it is a pleasure greater than discourse. It loathes articulated meaning and sets it free in a meaningless stammer. In so doing, it recognizes the supremacy of delirium over meaning, or rather, complements it. In Spanish, the loudest and merriest laughter is called a "carcajada", a stammering onomatopoeia (infrequent in Spanish) whose closest English equivalent is "guffaw."

Laughter —says Paz in the same essay— is a parenthesis within order as well as a critique of order. "It negates work, interrupts tasks, and above all, questions its seriousness. Laughter is a suspension and at times an outright loss of judgment." If work humanizes the world and

---

[17] *Ibid.*, 523.
[18] "En el filo del viento: México y Japón" in *OC* 8:471.

gives meaning to nature, laughter —writes Paz— "restores the universe to its original indifference and strangeness. (…) Through laughter, the world once again becomes a playground, a sacred enclosure, not a place of work. The nihilism of laughter serves the gods… Through death and laughter, the world and men become toys again," objects and subjects of the essential game at the origin of any artistic endeavor.

Paz's speculation follows a singular course in which he explores the meaning of divinity and the role laughter plays in its inexorable dominions: magical laughter, the laughter of the cosmos would seem to be the first language of creation. "In the beginning was the Laugh; the world begins with an indecent dance and a guffaw," he says, referring to a Japanese creation myth. Before another pre-Hispanic statuette that represents "God Who Comes Forth from a Ceramic Orchid,"[19] he says:

> Among clay petals
> is born, smiling,
> the human flower.

In "Risa y penitencia" he also insinuates that laughter is what remains of the language of Creation, a kind of embryonic language, the Big Bang of the Logos: "Today, only children laugh with a laughter that resembles the statuette's. Laughter of the first day, wild laughter and still close to the first whimper: agreement with the world, wordless dialogue, pleasure. It suffices to stretch forth our hand and pluck a fruit, it suffices to laugh in order to make the universe laugh…"

Paz seems to accept that play, poetry, and all aesthetic creation spring from the pleasure principle. If this is so, smile is the verification of that principle, its face. Poetry has one foot in the vertigo of reason and the other in wild babbling; together, they aim at knowledge as enjoyment, from and toward enjoyment. Paz brings to mind Freud and his notion that "jokes and art have the same origin. Jokes and poems are expressions of the pleasure principle, victorious for a single moment over the reality principle. In both cases, this triumph is imaginary, but while the joke fades, in art there is a will toward form."

[19] *Object Lesson*, trans. Muriel Rukeyser, *Early Poems 1935-1955* (New York, New Directions: 1973), 43.

In no way am I saying that Paz is a humorous or "amusing" poet. Obviously, his poetry always avoided flirting with jokiness or the easy laugh, the "killing joke" Verlaine warned against in his *Art Poétique*. On the other hand, the light spirit of play and its expression through the smile is perceptible, if subtle. Play in the Mexican sense of taking risks, in the sense in which "love of games moves us...to gamble life on a word."[20] There are also times in which this game allows guffaws, but not the guffaw aroused in the reader by the poem, but emulated and celebrated through poetic labor. This celebration —imitation, contagion of the guffaw— is shown in Paz by means of puns.

The rhetorics and poetics of wordplay in the poetry of Paz naturally exceed the scope of this essay. I have the impression that it is a game he plays on various, complex levels of meaning, and perhaps, more so, on a level of non-meaning prior to the *sui generis* meaning of the poem. The stammer of a pun seems to parody phonetically a generative guffaw, a proto-language infused with nonsensical meaning. Puns, an extreme instance of the pleasure of rhyme, rhythm and free association, are one of the forms of language's laughter. I insist: not the laughter of the poet, and less still an attempt to get a laugh out of the reader, but a representation of language in the act of laughing.

Let us cite some examples. There is a pun by Paz that describes laughter and at the same time mimics it: "La risa: rezo de posesa pitonisa" (Laughter: the prayer of a possessed pythoness).[21] Again, he insists upon the divine nature of laughter, a wisdom of a superior order that flirts with the dispossession of oneself and therefore supposes that one is possessed by a superior force. Another play on words operates at a distance from human beings, but on the same principle of the origins of language: "El erizo se irisa, se eriza, se riza de risa" ("The thistle whistles, bristles, buckles with chuckles"). "Sopa de sapos, cepo de pedos, todos a una, bola de sílabas de estropajo, bola de gargajo, bola de víceras, de sílabas, badajo, sordo badajo..." ("Broth of moths, charts of farts, all together, ball of syllables of

---

[20] *Eagle or Sun?*, trans. Eliot Weinberger (New York: New Directions, 1976), 13.

[21] *Totalidad y fragmento*, *Vuelta* (Barcelona: Seix Barral, 1976), 29; untranslated in *The Collected Poems*.

waste matter, ball of snot splatter, ball of the viscera of syllable sibyls, chatter, deaf chatter...").[22]

On several other occasions, that ludic possession that makes language express itself in boasts that, by dint of associating rhymes and homophonies, in a sort of automatism, creates a kind of pre-signification, of pre-scriptoral and pre-significant scrawl, characterized by "dumbfoundedness," the linguistic confusion of the primogenetic babble:

> La filfa el filmo el figo
> El hipo el hilo el filo
> Desfile baboso de bobos bubosos
> Tarántula tarantela
> Tarambana atarantada [23]

Laughter is beginning and, at the same time, is *a* beginning.

Laughter and the smile are recurrent themes in Paz's poetry. He starts early. From the beginning, laughter is one of the poet's tasks. In *Palabra*, one of the first poems devised to hatch a poetics,[24] Paz defines the attributes of the word: its essence is "exact / yet erroneous; / dark and luminous," and it also is

> laughing and pure, free
> like cloud, like water
> like wind and light,
> like eyes wandering through the world
> like me, if I forget myself.

The laughing quality of the Word seems to guarantee from the outset the privilege of being able to divest oneself, with them and within them. From the outset, the Word/Laughter is a liberty capable of eradicating the burden of contingency. This conviction will prevail unchanged throughout the years, as seen in the strophe of *Entrada en materia*:[25]

---

[22] *Eagle or Sun?, op. cit.*, 12 & 13.
[23] *Totalidad y fragmento, loc. cit.*
[24] In *Bajo tu clara sombra, OC* 11:40. This poem is dated 1939; no English translation is available.
[25] *OC* 11:266; no English translation available.

The names are not names
They don't say what they say
I must say what they don't say
I must say what they say
Stone blood sperm
Rage city clocks
Panic laughter panic...

In what way do names speak/not speak this laughter between the parenthesis of contingency? In a poetry so grounded in nature, experience, and celebration of the moment, the smile, the laughing word has singular responsibilities. It is frequently a cipher of the instant, a metaphor for its perfection or the pleasure of its statement. In this sense, the smile has its place in Paz's repertoire of images and meanings which he uses to lay siege to and capture those moments, along with music, sunrise, the empty street, and the bird suspended in flight, among other images for which Paz has a predilection.

The smile is to the face what the revelation is to the moment: it is the preface to its imminence, the register of its presence or its consequence: a sign of gratitude. In any case, it functions as a ceremony for the revelation of the moment and verifies its order or expresses its essential, founding harmony. This harmony, be it at dawn or noontime, always inaugurates a separate time. The inaugural connotations of the smile are repeatedly observed. Just as the sun and the smile on the statuette launch the morning, a woman's laughter is "the sun buried in the suburbs."[26] In *Walking Through the Light*,[27] daybreak begins like this:

You lift your left
foot forward the day
stops and laughs
and starts to step lightly
while the sun stands still

---

[26] *Sleepless Night, Collected Poems, op. cit.*, 101
[27] *Ibid.*, 103.

In *Day*[28] (*Spring*), describing the daily entrance into the morning measured by the clock, a woman's smile inaugurates the day both as poetic time and as a prolonged instant:

> ...You laugh and do your hair not noticing
> A day begins at your feet [...]
> A day begins in your mouth.

The same situation recurs in *Native Stone*:[29]

> Joy ripens like fruit...
> The trees, the streets, the mountains
> Unfold in translucent waves
> A girl laughs as the day dawns...

An interesting sub-theme appears in the former stanza, that of the wave. Just as the sun illuminates the library, the sun of the smile illuminates the intimate day of the lover. In a poem entitled *Elogio* (*Praise*),[30] the day begins:

> ...Like the wave that comes forward and swells and unfolds
> into a wide smile...

This identification between smile and waves is an early one (if one takes into account that the lines cited above belong to a poem written before 1950) and reappears through the years, sometimes shifting towards the waterfall, that full-time wave. Curious association: apparently, the metaphor proposes that laughter is to the body what waves are to the sea. When we laugh, our body is a sea and our laughter its waves. Or else, laughter is born, advances, implodes and recedes in the face with a rhythm similar to that of waves, which are also an expression of time.

In Paz's famous poetic narrative, *My Life with the Wave*, the beneficiary of the smile-wave is the lover-swimmer. This enigmatic text

---

[28] *Early Poems 1935-1955, op. cit.*, 35.
[29] *Semillas para un himno, OC* II:126; no English translation available.
[30] *Ibid.*, 133.

from *Eagle or Sun?*[31] proposes a basic plot to describe the evolution from romantic love to married life: a man falls in love with a wave and takes it/her home with him. At first, when they embrace,

she would swell with pride, incredibly tall like the liquid stalk of a poplar; and soon that thinness would flower into a fountain of white feathers, into a plume of laughs that fell over my head and back and covered me with whiteness.

The implications of this exaltation are evident: laughter, as it falls over the head, baptizes the lover with joy; by covering the lover with the sea's sexual whiteness, he is purified and made holy. But once love fades and is substituted by routine, the wave goes insane: "her sweet arms became knotty cords that strangled me" and her beneficent laughter of the beginning becomes a sinister omen: "she cursed and laughed, filled the house with guffaws and phantoms."

Within this analogy between smile and wave, there is a variant, also reiterative, in the visual imagination of the poet: the smile is wave, the wave causes a foam that becomes a plume of white feathers. It appears, for instance, in *Sunstone*, in a list of the attributes of the beloved:

...you throb like a squirrel between my hands,
you fly like a thousand birds, and your laugh
is like the spray of the sea [...][32]

The image "laugh like a spray / wave like foam / foam like feathers" elaborates a cenestecy that translates the sound of laughter into a visual image: a shower of generative foam, a shower of amniotic phlogiston, a welcome. An inaugural celebration, laughter crowns the moment with its delight and covers those who smile, and those who bear witness to it, in an amorous baptism.

There are other images and metaphors, reiterated to decipher and cipher a smile. An interesting one identifies the smile with citrus fruits,

---

[31] *Eagle or Sun?, op. cit.,* 44-57.
[32] *Sunstone, Collected Poems, op. cit.,* 25.

doubtless the most poetic of Paz's fruits: cipher of the day ("of twenty four sections"), a living ball, the Host of the agnostic, a manageable planet. In *Sunstone*, "...the world / grows green again when you smile/ eating an orange."[33] The smile is substituted with "sections of joy" (*Ser natural*).[34] The metaphor equates the shape of the section of a citrus fruit with the shape of the mouth, and the smile itself with the fruit's nutritious coolness, just as the slice of watermelon in Tablada's famous *haiku* is the laugh of summer.[35] Does this analogy derive from one of the images that marked his adolescence, enumerated in *1930: Scenic Views*: an image of Indian women selling fruit in the market, laughing, submerged in the river of their wares?:

...limes and lemons: sudden freshness of laughter of women bathing in a green river...:

On another level, laughter is an ingredient of Eros silent language: it makes the woman an instantaneous Shiva, as in *Maithuna*,[36] where laughter is:

A cage of sounds
open
to the morning...

[...]

Your laughter burns your clothes
your laughter
soaks my forehead my eyes my reasons...

[...]

You laugh over your ashes...

---

[33] *Loc. cit.*
[34] *OC* 11:189; no English translation available..
[35] José Juan Tablada, *Un día...* (1928), *Poesía completa* (México: UNAM, 1972).
[36] *Collected Poems, op. cit.*, 275-283.

Once again, laughter belongs to the early morning and is compared to freedom and birds (now with their song, not with their feathers). And now not to the water of baptism, but also to fire with it's healing "tongues" that burn reasons and light up the lover (it is impossible not to remember the tongue "like a damned flame sticking out of an oven," which appears in López Velarde). It is particularly interesting that the beloved's laughter is perceived with his lover's brow, rather than with his eyes or ears. Because the brow is a sum of sight and hearing, it is the site of a higher sense, the proper zone to receive the cleansing waters of love.

In *The Monkey Grammarian*, driven by the need to go deeper into the nature of erotic laughter, Paz explains the process of those metaphors. Why identify laughter with fruit, water, wave, cascades, feathers, the brow? He writes:

> This laughter that scatters itself about here like the pearls of a broken necklace is the same laugh as always and always another, the laugh heard on a Paris street corner, the laugh of an afternoon that is drawing to a close and blending with the laugh that silently, like a purely visual cascade, or rather an absolutely mental one —not the idea of a cascade but a cascade become idea— plunges down onto my forehead and forces me to close my eyes because of the mute violence of its whiteness. Laughter: cascade: foam: unheard whiteness.[37]

The descending scale of laughter that falls as foam/cascade/whiteness appears again in *A Fable of Joan Miró*[38], (a poem defined by Paz as "epic-comic")[39] which openly states: "a waterfall is a girl coming down the stairs dying of laughter."

There are other poems written with a light heart, of a good mood bordering on amusement, but there are only a few of them. The most obvious examples are the epigrams in which he experimented with the blend of humor, cleverness, irony, and brevity of the *Greek Anthology*. These poems are found in *East Slope* (1969), the most joyous book of all his poetic works. Let us recall two:

---

[37] *Monkey Grammarian*, trans. Helen Lane (New York: Seaver Books, 1981), 138-139.

[38] *Collected Poems, op. cit.*, 566-571.

[39] In *Travesías: tres lecturas*, 189. Untranslated into English.

Royal Hunt

The woes of a taxidermist:
His Highness has sent him,
for the trophy room,
the skins, not well cured,
of his father and his brother, the first born.
Epitaph for an Old Woman:

They buried her in the family tomb
and in the depths the dust
of what was once her husband
                    trembled [...]⁴⁰

It is interesting that, in both examples, the humor of the situations derives from the helplessness of the deceased protagonists.

In the work of Paz, laughter also has a moral dimension: in fulfilling a subversive mission (to the extent that this presumes a critical distancing from reality), it is also a peculiar exercise in freedom. In *Proem*⁴¹ he points out that poetry is "laughter that sets fire to rules and the holy commandments." Laughter is a sign of the celebration of life and is grateful for all its gifts, but because it belies intelligence and the analytical, it is one of the definitions of modernity. Laughter is a non-articulated philosophical attitude that is both the instrument of irony and the acknowledgment of the devastating nature of Evil. It is also a declaration of absurdity and a remedy for its exactions. "Laughter is a defense against the intolerable," he points out in another essay. "It is also an answer to the absurd. A no less absurd answer."⁴²

At the same time, however, laughter is an element in a definition of modernity that strives to become abstracted from it, acting from its margins. The absurdity of its answer is that it answers without saying anything, although it carries a great deal of meaning. In "Risa y penitencia",

---

⁴⁰ *Ibid,* 189, 191.
⁴¹ *Ibid,* 483.
⁴² "Una novela de Jorge Ibargüengoitia," *OC* 4:368; untranslated into English.

Paz says that "laughter is the beyond of philosophy. The world began with a guffaw and ends with another," which would appear to endow laughter with stoic combativeness. Laughter is the frontier where intelligence and intelligent intuition recognize their limits, as in Nietzsche.[43] "When facing the dizzying vision of the void," says Paz, "the only answer is laughter."

Paz also identifies this laughter before the void with the *atheology* that Bataille speaks of in his work on eroticism, which Paz cites in his essay on Charles Fourier.[44] Interestingly enough, when he speaks of his beloved Francisco de Quevedo, at the moment the poet contemplates his own face and discovers the "abyss," Paz criticizes him for neither smiling at it nor feeling pity for it.[45] The hollow laugh of terror and surprise before the void is a final reconciliation, this time with death. It deals with a ridiculous proposition, admits Paz, since… "Who laughs himself to death? Everyone and no one. The old rational and stoic recipe was to laugh at death. But if when we laugh, we die…is it death or we ourselves who laugh?"

The laughter of the beginning and the end: a parenthesis of senselessness that demands all our efforts to clothe ourselves with an evanescent feeling. This parenthesis, this interim, is peopled by other laughs, partial, affirmative, liberating: the laughs enumerated by the philosopher Kostas Papaioannou, according to the evocation of his friend Paz,[46] as preparation for an indefinable freedom, laughter that allows us to

> … it unchains the prisoner free, says *no* to the monstrous, says *yes* to the sun of this moment, freedom is
> and you never finished: you smiled […]

Laughter is origin, and also the adequate way to end. A proto-idiomatic babble and a dissolution of cognitive toil. Maybe these are the remains of that transrationality that Paz foretold in Buddhism. Our way

---

[43] "Nihilismo y dialéctica," *OC* 10:573-577; no English translation available.

[44] "La mesa y el lecho", *OC* 10:92-94; no English translation available.

[45] Paz writes, "…on seeing himself, [he] neither smiles nor takes pity on himself, but freezes into a hideous grin." "Quevedo, Heraclitus, and a Handful of Sonnets," *Convergences: Essays on Art and Literature*, trans. Helen Lane (San Diego: Harcourt Brace Jovanovich, 1987), 246.

[46] *Kostas Papaioannou (1925-1981), Collected Poems, op. cit.*, 537-543.

to end, and not to end, is by smiling, as he strived to do himself. The smile is a beyond. It is what is not said, what cannot be said, what is said by not saying it: the dawn of the face in a world that dispenses with words. It is our humble way to emulate, in a fleeting instant, the eternal wisdom of Buddha, on whose face Paz reads:[47]

> Still intact,
> the smile, that smile:
> a gulf of pacific clarity.
> And I was, for a moment, diaphanous,
> a wind that stops,
> turns on itself and is gone.

No longer the wave or the waterfall, but a gulf of pacific clarity. The troubled waters of thought are dammed in quietude. On Buddha's face, Paz sees:

what is most needed in the 20th century: a resurrection of piety. One of the most beautiful things of Buddhism is that Buddhist saints are always smiling. And that smile is irony and piety.[48]

Piety: one of the values Paz loved most, above all in his later years, under different names: solidarity, fraternity. Between the tiny face of the Meso-American statuette that laughs with the cosmos, and Buddha's face that smiles because it knows itself and has compassion for itself, vibrated the smile of Octavio Paz. The poet —whose task it is "to water the parks with a solar and lunar laughter"— knows that the way to end is the beginning of a smile. Octavio Paz ended with that smile, and it carried him into the long moment of eternity.

Translated by Tanya Huntington and Álvaro Enrigue

---

[47] *The Face and the Wind, ibid.,* 565.
[48] "Nosotros, los otros", *OC* 9: 28.

THE COMPLETE WORKS
OF OCTAVIO PAZ

THE HOUSE OF TIME
OR THE FOUNDATION OF POETRY:
THE HISTORY OF AN EDITION

NICANOR VÉLEZ

To Gruchenkita

I would like to think that we are in a sort of *Casa de la presencia* (House of Presence), a sort of enclosure outside time that lends its name to the first volume of Octavio Paz's complete works. Somewhere in his prose writings, Paz said that poetry is "undated antiquity." It is no surprise, then, that among the first titles he proposed for his works in 1990, he wished to call this volume *La casa del tiempo. La fundación de la poesía* (The House of Time. The Foundation of Poetry). As Paz says in his prologue: "The present of poetry is a transfiguration: time becomes incarnate in a presence. The poem is the house of presence." Hence, the final title for this volume.

The idea of publishing his complete works, as Paz recounts in the first of his prologues, emerged from a conversation with Hans Meinke, who at the time was director of the Círculo de Lectores and who is now managing director for the Galaxia Gutenberg publishing company. Valencia, the site of their first meeting in 1987, marked the point of departure. Our publishing house had already published an anthology of Paz's poetry under the supervision of Juan Luis Panero in 1985. There was talk of the possibility of publishing one of his books of essays, but discussion quickly shifted to the idea of including a significant selection of Paz's work in seven volumes. The texts would be organized according to thematic criteria. However, once the distribution of texts had been determined, Paz thought it necessary to increase the number of volumes to eight, in order to devote one volume exclusively to his general reflections on poetry (*The Bow and the Lyre, Children of the Mire*, etc.).

The first book was slated to appear on March 31, 1989, in order to commemorate his 75th birthday, and publication of the entire series was to be concluded on December 31, 1990. However, various sorts of difficulties, such as the organization of the texts, the order of appearance, and the drafting of the prologues, delayed publication until February 1990, when the decision was made to publish the complete works. Once this was resolved, we felt that there should be 12 volumes, but while preparing the eighth volume, we were forced to reconsider, and we opted for 14. The news, which you may have anticipated, is that there will now be 15. It was my task to oversee the development of these works over a ten-year period and oversee the entire process of preparing the edition. It is worth noting here, however, that in this process, various people have played an important role: first and foremost, Hans Meinke, the father of the idea; the designer, Norbert Denkel; the production supervisor, Susanne Wherthwein, and the current director of the Círculo de Lectores, Albert Pèlach, who made it possible to continue the project.

In 1993, Adolfo Castañón, of the Fondo de Cultura Económica in Mexico, contacted the Círculo de Lectores in order to express the Fondo's interest in publishing the complete works in the Americas. After a meeting in Barcelona, we agreed that the FCE would publish our edition, maintaining the same format and the same external characteristics. It was thus that the project became an adventure between the two shores. The FCE's first volume appeared in 1994. By then, the Círculo had already published the first six volumes, which were once again corrected by Octavio Paz, Ana Clavel of the FCE, and myself, in order to "completely" cleanse them of errata. Starting with the seventh volume, we decided that both Paz and the FCE would read each volume in its second draft form, without waiting for our edition to be printed, in order to expedite the publication of the volumes in Mexico.

No set of works in the history of literature, as least as far as I know, has gone through such a substantial restructuring by the author when it was being published as the "complete works." Although this is significant, because most authors simply assemble their books into volumes, what is truly important and surprising is the realization that this restructuring is, in a certain way, the type one uses to solve a puzzle. In

Paz's case, each element, each text has an important value in and of itself, but in undergoing this type of metamorphosis, not only does each text maintain its value, each text highlights the consistency of an ever-active thought process. What I understand here by "consistency" must not be confused with a static or immobile condition. It is, rather, a critical consistency, mingled with passion and lucidity, that brings to light the "ardent power of reason".

I must emphasize the importance of it having been Paz himself who subjected his entire prose work to thematic restructuring, while partially maintaining a chronological order. The prose work of a poet is nothing more than, on the one hand, his coming into consciousness, and on the other, the recreation of his own tradition. If this is true, the structure of the complete works of Paz invites us to view multiple figures as possible. I would like to take up one of these figures, which, although it precedes these huge tomes, is still one of the most effective and expressive ways of defining them. I should point out, nonetheless, that we should view it as a figure that tends to resemble a sketch more than it does something fixed.

Those familiar with Borges writing will perhaps not have forgotten that character who "takes upon himself the task of drawing the world (…) and over the years populates a space with images…" "Shortly before his death," according to the narrator, "he discovers that this patient labyrinth of lines is tracing the image of his face." This said, Paz, who like the Argentine writer knew from very early on that his destiny would be a literary one, began to draw a vision of a universe through the spiral, which is the geometric figure that best defines the rhythm of his prose, and through the sequence of his verses, until he formed the figure described by Cortázar in his work: "A starfish". We are all aware that the subjects encompassed by the work of Octavio Paz are multiple and diverse. Their most important characteristic: lucidity; their spinal column: poetry; and their vertebrae: the world of ideas. Poetry is at once the center and the exploding point. The world of ideas is the set of edges that trace the figure that Cortázar saw through his prose and poetry. His essays, the points on that starfish, are adjacent to history, sociology, anthropology, the history of ideas, and literary criticism. It would seem that, as Terence would say, "nothing human is alien to him."

It should not surprise us, then, that in the presentation of these complete works in Barcelona in 1991, and in Madrid and Oviedo in 1993, the figure of the "humanist", a figure so alien to this century of watertight compartments and specialists, was evoked in order to define Octavio Paz.

It is important to set forth, even if only superficially, the innovative aspects of these works. We will not go into detail and will give only a few examples because of obvious time constraints. First of all, we have already highlighted structure. Secondly, there are two books that take shape with the publication of the complete works: *The Double Flame* and *In Light of India*. Both had been conceived as 100-page essays that would make up part of *Ideas y costumbres* (Ideas and Customs); however, these texts followed a path of their own and became books, as Paz recounts in his prologues and correspondence. In addition to these central books, there are new texts with which Paz aimed to expand on an idea or outline a theme. For example, in regard to *Excursiones/Incursiones* (Excursions/Incursions), the second volume, and the third, *Fundación y disidencia* (Foundation and Dissidence) Paz says in a letter to Meinke: "Searching for, compiling, and reviewing the texts was very laborious. I did not confine myself to correcting the errata but, in some cases, I added pages and even wrote a small essay to fill out what I say about Ezra Pound ("Afterthoughts"). I am also satisfied with the two and a half pages that I added about Neruda." Aside from this, some of the volumes contain hitherto unpublished texts.

The prefaces to each volume are among the most valuable features of these works. Taken together, they are undoubtedly a veritable intellectual biography. A simple perusal of "Entrada retrospectiva" (Retrospective Entrance) and "Itinerario" ("Itinerary"), the prologues to *El peregrino en su patria* (The Pilgrim in His Homeland) and *Ideas y costumbres I* (Ideas and Customs I), will suffice to confirm this fact.

For the first time, all the scattered texts and poems from Paz's youth appear in Volume 13, *Miscelánea I. Primeros escritos (Miscellanea I: First Writings)*. For years, many people criticized Paz for having revised or suppressed some of his youthful works for political reasons. Although not all were willing to listen, Paz explained on various occasions his motives for his suppressions and alterations *(Entre la piedra y la flor [Between Stone and Flower])*. Now, in this volume, not only do the scattered texts appear; so also do the first versions of the poems of Paz's youth. In a fax dated February 2, 1994, he tells me,

I am sending you the first part of Volume II, i.e., the poems from my adolescence and my youth, excluded from (or never collected in) my *Obra poética*. You can imagine the mixed feelings I have in making this collection. If I had let myself be guided by poetic justice, I would have destroyed these texts. But it is impossible; all but one were published. I just found out that *El tamaño de mi esperanza*, a book whose reprinting Borges had expressly prohibited, reappeared. It is useless to rebel against these practices *post mortem*.

And in his preface, he adds,

And there is another circumstantial reason: some critics and journalists, censors who write with bile, have reproached me for suppressing various poems and correcting many others. They have said that those modifications and corrections were for reasons of an ideological nature; through them, I was trying to erase the traces of the ideas and feelings that moved and stirred me in my youth. These critics, if they can be called that, voluntarily ignore the fact that the impulse that led me to correct and suppress some of my poems has been my dissatisfaction with my work and its defects. I corrected and suppressed not out of sordid considerations of political ideology, but by a thirst for perfection. I have not been the only one; countless writers have felt and done likewise.

Attention should also be called to Volumes 14 and 15, which collect the final writings and include a selection of about 35 interviews chosen by Octavio Paz, with the assistance of Ana Clavel and Adolfo Castañón. As to the more specific and concrete corrections, in some instances we find a note that nuances or expands upon an idea. In a very limited number of cases, one word replaces another, not to deny, but to concretize or pinpoint. In a way, in these cases, it is simply a matter of restoring the proper name for each thing. On the other hand, by mutual agreement, we unified the etymological forms of many words, the Chinese, Japanese, and Russian proper nouns, or the terms for the Oriental philosophies and religions. The corrections to the poetry were minimal; however, there is one exemplary case I would like to mention here. When we were preparing the edition of *Delta de cinco brazos* (Delta with Five Branches) (a book which includes his five most important long poems and ten short poems), I received a fax from Paz dated February 23, 1994. Among other things, he said:

> It had literally been years since I last read *Sunstone*. Last Saturday, I was imprudent enough to go back to that poem and found, aside from other things which at this point are beyond repair, two lines which were asking to be amended. I am referring to the passage that speaks of death (pp. 273-275); there is a moment when, guided by the similarity between the sounds —animal sounds, physiological sounds— that we make in dying and at birth, I refer to "ese jadeo / de la vida que nace" ("that pulsebeat of life / as it's born"). In and of itself, the phrase is not entirely reprehensible (it alludes to a fact, nothing more), but in this case it is an intrusion that breaks the flow and, in turn, is abruptly interrupted. Although I have not touched the poem since it was first published 36 years ago, I gave in to the temptation, a temptation that was truly insurmountable, and changed those lines. On page 274, lines 12, 13 and 14 of the *Obra poética*,[1] where it used to say:

> el delirio, el relincho, el ruido obscuro
> que hacemos al morir y ese jadeo
> de la vida que nace y el sonido
> de huesos machacados en la riña

> the raving, the dark sound we make
> when dying and that pulsebeat of life
> as it's born, and the sound of bones being crushed
> in the fray [...]

> it should now read:

> el estertor del animal que muere,
> el delirio, el jadeo, el ruido obscuro
> de la piedra que cae, el son monótono

---

[1] Ed. note: The passage in question corresponds to p. 27, lines 24-27 of Eliot Weinberger's English translation of *Sunstone* in *The Collected Poems of Octavio Paz, 1957-1987*, ed. Eliot Weinberger (New York: New Directions, 1991).

[de los huesos machacados en la riña]
the death-rattle of the dying animal,
the raving, the pulsebeat, the dark sound
of the falling stone, the monotonous sound
[of the bones being crushed in the fray]

I hope you don't find this last-minute correction absurd. And I hope it arrives on time.

On March 3, 1994, Paz took up the subject once again:

I am delighted that you liked the correction. Hopefully, there is time to insert a small variation, which will improve one line and avoid repetition. Where *Obra poética*, p. 274, line 12, says, "el estertor del animal que muere" ("the death-rattle of the dying animal"), it should say, "la mirada del animal que muere" ("the gaze of the dying animal").

And on March 6, 1994, he wrote to me again:

Poetic gestation is at once slow and rapid, contradictory and definitive. You have had the dubious privilege of witnessing one such period [...] The three lines will not leave me. I found the two versions I sent you to have repetitions of words and ideas. In the first version, "estertor" ("death-rattle"), in the second, "mirada" ("gaze"). The version below will, I promise, be the definitive one, not only because I find it better than the previous ones, but because there will no longer be any possibility of changing it:

el animal que muere y que lo sabe,
saber común, inútil, ruido obscuro
de la piedra que cae, el son monótono
[de los huesos machacados en la riña]

the animal that dies and that knows it,
a common, useless knowledge, the dark sound
of the falling stone, the monotonous sound
[of the bones being crushed in the fray]

The knowledge that we are going to die is universal, common to all living beings. Most —perhaps all— of the animal species share that with us. Consciousness, the realization of one's own existence, appears in all animals, even
if it is shapeless, as a sensation; in turn, this awareness is inextricably linked to
the dark knowledge of death. It is enough to have seen a dog, a bull, a bird, a
butterfly, or any other insect die to confirm that the knowledge of one's own
mortality is an attribute or consequence of living animal beings (I am not getting into the enigma of the other live organisms, such as plants). All animals
know (feel) that they are alive and all know (have a feeling, a premonition)
that they are going to die. This is the root of animal *fear*, the root of the reaction of the animal in the face of fear: flight or ferocious aggression. And this
is what makes the marvelous spectacle of nature so sad —the intangible presence of death floats over life like a veil or a shadow. But that knowledge is useless for the individual (although perhaps not for the species); it does not avoid
death. On the contrary, it informs us that we are returning to the place from
where we come, raw matter: stones, atoms, or suns and galaxies. I am sure that
neither an electron nor a sun has the awareness of men, cows, snakes, and
flies. Finally, this knowledge is doubly useless, because it does not prevent
man, like all animals, from daily crushing the bones of his neighbor... Pardon
this digression to justify three lines of a poem. Hadn't we agreed that poetry
needed neither justification nor explanation?

Among the many examples that we could take from our correspondence, I choose this one deliberately, not only because it reflects a form
of respect towards others, but because it also represents one of his most
constant ambitions: perfection, constant reflection, but above all, the
essential trait for this to happen: doubt, that is, uncertainty. Only the
man who doubts can maintain a state of exaltation, which, as Stefan
Zweig says, is the other term for youth.

To a large extent, the series of parallel projects that we undertook
with the Círculo de Lectores and are now carrying forward jointly with
the Galaxia Gutenberg publishing house can be considered a fruit of
these complete works and of the ongoing work carried out over the last
ten years. Among these projects are, on the one hand, the illustrated
editions of books such as *The Double Flame, In Light of India, The Monkey Grammarian, East Slope,* or special books like *Delta de cinco brazos*

(Delta with Five Branches); without forgetting the recording of his voice on *Travesía: tres lecturas* (Crossing: Three Readings), or the new edition of his complete works that we prepared on Bible paper. Lastly, I should mention the bilingual edition we prepared of *Versiones y diversiones* (Versions and Diversions), and above all, the recent publication of *Figuras y figuraciones* (Figures and Figurations), a book that is a sort of dialogue between art and poetry, between Marie-José Paz and Octavio Paz. Ten of the twelve poems in the book emerged from Marie-José's box-*collages*, and two box-*collages* were born out of two short poems. It was in 1991 that Octavio Paz first expressed to us his desire to do this book, and it was always thought of as a dialogue between figures and figurations.

Here, I would like to point out a few constant traits that emerge from the reading of his works. I would start with their most visible characteristic: his prose is suffused with intuition and lucidity. And when I say this, I do not purport to engage in gratuitous attributions or Homeric epithets. That is why I have said elsewhere that often what is important in Paz is not so much the conceptual idea he develops, but rather how he makes us participate in his own sensations. There are felicitous turns of phrase and encounters in his prose that could only be produced from poetry and through poetic language. One example of intuition and lucidity is *The Labyrinth of Solitude* (and although I might think it is not the best example, I choose this text deliberately, because of its controversial nature, and because it is one of his most widely read books, at least in Mexico). A specialist in Mexican history, or in one of the branches of the social sciences, will discover gaps, partial elements that are missing, problems that are barely enunciated, etc. Since this is not the work of a specialist, the result is similar to most creative works; one of its essential values is to be found in what it reveals, discovers, insinuates, profiles, or awakens, more than in what it demonstrates. There is a series of issues in *Labyrinth* that Mexicans, in the wake of the book, can no longer approach in the same way. If one of the great virtues of his work is that it constantly suggests, I am not unaware that one of the risks of intuition is the temptation to generalize. Not for nothing did Bachelard include it as one of his epistemological obstacles. And as the author of *La flamme d'une chandelle* says in one of his talks: "Generalization is only possible if reality allows it." I point this out because in books like

The Double Flame or *In Light of India*, the small slip-up of generalization, which at times disorients truth, can be forgiven if we understand
intuition more as a universe of questions than a system of answers.

And since we are talking about recurring patterns in his complete
works, there is one trait, with a particular relation to how one listens to
someone else, that cannot be left out: generosity. As far as I know, no
one has expressed Paz's generous character more accurately than Ale-
jandro Rossi, who, with the intuition of the creator and the acuity of
the philosopher, says of his prose: "Prose that does not forgive errors,
but does forgive the man who made them."

But generosity, of course, is not in contradiction with criticism. When he
was awarded the Nobel Prize, Paz, in response to one of the many questions
put to him, said that he did not accept public posts because it was more
beneficial to him to work on what he believed in, away from a public post.
This, he said, would allow him to refine his criticisms and accolades.

Nonetheless, when we are totally critical, we run the risk of our
thoughts being more easily manipulated. No one is unaware that institutions are always wary of the poets' voice. And applause is often the
most elegant way to silence them.

Paz was always aware that the writer's trade is a trade of words. Conse-
quently, the writer's offensive and defensive weapon is language, and within language, the best shield against the State or any other type of reductive
power is undoubtedly one of the shortest words in the dictionary, the
monosyllabic NO. A writer must be first and foremost a *consciousness*; as
Paz would say, "he is not the man of power or the party politician: he is
the man of *consciousness*." And nothing surpasses this consciousness as an
antidote to ideologies. In a way, it is nothing more than poetry's great NO
to the powers of society. Let us once again recall the words of the author
of *Libertad bajo palabra*, in an interview with Braulio Peralta: "Hostility
to poetry is moral in origin: poetry is dangerous because it expresses the
irrational part of man, his passions, his desires, his dreams. The poet invents images and figures that are more or less real with feelings and human passions that break the social order. All of a sudden, a poetic myth,
Don Juan, becomes more real that a treatise on sociology"[2] In a word, it

---

[2] Interview with Braulio Peralta, *La Jornada*, October 12, 1990.

has to do with the possibility of saying NO, or of saying, "This is not that." During the presentation of the complete works in Madrid in 1993, Paz said, "A literature that has forgotten the power of the word *no* is a literature that has abandoned its principles." Whether right or wrong in his ideas, "Octavio Paz," as Álvaro Mutis says, "has taught us all not to swallow things whole, to meditate on each step of our destiny, on each phase of our human condition".[3]

The best way to reward a writer is to "publish" him, because, when all is said and done, the greatest homage that can be rendered him is for him to be "read", to make possible a direct circuit between the "writer" and his "readers", without going through all sorts of intermediaries, superfluous praise, or malicious attacks. The idea, therefore, is to reach a point where we can speak more about the work than about the man, more about his thought than about his personal circumstances, more about the ideas and feelings of his that are present in his work than about day-to-day intrigues.

And I return once again to the presentation of his complete works in Madrid. On that occasion, he said, "I am thinking about so many poets who never got to see their works published. I am thinking about Góngora, Quevedo, Bécquer, and I feel embarrassed." And according to the story that appeared in one newspaper, "He asserts that the publication of a mere book is a risk, and the collected works are 'an even greater challenge, a suicidal risk. But I don't think that seeing my works collected and edited will mummify me alive'."

This said, are we in the presence of a classic? I don't know. But if this is the case, I believe it only remains for us to wish that his work not fall into that definition of a classic that Borges used to put forward: a writer whom everyone mentions, but no one reads. The reader decides, but in order to make the decision, at the very least, he must have access to the writer's works. This is where publishers can make a small contribution.

However often one may argue the contrary, Paz's poetry is the center of that starfish that felt at home in every ocean. Therefore, in closing, I want to share with you two of Paz's reflections on his own work. In his fax of February 17, 1997, he tells me:

---

[3] March, 31, 1994

I am waiting for the contract for *Versiones y diversiones.* I am really happy to be able to publish that book with you —it's one of my favorites. Perhaps because this is only half mine, and in recent months I am looking at everything I have done with apathy and melancholy. For example, the first volume of my poetic works (the book is very beautiful) caused a strange —or not so strange— reaction in me: are some of its pages really worth it? I perceive the shortcomings and defects but I cannot clearly see the achievements. Has everything been a mistake? I believe that this doubt has been and is felt by practically every author of a work of the imagination. Bolívar was right: we're plowing the sea. And yet I am happy. We should write (and in general create) disinterestedly, as Krishna says— not in search of more or less illusory results, but because it is our destiny, our duty, our *dharma.*

I hope that more than the portrait of a man, in this case a poet, I have left you with a few brushstrokes that might suggest profiles, traits, which in turn are, of course, sensations, emotions, feelings that because they are moments in time are human, the antidote for that other face, the divine one, that is our obsession: eternity. I might point out in passing, as Paz suggested on so many occasions, that it is not a question of saving the world, but of accompanying the rest of mankind and walking down the road together.

And I would not want to conclude this presentation without recalling the author who gave his name to this Institute (the Instituto Cervantes). When we were preparing the volume of his poetry in September 1996, he wrote to me in a fax:

I have read the proofs twice. I very quickly went from natural happiness to doubt, later to fear, and finally, to a sense of uneasiness and despair. The experience was like reading the sentence of my own private Last Judgment. Will something remain of all this? Did I labor in vain? How could I know? That book is not what I am and much less what I would have wanted to be, but rather what I was able to be. In thinking about this, I was reminded once again of Alonso Quijano, already cured of illusions, back in his town and putting his soul in order. But he tried to right wrongs and I merely tried to write verses. In short, reading the proofs has not been so much an exercise in humility —what more could I want than that!— as in resignation. Now I feel lighter, almost happy.

Translated by Daniel Sherr

THE DOORS OF THE HOUSE

ADOLFO CASTAÑÓN

While it is true that a man is not a bird except in the realm of poetry, it is undeniable that a man is a word, a fistful of sounds and silences. As an author, Octavio Paz was very demanding with his editors. He was not unaware that, if a man is a phrase, the editor has an enormous moral responsibility, since it depends on him to ensure that the bridge erected between words and men is not broken. Because he has asked much of them, words give much to Octavio Paz; he makes them sing and think, weep and cry out. He knows how to turn them into water, or wind, or birds. For him, the word is both bread and stick, charity and horseflies, river and laughter. And the editor must follow him when the book is an overcoat and when it is a labyrinth, when it is a pillow and when it is a sword.

In the first volume of his *Obras completas* (Complete Works), Octavio Paz recalls that when Hans Meinke, Director of the Círculo de Lectores, proposed the project, his first reaction was one of surprise. The very notion of an *oeuvre*, he says, was alien to him. He, who is kept awake only by poetry and, above all, by embodying the figures of poetry in our time, in order to draw a radius from there towards the Museum, the Library, and the City, finds the idea of an *oeuvre* strange —trivial and archaeological at the same time. In any case, if the *oeuvre* is a construction, as Kafka thinks, Paz's work has neither one nor two doors. Octavio Paz's complete works are a document crisscrossed by the cultural and critical history of the 20th century. Paz's work is a review of modernity, encompassing politics, the history of ideas, visual arts, the vanguardist movements, anthropology, and philosophy, but —and this is perhaps the most relevant aspect— always from the perspective of poetry. This means that whatever subject Paz decides to address, whether Buddhism or the history of painting, his language will always be magnetized by a wandering clarity, tensed by a peculiar intellectual energy. The publication of the *Obras completas* of Octavio Paz does not represent a mere compilation, a chronological hodgepodge. The edition reveals the overarching characteristics of an intellectual architecture that was not immediately visible from the reading of the approximately 30 books of poetry and 30 collections of essays. In undertaking the edition of his works, Paz dares to take on a task that for others would be unthinkable and rash: to break up, reorganize, and recast his work in order to give it a thematic format. Because of the effect of this new composition, of this editorial rereading, the outline of this dazzling literary tapestry is clearly exhibited. We see the six doors of the *Casa de la presencia* (House of Presence) open wide: 1) literary and historical criticism; 2) history of culture; 3) political and moral criticism; 4) anthropology and philosophy; 5) art; and —*last but first*— 6) poetry. We shall recognize, however, on a deeper level, that the editorial sketch is also a clock; the *Obras completas* of Octavio Paz are truly a time-producing and history-making machine. In that reconstruction of the calendar, in that reconstruction of the slavish phrases of institutional chronology, we notice how the search for a time that would be embryonic and perennially dawn-like is propagated from the inner space of poetry onto external spaces and forums through that amorous connection called Analogy.

However, if the work of Octavio Paz is a time machine (or a "timeless" critical machine), his poetry is the meridian that marks the hours of contemplation to be inserted in history. For me, on the most personal level, perhaps the most valuable lesson of Octavio Paz as a teacher (a teacher of wisdom) is to have shown us that an active life and a life of contemplation are not divergent, that action can only escape mechanical routine and epileptic activism if it is illuminated by contemplation, and that the life of contemplation is nourished by parentheses of dizzying intellectual action.

For this reason, the *Obras completas* of Octavio Paz represent a new book of hours. I like to think that they are also an image of his bustling day: looking at the sky at dawn; writing a love poem or a contemplative poem in the morning; reading the newspapers from Mexico and the world; gazing at the paintings from a modern art exhibition or from an exhibition of that ancient art where the primordial adoration of the Cosmos unfolds; playing cat-and-mouse with public opinion; engaging in endless conversations with friends from around the world; translating a poem in the afternoon; traveling with his imagination and thoughts to the Orient or to ancient Mexico through the contemplation of a mandala; pruning his garden of fine arts and returning one more time to gaze with sagacious eyes at the sunstone, the Aztecs' sacred calendar that still continues to arrange, on the deepest level, the national banquet with its macabre festivities and its dishes of blood.

Because they set forth an "order of the day", the works of Octavio Paz are a lesson. That is why we are grateful to him: for having taught us to (re)organize our time lived, our time thought and our time dreamt; for having opened our eyes to the short reading from the Long Count —as the Maya used to call it— and vice versa.

This lesson of vital and critical architecture came to complete fruition thanks to editorial consummation. Because between the words that have a life of their own —like a bird— and the Poet-Philosopher, there was a third man, no less impassioned: Octavio Paz the editor, who not only knows how to make books, but knows how to read the silent language of stones and empires. His politics are derived from his poetics; his grammar merges into a syntax: it is a relationship of languages and parlances, a rotation of ideas and correspondences. Poetry or criticism, art or translation; it is time, Octavio Paz tells us, to discover the present and from there start the incessant search for the beginning. Therefore, upon concluding the publications of the *Obras completas* of Octavio Paz, the true task will begin: reading him with a fresh and limpid perspective.

Not only does an encyclopedic and clear-sighted witness of our culture and of the twilight of the modern idols await us; a Master awaits us. But in truth, it is an unknown Master, as is demonstrated by that unpublished book made up of the prologues to the various volumes.

Translated by Daniel Sherr

A FIRST ENCOUNTER WITH OCTAVIO PAZ'S *COMPLETE WORKS*

CARLOS MONSIVÁIS

Was Octavio Paz a graphomaniac, a man dedicated solely to the production of these 14 volumes? Surely not. He devoted a great deal of time to carrying out his diplomatic functions, editing a magazine, reading avidly, holding lengthy conversations, debating at even greater length, traveling around the world, cultivating innumerable friendships, teaching for a short time, directing a TV cultural series with himself as the expert and contentious center, carrying out his duties as an international celebrity unenthusiastically albeit with discipline, and editing his works. But if he was not a graphomaniac, he was indeed, like his Mexican predecessor Alfonso Reyes, a professional writer who carefully conceived his *oeuvre*, even if he never called it that. "He traced the map of sympathies and differences," said Reyes. Paz might have chosen "admirations and rejections." He carefully studied the basic themes that he needed for his national and international trajectories and tried to write about them to the best of his ability. And throughout, he constructed his work in accordance with the highest standards of artistic and intellectual rigor. This explains, for example, his revision of his poetry; his reordering of material; his clear intention of building a legacy; his rediscovery of the profound unity of themes and texts; his pleasure in obsession. What impressions do the *Complete Works* of Octavio Paz transmit to me upon my brief initial encounter with them? I will set down a few of these, in no particular order.

1. Paz believes in the generations of readers and grants them successive respect. If a poetic text was important to a given generation, Paz does not feel bound to a similar loyalty and instead believes in the need to reconsider that text, in order to honor his basic commitment to the following generations and thus comply with the demands of a highly critical reader: himself. In prose, his reconsideration is less radical, even though he is constantly preoccupied with achieving greater precision

and coherence. That is why in his retrospective prologue to Volume 8, *El peregrino en su patria* (*The Pilgrim in His Homeland*), Paz confirms that "ultimately, my opinions today are not always the same as those I held in 1949 when I wrote *The Labyrinth of Solitude*. On the other hand, some have become firmer over the years. It was impossible to fill the text with notes and clarifications. I preferred to trust the good sense of my readers."[1]

2. Paz, detached from localism, sets out to organize the landscape of international and Latin American tradition that is important to him. And for obvious reasons, in this endeavor he is at his most thorough when writing about Mexico. This results in an intense exploration of modern poetry, its tendencies and achievements, its limitations and major writers. The first five volumes deal with this: *La casa de la presencia* (The House of Presence), *Excursiones e incursiones* (Excursions and Incursions), *Fundación y disidencia* (Foundation and Dissidence), *Generaciones y semblanzas* (Generations and Portraits), and *Sor Juana Inés de la Cruz, o las trampas de la Fe* (*Sor Juana, or, The Traps of Faith*). The contents of various books are assembled here, among them two fundamental texts, *The Bow and the Lyre* and *Children of the Mire*. If for Paz the analysis of modernity is basic, he also examines the works of poets he considers essential for their experimental vigor, their relationship to eroticism, and their experiments with language: the poets of the Spanish Golden Age, Nerval, Blake, Mallarmé, Cernuda, Pessoa, Huidobro, Neruda, among others. To this analysis, he adds his poetic translations, which both pay homage and insist upon the international circulation of a single great poetry. Otherness, so important to Paz in society and human life, is for him inconceivable in poetry, in spite of linguistic barriers.

Following a crystal-clear strategy since the 1950s, Paz puts together his map of genuine and legible traditions, both in poetry and the visual arts. He hardly ever deals with music and, for all his acuity, he makes comparatively few references to fictional narrative. Paz sets out to cover that which is essential, including those sometimes paternalistically considered minor poets and painters. And in the case of Mexican tradition, Paz wishes to repay the great debt of his own and the following

---

[1] Obras Completas (*OC*) 8: 15.

generations to that extraordinary figure of the Viceroyalty, Sor Juana Inés de la Cruz, which he fulfills during the 1980s. Regarding Sor Juana, Paz unveils yet another of his purposes: by offering a reading of the canon, he offers, perhaps indirectly, his own intellectual biography composed of admirations and approximations:

> I see in Sor Juana the intellectual who, because of her fidelity towards her vocation, has a difficult, even unfortunate relation with her surroundings. Sor Juana was defeated, but her defeat was that of an independent writer, confronting a closed ideology and a despotic clergy. Her defeat, as she writes in a poem, was also a victory. In this sense, Sor Juana is an absolutely modern figure; the same cannot be said about Lope de Vega, Góngora, Quevedo, nor any of the other great poets of her times in Spain. Thus, I could not say what Flaubert said about Madame Bovary: *Madame Bovary, c'est moi.* But I can say that I see myself in Sor Juana.[2]

Obviously, there is no otherness here.

Paz also recognizes himself in such ancestors and contemporaries as Ramón López Velarde, Rufino Tamayo, Xavier Villaurrutia, and Pablo Neruda, as well as integral parts of the canon in Mexico like Quevedo, Rubén Darío, and T.S. Eliot, among others. He recognizes and does not recognize himself, because for Paz, the need to establish distances is another way of getting closer. He always locates nuances, even in the inevitable generalizations.

3. The insistences and obsessions in Paz, and his way of enriching his thought by means of divergence, can be readily seen in the *Complete Works*. When dealing with morality and politics, his dominant theme is the totalitarian lie, the relinquishing of intellectual independence to the more-than-deceitful cause of real socialism. His persistent denunciation, born of his disappointment with a militancy incapable of seeing the realities of Stalinism, is the most visible aspect of his project of democratic normalization. Whether in the USSR, the socialist republics, Castro's Cuba, or Sandinista Nicaragua, Paz finds the ruth-

---

[2] "En el filo del viento: Dos puntos, México y Japon," conversation with Tetsuji Yamamoto and Yumio Awa, from *Iichiko #1*, in *OC* 8: 462.

less abolition of freedoms, and feels that these repressions are extended, by means of intellectual complicities, to countries free of totalitarianism even though their governments are far from democratic. *El peregrino en su patria* and the two volumes of *Ideas y costumbres* wage that battle against ideologies and bear witness to the energy of commitment, even though Paz would not have accepted the word "commitment" due to its somber undertones. Has this battle become outmoded? I am sure it has not, not only because of the quality of Paz's writing, but because of the method his essays utilize and inherit, their resistance to self-deception, their indifference to the results of dissenting from dissidence, and their awareness that a bright future is not reached by enslaving the present. The moral lesson in these volumes is also an overview of modern history.

4. The two volumes of *Los privilegios de la vista* contain the other major Paz theme: the search for a literary equivalent of the visual arts. Paz is not, nor does he intend to be, an art critic. He is a writer who brings to literature, and frequently strictly to poetry, his impressions of the varied universe inhabited by Picasso, de Kooning, the Mexican painters, especially Tamayo —the solar painter who had such an effect on Paz, who resolved, even if he only acknowledged it towards the end of his life, during his last public appearance, to be a solar writer— Matta, Richard Dadd, Hindu art, the impressionists, Klee, the avant-garde —respectfully acknowledged, but at a distance— Orozco, and, now and again, Siqueiros and Rivera. Painting, engraving, sculpture, architecture, ceramics, and pre-Hispanic art in particular forced Paz to see and think poetically in another way. Without the visual arts, much of his lyric imagery cannot be understood.

5. The Orient attracts him for its wealth of ideas and imagery, and for the purpose of establishing unexpected links between one culture and another

6. Eroticism, the reflection of the Shakespearean beast with two backs, is an inescapable theme of Paz's work. To love is to struggle. If two people kiss, the world changes. Entwined naked bodies take diverse forms that, among other things, express the demand for population control, one of the intellectual and poetic demands of Paz, whose concept of the sacred includes, first and foremost, copulation.

The *Obras completas* of Octavio Paz, this magnificent effort of the Círculo de Lectores and the Fondo de Cultura Económica, are an editorial success and a generous invitation to come closer to a great writer. Unlike other complete works, even by other first-rate authors, these do not constitute a mausoleum, but an immense opportunity to continue the dialogue and —as often happens— the debate with Octavio Paz.

Translated by Cyretta Chaput

Octavio Paz:
Selected Poems

Metropolitan Museum of Art
Poetry Reading
October 24, 1999.

PHILIPPE DE MONTEBELLO

The program, as you know, is the combination of several days of events
that honor this genial man who spoke for the Mexican ethos, of course,
but for all of mankind as well, as one of the leading literary figures of this
century. The program is held under the auspices of the Mexican Cultural
Institute, both in Washington and in New York, and we are indeed most
grateful to them. We are especially pleased to have this event at the Metropolitan, not only because Octavio Paz represents the highest standards
of his craft as a writer and a level of inspiration and creativity rarely
achieved, but because he was also deeply concerned with the visual arts.
Indeed, I should remind you that Octavio Paz was a good friend of the
Metropolitan and as such he was enormously helpful in shaping the exhibition "Mexico: Splendors of Thirty Centuries" that was held here in 1991,
a show to which he contributed a major essay entitled "Will to Form,"
which was at a level of humanism rarely found, I'm afraid, in exhibition
catalogues. He wrote the piece, he said, "...under the auspices of three
emblems: the eagle, the jaguar and the virgin," emblems which clearly
said much to Octavio Paz about the multifaceted character of Mexico. It is
my pleasure and my role now to express my appreciation to the co-sponsors
for today's event, to the distinguished personalities, friends, and admirers
of Octavio Paz who will presently come to this podium to read from his
poetry. And I would like to thank the institutions that have collaborated
with us and the Mexican Cultural Institute, namely, the Fundación Octavio Paz, the Instituto Cervantes, the Academy of American Poets, the Poetry Society of America, the Secretaría de Relaciones Exteriores, and the
Instituto Mexicano de Cooperación Internacional. I would also like to
acknowledge the presence here of His Excellency Jesús Reyes Heroles,
Ambassador of Mexico to the United States, and, of course, Mrs. Marie-
José Paz. After my reading of the start of the poem "Sunstone," its conclusion will be read at the end of the program by Eliot Weinberger, whose
translation incidentally it is.

Sunstone
(fragment)

a crystal willow, a poplar of water,
a tall fountain the wind arches over,
a tree deep-rooted yet dancing still,
a course of a river that turns, moves on,
doubles back, and comes full circle,
forever arriving:
                    the calm course
of the stars or an unhurried spring,
water with eyes closed welling over
with oracles all night long,
a single presence in a surge of waves,
wave after wave till it covers all,
a reign of green that knows no decline,
like the flash of wings unfolding in the sky,

a path through the wilderness of days to come,
and the gloomy splendor of misery like a bird
whose song can turn a forest to stone,
and the imminent joys on branches that vanish,
the hours of light pecked away by the birds,
and the omens that slip past the hand,

a sudden presence like a burst of song,
like the wind singing in a burning building,
a glance that holds the world and all
its seas and mountains dangling in the air,
body of light filtered through an agate,
thighs of light, belly of light, the bays,
the solar rock, cloud-colored body,
color of a brisk and leaping day,
the hour sparkles and has a body,
the world is visible through your body,
transparent through your transparency...

DORE ASHTON

> Me han pedido un prólogo
> corto, me dijeron, pocas palabras…
> —OCTAVIO PAZ

Octavio's thoughts and poems have accompanied me all my adult life —I met him in my mid-twenties. We often talked about painting and sculpture, argued, corresponded, and occasionally had monumental disagreements. But through it all, I listened for Hermes, the messenger who was also the god of boundaries. Octavio's unerring sense of form, which is to say boundaries, guided me. He was truly my Hermes.

When I thought about reading a poem, I chose the most succinct I could find, which has bearing on my almost lifelong conversation with Octavio. "The other," it has always seemed to me, is a perfect linguistic counterpart to the late drawings of Picasso, in which he masked and unmasked not so much his self as the self of all painters who cast themselves into space in order to retrieve sensed forms.

The Other
(trans. Eliot Weinberger)

He invented a face for himself.
                    Behind it,
he lived, died, and was resurrected
many times.
        His face now
has the wrinkles from that face.
His wrinkles have no face.

                    [East slope]

BEI DAO

Octavio and I met each other in 1989 in New York City. After the shocking events that happened in China, he attended a panel discussion about Chinese literature to share the sadness and loss with us. Octavio's poems entered Mainland China about twenty years ago. I still remember how excited I felt when I read his work for the first time. The poem "The Street," was especially influential on Chinese poets. Five years ago, I recited this poem in a tribute to Octavio's eightieth birthday here, at this museum, when he was among us. I am going to recite it again today.

The Street
(trans. Muriel Rukeyser)

A long and silent street.
I walk in blackness and I stumble and fall
and rise, and I walk blind, my feet
stepping on silent stones and dry leaves.
Someone behind me also stepping on stones, leaves:
if I slow down, he slows;
if I run, he runs. I turn: nobody.
Everything dark and doorless.
Turning and turning among these corners
which lead forever to the street
where nobody waits for, nobody follows me,
where I pursue a man who stumbles
and rises and says when he sees me: nobody.

[*Calamities and Miracles*]

FRANCESCO CLEMENTE

I met Octavio Paz in recent years with Marino and Francesco Pelizzi. I've always admired his sense of history and of geography; he was someone from the South who wanted to talk to the North and travel East. We shared a passion for India, and I'm going to read from one of the rare and sentimental books written about India, *The Monkey Grammarian.*

The Monkey Grammarian
(trans. Helen R. Lane)

I walk over to the opposite edge of the terrace and from there I see in the distance the bony crest of the mountain outlined with cruel precision. Down below, the street and the fountain, the temple and its two priests, the booths and their elderly vendors, the children leaping about and screeching, several starving cows, more monkeys, a lame dog. Everything is radiant: the animals, the people, the trees, the stones, the filth. A soft radiance that has reached an accord with the shadows and their folds. An alliance of brightness, a thoughtful restraint: objects take on a secret life, call out to each other, answer each one, they do not move and yet they vibrate, alive with a life that is different from life. A universal pause: I breathe in the air, the acrid odor of burned dung, the smell of incense and poverty. I plant myself firmly in this moment of motionless: the hour is a block of pure time.

JOHN KENNETH GALBRAITH

Diplomacy has its wonderful, even exotic aspects. Even thus, it was a bit at the extreme in bringing two friends, Octavio Paz and myself, as ambassadors to India. I found there that in days of peace or relative calm, by not doing what my staff could do as well or better, I could complete the day's business in not over three hours. Octavio could do it all in, I would judge, around thirty minutes. Thus, we both had time to survey the compelling Indian culture and scene. A special, even spectacular example of the latter is the glowing city of Udaipur, capital of the princely state of Mewar.

By our time, the princes had mostly suffered the inevitabilities and, I hasten to add, the compelling virtues of democracy. Or most of them. But in Udaipur, the princely family was still a dominant and valued presence. They occupied, on a hill by the lake, the splendid palace that looked over and down on a smaller but equally splendid palace on an island in the lovely lake. A visit there was artistically, architecturally, and socially a return to the Indian past. (It was chosen to take Jacqueline Kennedy, visiting India, into that past.) And there on a special occasion came Octavio Paz. It was a reward for him and later for all who loved Octavio and his verse. Looking out from the great palace to the lake, the island, and the Lake Palace, he wrote *The Day in Udaipur.*

The Day in Udaipur
(trans. Eliot Weinberger)

White palace,
white on the black lake.
Lingam and yoni.
        As the goddess to the god,
        you surround me, night.
Cool terrace.
You are immense, immense —
made to measure.
        Inhuman stars.
        But this hour is ours.
I fall and rise,
I burn, drenched.
Are you only one body?
        Birds on the water,
        dawn on eyelids.
Self-absorbed,
high as death,
the marble bursts.
        Hushed palaces,
        whiteness adrift.
Women and children
on the roads:
scattered fruit.
        Rags or rays of lightning?
        A procession on the plain.
Silver running cool
and clanking:
ankle and wrist.

In a rented costume
        the boy goes to his wedding.
Clean clothes
spread out on the rocks.
Look at them and say nothing.
        On the little island
        monkeys with red asses screech.
Hanging from the wall,
a dark and angry sun:
wasps' nest.
        And my head is another sun,
        full of black thoughts.
Flies and blood.
A small goat skips
in Kali's court.
        Gods, men and beasts
        eat from the same plate.
Over the pale god
the black goddess dances,
decapitated.
        Heat, the hour split open,
        and those mangoes, rotten . . .
Your face, the lake:
smooth, without thoughts.
A trout leaps.
        Lights on the water:
        souls sailing.
Ripples:
the golden plain — and the crack . . .
Your clothes nearby.
        I, like a lamp
        on your shadow body.
 A living scales:
bodies entwined
over the void.

The sky crushes us,
the water sustains us.
I open my eyes:
so many trees
were born tonight.
What I've seen here, what I say,
the white sun erases.

[*East slope*]

ROBERT GARDNER

From the moment I met Octavio exactly thirty years ago, I never doubted I would come to know not only a great poet but an indisputable shaman. The certainty of this became evident as he showed me, time after time, that he could see what was invisible to everyone else —a sure sign of shamanic powers. Octavio was too good a shaman to ever reveal his shamanhood, but there was no question he possessed all the classic attributes of his calling, including the capacity for magical flight. Today, I would like to let his words convey you to one of his favorite geographies by reading *Sunday on the Island of Elephanta.*

Sunday on the Island of Elephanta
(trans. Eliot Weinberger)

IMPRECATION

At the feet of the sublime sculptures,
vandalized by the Muslims and the Portuguese,
the crowds have left a picnic of garbage
for the crows and dogs.
I condemn them to be reborn a hundred times
on a dungheap,
and as for the others,

for eons they must carve living flesh
in the hell for the mutilators of statues.

INVOCATION

Shiva and Parvati:
                    we worship you
not as gods
                    but as images
of the divinity of man.
You are what man makes and is not,
what man will be
when he has served the sentence of hard labor.
Shiva:
        your four arms are four rivers,
four jets of water.
                    Your whole being is a fountain
where the lovely Parvati bathes,
where she rocks like a graceful boat.
The sea beats beneath the sun;
it is the great lips of Shiva laughing;
the sea is ablaze:
it is the steps of Parvati on the waters.
Shiva and Parvati:
                    the woman who is my wife
and I
        ask you for nothing, nothing
that comes from the other world:
                                only
the light on the sea,
the barefoot light on the sleeping land and sea.

[*Toward the beginning*]

ALMA GUILLERMOPRIETO

I chose a short poem that succinctly presents some of Octavio Paz's favorite words, words that in my opinion become miraculously beautiful when they are intertwined in his poetry.

Wind, Water, Stone
(trans. Eliot Weinberger)

for Roger Caillois

Water hollows stone,
wind scatters water,
stone stops the wind.
Water, wind, stone.

Wind carves stone,
stone's a cup of water,
water escapes and is wind.
Stone, wind, water.

Wind sings in its whirling,
water murmurs going by,
unmoving stone keeps still.
Wind, water, stone.

Each is another and no other:
crossing and vanishing
through their empty names:
water, stone, wind.

[*A tree within*]

EDWARD HIRSCH

Octavio Paz practiced poetry like a secret religion. He dwelt in its mysteries, he invoked its sacraments, he read its entrails, he inscribed its revelations. Writing was for him a primordial act, and he stared down at the blank page like an abyss until it sent him reeling over the brink of language. The poems he brought back are filled with ancient wonder and strangeness, hermetic knowledge, a dizzying sense of the sacred. They are magically —sometimes violently— uprooted from the flow of linear or successive time.

I'm struck by how many of Paz's poems seem to unfold and take place in liminal spaces, in pauses and intervals, odd crossings, interrupted movements. He finds a poetic space opening up in gaps and ruptures, in the realm of the betwixt and between. Think of all the arches and bridges in his poems, the shadowy tunnels and endless interior corridors, the elemental passageways, vertiginous heights. He is a seeker, a pilgrim, a poet of crossings and thresholds, of portals to the other side. He said: "For the poem is a means of access to pure time, an immersion in the original waters of existence."[1] He defined the poetic experience as "an opening up of the wellsprings of being. An instant and never. An instant and forever."[2]

Paz's inspired poetic gift opened up deep wellsprings of being and delivered eternal pauses, what Virginia Woolf calls "Moments of Being." He consecrates an endless instant, an elusive clarity, a wavering stillness, a superabundance of time and being. It is "Within a Moment: The Pulsation of the Artery," William Blake writes, "When the Poet's Work is Done." I find such a luminous moment of revelation in *Between Going and Staying*.

Between Going and Staying
(trans. Eliot Weinberger)

Between going and staying the day wavers,
in love with its own transparency.

---

[1] *The Bow and the Lyre*, trans. Ruth L. C. Simms (Austin: University of Texas Press, 1973), 15.
[2] *Ibid.*, 139.

The circular afternoon is now a bay
where the world in stillness rocks.
All is visible and all elusive,
all is near and can't be touched.

Paper, book, pencil, glass,
rest in the shade of their names.

Time throbbing in my temples repeats
the same unchanging syllable of blood.

The light turns the indifferent wall
into a ghostly theater of reflections.

I find myself in the middle of an eye,
watching myself in its blank stare.

The moment scatters. Motionless,
I stay and go: I am a pause.

[*A tree within*]

WILLIAM LUERS

During my early years in the 1970s as a diplomat serving in Latin America, I read *The Labyrinth of Solitude*. It opened pathways in my mind that over the years helped me comprehend the complexities and mysteries of the most ancient and most intricate civilization in the Western Hemisphere. My fascination with the essays of Paz were reinforced by my friend, the Venezuelan writer Carlos Rangel, who considered Paz to be one of the giants of Latin American letters and thought. Over the years, I revisited Octavio's essays, which provided insights into the history, culture, and politics of Mexico. For years I carried with me extra paperback editions of his essays to give to friends and colleagues. I believed that no other nation, no other people had produced such a writer and philosopher capable of grasping and interpreting for others the wide range of his country's cultural, political, and social makeup. Paz was unique.

Then in the 1980s, while I served as Ambassador in Prague, I came to know the Mexican Ambassador, who was a prominent Mexican writer. He said, "Bill, it is the poetry of Octavio Paz that you must read." In that poetry, I began my real journey with this amazing writer. I was stunned by the ambition and reach of his mind.

I had met Paz during the mid 1970s while dealing with Mexico as a diplomat in Washington, but had more frequent contact with him as President of the Metropolitan Museum of Art as we prepared the great exhibition on Mexican civilization in the late 1980s. I introduced him to an audience in this auditorium in the fall of 1990, just days after the announcement that he had won the Nobel Prize in Literature. A few years later I helped organize, in this same hall, an evening dedicated to Paz's poetry. I introduced the evening and listened for the first time to many of his poems in Spanish and read in English translation. It was one of the most memorable evenings of my time in New York and sent me back to Octavio's poetry. Hearing his art in the two languages reinforced for me the sense that Paz was both the finest interpreter of Mexican civilization and one of the world's greatest artists.

Bang
(trans. Eliot Weinberger)

A Lasse Söderberg

The word leaps
ahead of thought
ahead of sound
the word leaps like a horse
ahead of the wind
like a sulfur bull
ahead of the night
it's lost in the streets of my skull
the tracks of the beast are everywhere
the scarlet tattoo on the face of the tree

the ice tattoo on the tower's forehead
the electric tattoo on the sex of the church
its claws in your neck
its paws on your belly
the violet sign
the sunflower that turns toward white
toward the scream toward enough!
the sunflower that turns like a flayed sigh
the signature of the nameless across your skin
everywhere the blinding scream
the black swell that covers thought
the angry bell that clangs in my head
the bell of blood in my chest
the image that laughs at the top of the tower
the word that explodes the words
the image that burns all the bridges
the woman who vanished in the middle of a kiss
the derelict who killed her children
the idiot the liar the incestuous daughter
the persecuted doe
the prophetic beggarwoman
the girl who in the middle of my life
wakes me and says *remember*.

[*Days and occasions*]

MICHAEL PALMER

Why did I select this poem to read on this evening? It's very simple. I did
not select this poem. Some weeks ago, I sat down with *The Collected Poems of Octavio Paz (1957-1987)* at hand, lit a small candle scented with ver-
bena and said the following, "Octavio —can you hear me, Octavio?
Octavio, we have to make a deal. I have agreed to give a talk in Washington on your relation to vanguardism. I do not like to give talks. They
are difficult for me to prepare, and I am an anxious and private person,

but I have agreed. The way I see it, you owe me one. I have also consented to read from your work at The Met, the Big House. Important people will be there. Friends will be there. The famous will be there. Monumental statuary will be in evidence. You are a believer in magic and in chance. You must select a poem for me, one that breathes in and out, one that speaks of the making, and of first and final things, and of sun and stone." At that I placed the book on my desk and allowed it to fall open wherever it might, in the slight breeze that had inexplicably arisen. Hence *La palabra escrita* (*The Written Word*).

The Written Word
(trans. Eliot Weinberger)

Written now the first
word (never the one thought of,
but the other—this
that doesn't say it, contradicts it,
says it without saying it)
Written now the first
word (one, two, three—
sun above, your face
in the well water fixed
like an astonished sun)
Written now the first
 word (four, five—
the pebble keeps falling,
look at your face as it falls, reckon
the vertical measure of its falling)
Written now the first
word (there's another, below,
not the one that's falling,
the one that holds face, sun, and time,
above the abyss: the word
before the fall, before the measure)
Written now the first

word (two, three, four—
you will see your face crack,
you will see a sun that scatters,
you will see the stone in the broken water,
you will see the same face, the same sun,
fixed above the same water)
Written now the first
word (go on,
there are no more words
than the words of the measure)

[*Days and occasions*]

ROBERT PINSKY

The object of our celebration and grief this evening is a person and a body of work that included international and domestic politics, visual art, philosophy, anthropology, and all of these things not only as a commentator —an incisive and memorable commentator— but as a participant as well.

The diversity and eminence of the people who are sharing in this celebration and mourning are evidence of the magical spirit of Octavio Paz's work: he could do these things not as one who moves outside the world of poetry to engage visual art or international politics or national politics— but rather in such a manner that the notion of poetry includes all of those other worlds.

That is the magic we salute this evening. My function will be that of the magician's gesturing assistant; that is, I will read for you the names of the speakers as they appear.

But first, it's my honor and privilege to begin by reading a poem, a great poem. I've chosen a short one because I've been given permission to read it in both English and Spanish, which will be a pleasure. First in English in Eliot Weinberger's superb translation, *Between What I See and What I Say.*

Between What I See and What I Say...
(trans. Eliot Weinberger)

for Roman Jakobson

1

Between what I see and what I say,
between what I say and what I keep silent,
between what I keep silent and what I dream,
between what I dream and what I forget:
poetry.
    It slips
between yes and no,
            says
what I keep silent,
            keeps silent
what I say,
        dreams
what I forget.
           It is not speech:
it is an act.
        It is an act
of speech.
      Poetry
speaks and listens:
           it is real,
And as soon as I say
          it is real,
it vanishes.
        Is it then more real?

2

Tangible idea,
        intangible

word:
    poetry
comes and goes
        between what it is
and what is not.
        It weaves
and unweaves reflections.
          Poetry
scatters eyes on a page,
scatters words on our eyes.
Eyes speak,
    words look,
looks think.
    To hear
thoughts,
    see
what we say,
    touch
the body of an idea.
       Eyes close,
the words open.

                [*A tree within*]

ROBERT RAUSCHENBERG

A Wind Called Bob Rauschenberg
(trans. Eliot Weinberger)

Landscape fallen from Saturn,
abandoned landscape,
plains of nuts and wheels and bars,
asthmatic turbines, broken propellers,
electrical scars,
desolate landscape:

the objects sleep side by side,
great flocks of things and things and things,
the objects sleep with eyes open
and slowly fall within themselves,
they fall without moving,
their fall is the stillness of a plain under the moon,
their sleep is a falling with no return,
a descent toward a space with no beginning,
the objects fall,
               objects are falling,
they fall from my mind that thinks them,
they fall from my eyes that don't see them,
they fall from my thoughts that speak them,
they fall like letters, letters, letters,
a rain of letters on a derelict landscape.

Fallen landscape,
strewn over itself, a great ox,
a ox crepuscular as this century that ends,
things sleep side by side—
iron and cotton, silk and coal,
synthetic fibers and grains of wheat,
screws and the wing-bones of a sparrow,
the crane, the woolen quilt, the family portrait,
the headlight, the crank and the hummingbird feather—
things sleep and talk in their sleep,
the wind blows over the things,
and what the things say in their sleep
the lunar wind says brushing past them,
it says it with reflections and colors that burn and sparkle,
the wind speaks forms that breathe and whirl,
the things hear them talking, and take fright at the sound,
they were born mute, and now they sing and laugh,
they were paralytic, and now they dance,
the wind joins them and separates and joins them,
plays with them, unmakes and remakes them,

invents other things, never seen nor heard,
their unions and disjunctions
are clusters of tangible enigmas,
strange and changing forms of passion,
constellations of desire, rage, love,
figures of encounters and goodbyes.

The landscape opens its eyes and sits up,
sets out walking followed by its shadow,
it is a stela of dark murmurs
that are the languages of fallen matter,
the wind stops and hears the clamor of the elements,
sand and water talking in low voices,
the howl of pilings as they battle the salt,
the rash confidence of fire,
the soliloquy of ashes,
the interminable conversation of the universe.
Talking with the things and with ourselves
the universe talks to itself:
we are its tongue and ears, its words and silences.
The wind hears what the universe says
and we hear what the wind says,
rustling the submarine foliage of language,
the secret vegetation of the underworld and the undersky:
man dreams the dream of things,
time thinks the dreams of men.

[*A tree within*]

GRACE SCHULMAN

Octavio Paz was acquainted with suffering and conversant with broad
social issues and yet at the same time believed that only art, and especially poetry, can reveal the wholeness of life, love, and nations. He
wrote: "Styles have never been exclusively national, and they leap

across walls and frontiers…" And again, "A writer is always a plurality of voices, every language is a plurality of languages." His great
poem, *Blanco*, has to do with a meeting between East and West, language and silence, the self and the other, opposites presented as dialogue that propels the poem forward. *Sunstone*, the poem named for
the Aztec calendar wheel whose elements, sun and stone, incarnate the
unity of life and death, invokes the myth that reforms the present moment, bringing new energy to earthly things.

Influenced early by the French Surrealists and later by the art and
culture of India, his poems embody a belief in pure time to which
only art has access. Where calendar time, the rhythm that governs
daily life, attaches an end to days and years, mythical time creates life.
The artist is a visionary who transcends daily time and in radiant moments can apprehend an unbroken world, unfragmented by time, un-
divided by "what I have been" or "what I will become." As he writes
in *Beyond Love:*

> Beyond ourselves,
> on the frontier of being and becoming,
> a life more alive claims us.

> [*Semillas para un himno*]

And in *January First*, the poem I will read today, these moving
lines appear:

> Tomorrow we must invent,
> anew,
> the reality of this world.

Paz has created an image of men and women going beyond
themselves, beyond human endeavor. Over and over again, he affirms that poetry lives on the deepest levels of the world's being. His
poetry is of a journey toward insight, his voyage my voyage, his passion my passion.

January First
(trans. Eliot Weinberger)

The doors of the year open,
like the doors of language,
onto the unknown.
Last night you said:
                              tomorrow
we must draw signs,
sketch a landscape, hatch a plot
on the unfolded page
of paper and the day.
Tomorrow we must invent,
anew,
the reality of this world.

When I opened my eyes it was late.
For a second of a second
I felt like the Aztec
on the rock-strewn peak,
watching
the cracks of horizons
for the uncertain return of time.

No, the year came back.
It filled the room,
and my glances could almost touch it.
Time, without our help,
had arranged
in the same order as yesterday,
the houses on the empty street,
the snow on the houses,
the silence on the snow.

You were beside me,
still sleeping.
The day had invented you,
but you hadn't yet accepted
your day's invention,
nor mine.
You were still in another day.

You were beside me,
and I saw you, like the snow,
asleep among the appearances.
Time, without our help,
invents houses, streets, trees,
sleeping women.

When you open your eyes
we'll walk, anew,
among the hours and their inventions,
and lingering among the appearances
we'll testify to time and its conjugations.
We'll open the doors of this day,
and go into the unknown.

[*A tree within*]

RICHARD SEAVER

Publishers have few, very rare accasions where the people they publish
are those they most adore, and Octavio Paz was certainly one of those.
I had the privilege of arriving at Grove Press just before we published
The Labyrinth of Solitude, so my relation with Octavio, my professional relation, goes back many, many, many years. When in 1970, ten years
later, we started an imprint called Seaver Books at the Viking Press,
Octavio Paz chose to come with us and for the next 20 years we published all his prose. His poetry was published by New Directions.

But in the real sense of the term, none of Octavio's work is really prose; all of it is so imbued with poetry that it is sometimes hard to distinguish one so-called genre from another. *The Monkey Grammarian* is the fourth of Octavio's works that we published at Seaver Books, in 1981. The book is, as someone has noted, a product of his long and very rich stay in a country he truly loved, India. I hadn't realized until Professor Galbraith had given us the rather astounding statistic tonight that Octavio was able to dispense with his ambassadorial duties within an hour. I had always thought that his ambassadorial duties consumed at least two or three of his waking hours, and that he devoted the rest of the time to study and writing.

The Monkey Grammarian is a prose poem —that was Octavio's depiction of it, the title comes from Hanumān, who was a red-faced-not red-assed, but red-faced monkey chief, and in the world of Hindi mythology, the ultimate grammarian. So I'm sure that Octavio was drawn to Hanumān for many reasons, both intellectual and otherwise, but the grammarian aspect was certainly part of it. Hanumān had many virtues and was a conspicuous figure in the *Ramāyāna*. He could leap from India to Ceylon in one bound, tear up trees carried away from the Himalayas, seize the clouds, and perform many other wonderful exploits. When I read of Hanumān I often think that Octavio was not far from accomplishing those exploits himself, near the end of *The Monkey Grammarian*, which is a journey, a mind journey, although I suspect that Octavio took that journey not only in his mind but on foot as well to the sacred city of Galta in India. Toward the end of the book, there is a short passage which I'd like to read.

The Monkey Grammarian
(trans. Helen R. Lane)

All poems say the same thing and each poem is unique. Each part reproduces the others and each part is different. As I began these pages I decided to follow literally the metaphor of the title of the collection that they were intended for, the Paths of Creation, and to write, to describe a text that was really a path and that could be read and followed as such. As I wrote, the path to Galta grew blurred or else I lost my bearings and went astray in the trackless wilds. Again and again I was obliged to return to the starting point. Instead of advancing, the text circled about itself. Is destruction creation? I do not know, but I do know that creation is not destruction. At each turn the text opened out into another one, at once its translation and its transposition: a spiral of repetitions and reiterations that have dissolved into a negation of writing as a path. Today I realize that my text was not going anywhere —except to meet itself. I also perceive that repetitions are metaphors and that reiterations are analogies: a system of mirrors that little by little have revealed another text. In this text Hanumān contemplates the garden of Rāvana like a page of calligraphy like the harem of the same Rāvana as described in the Rāmāyana like this page on which the swaying motions of the beeches in the grove opposite my window accumulate on this page like the shadows of two lovers projected by the fire on a wall like the stains of monsoon rains on a ruined palace of the abandoned town of Galta like the rectangular space on which they surge the wave upon wave of a multitude contemplated from the crumbling balconies by hundred of monkeys like an image of writing and reading like a metaphor of the path and the pilgrimage to the sanctuary like the final dissolution of the path and the convergence of all the texts in this paragraph like a metaphor of the embrace of the bodies. Analogy: universal transparency: seeing in this that.

LASSE SÖDERBERG

I first thought of selecting *Himno entre ruinas* because it is a central poem in Octavio's work, and also because it was the first poem of Octavio's that I ever read in a bilingual French edition in Paris in the early 50s. It was also the first poem that I translated shortly before I met Octavio, who was then secretary of the Mexican Embassy in Paris. But I thought, "That poem is too long." Then I thought of choosing *Disparo* out of sheer and shameful vanity, since I had the honor of having it dedicated to me. This poem, which you and I had the pleasure of already listening to, was called in English *Bang*. Finally I reflected upon a mysterious and mysteriously chilling little piece called *El otro*, but I was told that Dore Ashton already had selected it, so I chose another poem, *To Talk*.

To Talk
(trans. Eliot Weinberger)

I read in a poem:
to talk is divine.
But gods don't speak:
they create and destroy worlds
while men do the talking.
Gods, without words,
play terrifying games.

The spirit descends,
untying tongues,
but it doesn't speak words:
it speaks flames.
Language, lit by a god
is a prophecy
of flames and a crash
of burnt syllables:
meaningless ash.

Man's word
is the daughter of death.
We talk because we are
mortal: words
are not signs, they are years.
Saying what they say,
the names we speak
say time: they say us,
we are the names of time.
To talk is human.

[*A tree within*]

SUSAN SONTAG

I loved Octavio Paz. It was a great privilege to know him. To read a poem suggests, perhaps, that it is a favorite poem, and that would be impossible. This is not my favorite poem of Octavio's, although I have many, many favorites, but it is a poem that seemed particularly appropriate to read tonight because one of the extraordinary things about this man was that he was so alive, so alive mentally, so curious; he was full of appetites, and he understood that intellectual appetites are appetites, desires, passions. The range of his interests is extraordinary, the range of his achievement in these interests, the extent to which he was able to generate really interesting ideas, reflections. He was a great reader; he was extremely curious. Since this event is in Manhattan —Paz was Ambassador to India; unfortunately, he wasn't Ambassador to the United States of America, but he was interested in so many things that were and are central to the culture of the United States and particularly of New York —it seemed appropriate to read a poem of his called *On Reading John Cage.*

On Reading John Cage
(trans. Eliot Weinberger)

Read
    unread:
Music without measurements,
sounds passing through circumstances.
Within me I hear them
        passing outside,
outside me I see them
        passing with me.
I am the event.
Music:
    I hear within what I see outside.
    I see within what I hear outside.
(Duchamp: I can't hear myself hearing.)
        I am

an architecture
                    of instantaneous sounds
on a space that disintegrates.
                              (*Everything*
we come across is to the point.)
                              Music
invents silence,
                    architecture
invents space.
                    Factories of air.
Silence
        is the space of music:
a confined
        space:
                    there is no silence
except in the mind.
                    Silence is an idea,
                    the fixed idea of music.
Music is not an idea:
                    it is movement,
sounds walking over the silence.
(*Not one sound fears the silence*
                              that extinguishes it.)
Silence is music,
                    music is not silence.
Nirvana is Samsara,
                    Samsara is not Nirvana.
Knowledge is not knowledge:
                              a recovery of ignorance,
the knowledge of knowledge.
                              It is not the same,
hearing the footsteps of the afternoon
among the trees and houses,
                              and
seeing this same afternoon
among the same trees and houses now
                              after reading

Silence:
>Nirvana is Samsara,
>>silence is music.

(*Let life obscure*
>>*the difference between art and life.*)

Music is not silence:
>>it is not saying

what silence says,
>>it is saying

what it doesn't say.
>>>Silence has no meaning,
>>>meaning has no silence.

Without being heard
>>music slips between the two.

(*Every something is an echo of nothing.*)

In the silence of my room
>>>the murmur of my body:

unheard.
>>One day I will hear its thoughts.
>>>>The afternoon

has stopped:
>>and yet—it goes on.

My body hears the body of my wife
>>>>(*a cable of sound*)

and answers:
>>this is called music.

Music is real,
>>silence is an idea.

John Cage is Japanese
>>>and is not an idea:

he is sun on snow.
>>>Sun and snow are not the same:

sun is snow and snow is snow
>>>or

sun is not snow nor is snow snow

or
   John Cage is not American
(U.S.A. is determined to keep the Free World free,
U.S.A. determined)
              or
John Cage is American
                  (that the U.S.A. may become
just another part of the world.
                      No more, no less.)
Snow is not sun,
             music is not silence,
sun is snow,
        silence is music.
(The situation must be Yes-and-No,
                  not either-or.)
Between silence and music,
             art and life,
snow and sun,
          there is a man.
That man is John Cage
              (committed
to the nothing in between).
               He says a word:
not snow not sun,
          a word
which is not
      silence:
A year from Monday you will hear it.

The afternoon has become invisible.

                        [*East slope*]

MARK STRAND

As One Listens to the Rain
(trans. Eliot Weinberger)

Listen to me as one listens to the rain,
not attentive, not distracted,
light footsteps, thin drizzle,
water that is air, air that is time,
the day is still leaving,
the night has yet to arrive,
figurations of mist
at the turn of the corner,
figurations of time
at the bend in this pause,
listen to me as one listens to the rain,
without listening, hear what I say
with eyes open inward, asleep
with all five senses awake,
it's raining, light footsteps, a murmur of syllables,
air and water, words with no weight:
what we were and are,
the days and years, this moment,
weightless time and heavy sorrow,
listen to me as one listens to the rain,
wet asphalt is shining,
steam rises and walks away,
night unfolds and looks at me,
you are you and your body of steam,
you and your face of night,
you and your hair, unhurried lightning,
you cross the street and enter my forehead,
footsteps of water across my eyes,
listen to me as one listens to the rain,
the asphalt's shining, you cross the street,
it is the mist, wandering in the night,

it is the night, asleep in your bed,
it is the surge of waves in your breath,
your fingers of water dampen my forehead,
your fingers of flame burn my eyes,
your fingers of air open eyelids of time,
a spring of visions and resurrections,
listen to me as one listens to the rain,
the years go by, the moments return,
do you hear your footsteps in the next room?
not here, not there: you hear them
in another time that is now,
listen to the footsteps of time,
inventor of places with no weight, nowhere,
listen to the rain running over the terrace,
the night is now more night in the grove,
lightning has nesteled among the leaves,
a restless garden adrift–go in,
your shadow covers this page.

[*A tree within*]

NATHANIEL TARN

I met Octavio Paz exactly fifty years ago at Andre Breton's Surrealist Group meetings in Montmartre. We would often go on long walks back together to his place for food and drinks. I gradually drowned into Anthropology and so did not see Octavio after 1951. We made contact again when I had raised my head in Poetry a little and was working at Jonathan Cape Publishers in London. Octavio wanted a *Selected Poems* done to his specifications; Cape did not want to oblige. I was impressed by Octavio's minute attention to detail and his determination throughout an arduous correspondence.

We saw each other later with Marie-Jo in the sixties and seventies in London, at Harvard, at their place in the Zona Rosa. One time, there was a marvelous visit to the Cacaxtla frescoes with an enthusiastic picnic in a colonial churchyard. Perhaps the last time I saw them was in the 18th room of the great Matisse show at MOMA a few years ago. Octavio modestly apologized for not tarrying and explained that he was following an expert!

Apart from his strikingly handsome appearance (he was truly leonine), I was always struck by two things above all. First: he was one of the last representatives of a great but deliquescing human species: the Person of Letters. Nothing human or non-human was alien to him; the totalizing passion of the scholar without the heavy weight of scholarship; the prodigious activity (no one knows how he ever did it); the fervent defense of his beloved arts. Second: the generosity. To me, and doubtless to countless others, Octavio was always ready to give any and every kind of help in a very fraternal way. I never saw a cloud in any sky he stood under.

Trowbridge Street
(trans. Eliot Weinberger)

I

Sun throughout the day
                    Cold throughout the sun
Nobody on the streets
                    parked cars
Still no snow
                    but wind wind
A red tree
          still burns
in the chilled air
Talking to it I talk to you

2

I am in a room abandoned by language
You are in another identical room
Or we both are
on a street your glance has depopulated
The world
imperceptibly comes apart
                    Memory

255

decayed beneath our feet
I am stopped in the middle of this
unwritten line

3

Doors open and close by themselves
                              Air
enters and leaves our house
                         Air
talks to itself talking to you
                         Air
nameless in the endless corridor
Who knows who is on the other side?
                              Air
turns and turns in my empty skull
                              Air
turns to air everything it touches
                         Air
with air-fingers scatters everything I say
I am the air you don't see
I can't open your eyes
                    I can't close the door
The air has turned solid

4

This hour has the shape of a pause
This pause has your shape
You have the shape of a fountain made
not of water but of time
My pieces bob
at the jet's tip
what I was   am   still am not
My life is weightless
                    The past thins out
The future   a little water in your eyes

5

Now you have a bridge-shape
Our room navigates beneath your arches
From your railing we watch us pass
You ripple with wind   more light than body
The sun on the other bank
                              grows upside down
Its roots buried deep in the sky
We could hide ourselves in its foliage
Build a bonfire with its branches
The day is habitable

6

The cold has immobilized the world
Space is made of glass
                              Glass made of air
The lightest sounds build
quick sculptures
Echoes multiply and scatter them
Maybe it will snow
The burning tree quivers
surrounded now by night
Talking to it I talk to you

[*Return*]

CHARLES TOMLINSON

I shall read two extracts from *Airborn*, a poem Octavio and I wrote in collaboration. We had set out from our house, Brook Cottage, to put Octavio and Marie-José on to the London train at our local station. That day the train didn't run, so we retired to a nearby pub to get a snack and await the next connection. It was there that Octavio suggested we take two very basic words, "house" and "day," and collaborate in using them in a sequence of sonnets.

The choice of "house" was prompted by Brook Cottage, that of "day" by the fact that the day was so suddenly typically English, with Constable-like clouds scudding excitingly before the wind. I wrote the first four lines of "house" and sent it to Octavio to continue. Octavio wrote the first four lines of "day" and sent it to me to continue likewise. We wrote eight sonnets, four to each word, and then translated them into our own languages. The title *Airborn* implies a poem made possible by airmail between England and Mexico.

Airborn
(Fragment)

HOUSE

> Oh hermitage well found
> Whatever hours it be...!
> Luis de Góngora

I

One builds a house of what is there,
(horsehair bonded the plaster when horses where)
and of what one brings (the rhyme concealed):
space into its time, time to its space.

Yet we are born in houses we did not make.
(The rhyme returns, a bridge between the lines.)
The sun revolves its buried images
to restore to mind that ruined house once more

time and not I unmade —the rhyme revealed
only by the unheard pace of time,
and fragile yet dissonant against its space.

Time unmakes and builds the house again:
and rhyme, a sun brought, echo by echo, to birth,
illuminates, unspaces it back to time

DAY

Sweet day, so cool, so calm, so bright,
The bridall of the earth and skie.
George Herbert

I

Copious tree each day. This one
(July the fifth) grows hour by hour
invisible: a tree obliterated
to be freighted down with future leaves.

Coming to terms with day—light, water, stone—
our words extend a world of objects
that remains itself: the new leaves
gladden us, but for no motive of their own—

merely to be vegetable exclamations,
onomatopoeias of celebration
of the yearly chemical resurrection,

where evening already stains the finished page
and shadow absorbing shadow, day
is going down in fire, in foliage.

ELIOT WEINBERGER

I first read my translations with Octavio exactly 30 years ago, a few blocks
from here at the 92nd Street E, and over the years we read together many
times and in many places, and no matter how large the auditorium was,

it was always sold out. To read his poems publicly without him now is like being a translation without an original, a duet for a solo voice, as he might say. Though it's been extraordinary to hear these poems in so many different voices. It's what one hopes the poetry will become after the poet is no longer with us. It also makes me want to go home and rewrite all my translations. But I doubt I'll ever want to do this again —that is, read, not rewrite the translations. The first modern poem I read quite by accident, or perhaps not by accident, was Octavio's *Sunstone*. Before that moment it had never occurred to me to become a writer. "El presente es perpetuo" (The Present Is Perpetual). I thought I would end with the last page of *Sunstone*, where time and the poem itself returned to their beginnings.

Sunstone
(Fragment)

I want to go on, to go further, and cannot:
as each moment was dropping into another
I dreamt the dreams of dreamless stones,
and there at the end of the years like stones
I heard my blood, singing in its prison,
and the sea sang with a murmur of light,
one by one the walls gave way,
all of the doors were broken down,
and the sun came bursting through my forehead,
it tore apart my closed lids,
cut loose my being from its wrappers,
and pulled me out of myself to wake me
from this animal sleep and its century of stone,
and the sun's magic of mirrors revived
a crystal willow, a poplar of water,
a tall fountain the wind arches over,
a tree deep-rooted yet dancing still,
a course of a river that turns, moves on,
doubles back, and comes full circle,
forever arriving:

BIBLIOGRAPHY

BIBLIOGRAPHY OF OCTAVIO PAZ'S
WORKS PUBLISHED IN ENGLISH

The Labyrinth of Solitude: Life and Thought in Mexico, New York, Grove, 1961, 212 p. Trans. Lysander Kemp. Also published by London, A. Lane, Penguin Books, 1967, 199 p.

Sun Stone, New York, New Directions, 1963, 47 p. Trans. Muriel Rukeyser. Toronto, Contact, 1963, 67 p. Trans. Peter Miller. York, Ingl., Cosmos, 1969, 31 p. Trans. Donald Gardner. Texas Quarterly, vol. 13, núm. 3, (1970), 75-109. Trans. Laura Villaseñor. New York: New Directions, 1991, 59 p. Trans. Eliot Weinberger with ilustrations of the Aztec calendar by Mariano Fernández de Echeverría y Veytia.

Selected Poems, Bloomington, Indiana UP, 1963, 171 p. Trans. Muriel Rukeyser.

Marcel Duchamp: or, the Castle of Purity. London: Cape Goliard, 1970, 50 p. Other ed.: New York: Grossman, 1970. Trans. Donald Gardner.

Claude Lévi-Strauss: An Introduction. Ithaca: Cornell UP, 1970, 159 p. 2nd ed., New York: Dell Publ. Co., 1974. Trans. J. S. Bernstein and Maxine Bernstein.

¿Aguila o sol? Eagle or Sun? New York: October House, 1970, 125 p. 2nd ed., New York: New Directions, 1976, 121 p. Other ed.: London: P. Owen, 1990, 121 p. Trans. Eliot Weinberger.

Configuration. New York: New Drections, 1971 and London: Cape, 1971, 198 p. "Introduction" by Muriel Rukeyser, unpaginated. Trans. Muriel Rukeyser, G. Aroul, Denise Levertov, Charles Tomlinson, *et al.*

Renga: A Chain of Poems.. New York: G. Braziller, 1972, 95 p. Trans. Charles Tomlinson. "Foreword" by Claude Roy, 7-15; "Introduction" by O.P., 17-27; "The Transition of the Renga", by Jacques Roubaud, 24-34; "The Unison: A Retrospect", by Charles Tomlinson, 35-37.

The Other Mexico: Critique of the Pyramid. New York: Grove, 1972, 148 p. Trans. Lysander Kemp.

Early Poems, 1935-1955. New York: New Directions, 1973 and Bloomington: Indiana UP, 1974, 145 p. Trans. Muriel Rukeyser, Paul Blackburn, Lysander Kemp, Denise Levertov y William Carlos Williams.

Alternating Current. New York: Viking, 1973, 215 p. Trans, Helen R. Lane. Other ed.: New York: Penguin Books, 1970; New York: Seaver Books, 1983; New York: Arcade Books, 1990.

The Bow and the Lyre. Austin: University of Texas Press, 1973, 281 p. Trans. Ruth L. C. Simms. 2nd ed., New York: McGraw Hill, 1975.

Children of the Mire: Poetry from Romanticism to the Avant-Garde. Cambridge, Mass.: Harvard UP, 1974 186 p. Trans. Rachel Phillips.

Conjunctions and Disjunctions. New York: Viking, 1974, 148 p. Trans. Helen R. Lane.

The Siren and the Seashell, and Other Essays on Poets and Poetry. Austin: U of Texas P, 1976, 188 p. Trans. Lysander Kemp and Margaret Sayers Peden.

Marcel Duchamp: Appearance Stripped Bare. New York: Viking, 1978, 211 p. Trans. Rachel Phillips and Donald Gardner. 2nd ed., New York: Seaver, 1981, 206 p. Other ed.: New York: Arcade, 1990, 211 p.

A Draft of Shadows and Other Poems. New York: New Directions, 1979, 192 p. Ed. and trans. Eliot Weinberger; with additional translated by Elizabeth Bishop and Mark Strand.

Selected Poems. Middlesex, Engl.: Penguin Books, 1979, 207 p. Ed. and introd., "A Note on O. P.", by Charles Tomlinson, 13-14. Trans. Tomlinson, Elizabeth Bishop, Paul Blackburn, Eliot Weinberger, William Carlos Williams, Samuel Beckett *et al.*

Rappaccini's Daughter. In *O.P.: Homage to the Poet.* Ed. Kosrof Chantikian. San Francisco: Kosmos, 1980, 34-65. Trans. Harry Haskell.

Air Born. Hijos del aire. London: Anvil, 1981, 29 p. Sonnets written with Charles Tomlinson.

The Monkey Grammarian. New York: Seaver Books, 1981, 160 p. Other ed.: New York, Arcade, 1990, 162 p. Trans. Helen Lane.

Selected Poems. New York: New Directions, 1984, 147 p. Other ed.: Manchester: Carcanet, 1987. Ed. Eliot Weinberger. Trans. Weinberger, G. Aboul, Elizabeth Bishop, Paul Blackbum, Lysander Kemp, Denise Levertov, Muriel Rukeyser, Mark Strand, Charles Tomlinson, William Carlos Williams and Monique Fong-Wust.

The Labyrinth of Solitude; The Other Mexico; Return to the Labyrinth of Solitude; Mexico and the United States; The Philanthropic Ogre. New York: Grove, 1985, 398 p. Trans. Lysander Kemp, Yara Milos, Rachel Phillips Belash.

One Earth, Four or Five Worlds: Reflections on Contemporary History. San Diego: Harcourt Brace Jovanovich, 1985, 213 p. Trans. Helen Lane. Other ed.: New Delhi: Harper Collins, 1992.

On Poets and Others. New York: Seaver Books, 1986, 219 p. Trans. Michael Schmidt. Other ed.: Manchester: Carcanet, 1987; New Delhi: Harper Collins, 1992.

The Collected Poems of Octavio Paz, 1957-1987. New York: New Directions, 1991, 669 p. Ed. and trans. Eliot Weinberger; with additionals translations by Elizabeth Bishop, Paul Blackburn, Lysander Kemp, Denise Levertov, John Frederick Nims, Mark Strand and Charles Tomlinson. Other ed.: Manchester: Carcanet, 1994; New Delhi: Harper Collins, 1992.

Convergences: Essays on Art and Literature. San Diego: Harcourt Brace Jovanovich, 1987, 303 p. Trans. Helen Lane. Other ed.: London: Bloomsbury, 1987.

In the Middle of this Phrase and Other Poems. Helsinki: Eurographica, 1987, 82 p. Trans. Eliot Weinberger.

A Tree Within/Árbol adentro. New York: New Directions, 1988, 164 p. Trans. Eliot Weinberger.

Sor Juana, or, The Traps of Faith. Cambridge, MA.: Belknap, 1988, 547 p. Trans. Margaret Sayers Peden. Other ed.: *Sor Juana: Her Life and World,* London: Faber and Faber, 1988, 547 p.

In Search of the Present: Nobel Lecture, 1990 / La búsqueda del presente: Conferencia Nobel 1990. San Diego, CA.: Harcourt Brace Jovanovich, 1990, 68 p. Trans. Anthony Stanton.

The Other Voice: Essays on Modern Poetry. New York: Harcourt Brace Jovanovich, 1991, 161 p. Trans. Helen Lane.

Nostalgia for Death and Hieroglyphs of Desire. Port Townsend, WA.: Copper Canyon Press, 1992, 148 p. Trans. Esther Allen and Eliot Weinberger.

One Word to the Other. Mansfield, TX.: Latitudes, 1992, 43 p. Trans. Amelia Simpson, with a preface by Julio Ortega (7-8), an introduction by Juan Hernández-Senter (9-11), and an epilogue by Eliot Weinberger (41-43).

Essays on Mexican Art. New York: Harcourt Brace, 1993, 303 p. Trans. Helen Lane.

The Double Flame: Love and Eroticism. New York: Harcourt Brace, 1995, 276 p. Trans. Helen Lane. Other ed.: London: Harvill, 1996, 206 p.

In Light of India. New York: Harcourt Brace, 1997. 209 p. Trans Eliot Weinberger.

A Tale of Two Gardens: Poems from India, 1952-1995. New York: New Directions
Bibelot, 1997, III p. Ed. and trans. by Eliot Weinberger, with additional
translations by Elizabeth Bisop, *et al.*

Sade: An Erotic Beyond. New York: Harcourt Brace, to be published. Trans.
Eliot Weinberger.

First Letters. Austin: University of Texas Press, to be published. Trans. Enrico
Mario Santí and Melissa Simmermeyer.

PARTICIPANTS BIOGRAPHIES

Dore Ashton is an editor, art critic, and Professor of Art History, currently teaching at The Cooper Union. She was the art critic for *The New York Times* from 1955 to 1960. Among Ms. Ashton's numerous books on art and literature are *A Reading of Modern Art* (1970), *The New York School: A Cultural Reckoning* (1973), *American Art since 1945* (1982), and *Noguchi East and West* (1992).

Bei Dao was nominated for the Nobel Prize in Literature in 1996. After Mao's death and the defeat of the Gang of Four, Bei Dao joined with his friend and fellow poet Mang Ke in editing *Today* (Jintian), the best unofficial publication of the 1978 Democracy Movement in China. He became widely known on April 5, 1976 when, at a demonstration against dictatorship in Tiananmen Square, some of his poems were read. He has been in exile since the 1989 student revolt. He now teaches at the University of California at Davis. *Old Snow* (1991), *Forms of Distance* (1995), and *Landscape over Zero* (1996) are among his many books translated into English.

Adolfo Castañón is a poet, translator, and essayist. His most recent book of poetry is entitled *Recuerdos de Coyoacán*. He is the Editor-in-Chief of the Fondo de Cultura Económica.

Francesco Clemente's art has been shown in major retrospectives at the Philadelphia Museum of Art (1990), the Sezon Museum in Tokyo (1994), and currently at the Guggenheim Museum in New York. Clemente helps publish Hanuman Books, a collection of small-sized books by a variety of artists and writers, printed in India.

Christopher Domínguez Michael is a Mexican literary critic, cultural historian, and novelist. He has contributed to many newspapers and magazines, among them *Vuelta* and *Letras Libres*. Among his books are *Jorge Cuesta y el demonio de la política*, *Utopía de la hospitalidad*, *Literatura mexicana del siglo xx*, and the novel *William Pescador*.

Linda Downs has been the Director of Educational Programs of the National Gallery of Art in Washington, D.C. since 1989. She is the author of the monograph *Diego Rivera's Detroit Industry Murals*. In 1986, in collaboration with the Instituto Nacional de Bellas Artes, she organized a retrospective of Diego Rivera's works, which was exhibited in Detroit, Philadelphia, Mexico City, Madrid, Berlin, and London. She has published many articles and lectured widely in the United States and abroad.

John Kenneth Galbraith remains one of the better-known economists in the United States since the publication of *The Affluent Society* in 1958, and has worked in various sectors of the economy. Besides his work at Harvard and the Office of Price Administration, Galbraith was editor of *Fortune* magazine for several years, director of the US Strategic Bombing Survey, chairman of the Americans for Democratic Action in the late 1960s, television and newspaper commentator, advisor and speechwriter for John Fitzgerald Kennedy, Eugene McCarthy and George McGovern. He also served as the American ambassador to India in the early 1960s and has published two novels. His most recent book is *Name-Dropping: From F.D.R. On.*

Robert Gardner is a filmmaker and an anthropologist who has made feature-length and short films including *Dead Birds, Rivers of Sand* and *Forest Bliss*. He has served on the faculty and was Director of the Carpenter Center for Visual Arts at Harvard University for many years. He is presently preparing a feature for which he has written the script and is doing a series of short films about making art. The first, on the abstract painter Sean Scully, has recently been completed.

Yvon Grenier is Associate Professor of Political Science in Francis Xavier University, Nova Scotia, Canada. He edited the *Canadian Journal of Latin American and Caribbean Studies* and has written numerous studies of Latin American politics, including *Guerre et pouvoir au Salvador* and *The Emergence of Insurgency in El Salvador*. He is currently writing a book on the political thought of Octavio Paz.

Alma Guillermoprieto has written numerous articles on Latin America for *The New Yorker* and *The New York Review of Books*. Guillermoprieto's first book, *Samba*, an account of carnival life in a favela in Rio de Janeiro, was nominated for the 1990 National Book Critics Circle Award. Her second book, *The Heart that Bleeds*, is a collection of thirteen articles which originally ran in *The New Yorker* between 1989 and 1993.

Edward Hirsch is author of five collections of poems, among them *The Night Parade* (1989), *Earthly Measures* (1994), and *On Love* (1998). His most recent book is *How to Read a Poem and Fall in Love with Poetry*. He writes frequently for leading magazines and periodicals —among them *American Poetry Review*, *DoubleTake*, where he is the editorial advisor in poetry, and *The Paris Review*. He has received numerous awards, among them a MacArthur Foundation Fellowship, a Guggenheim Fellowship, and the Rome Prize from the American Academy of the Institute of Arts and Letters. He teaches at the University of Houston.

David Huerta is one of Mexico's major contemporary poets. He studied literature and philosophy at the UNAM. His books of poetry include *El jardín de luz*, *Cuaderno de noviembre*, *Huellas del civilizado*, *Versión*, and the long poem *Incurable*. He has translated works by Victor Serge, Maurice Blanchot, and Bernard Noël. Among the awards he has received are the Diana Moreno Toscano Prize for Emerging Writers, the Carlos Pellicer Prize, and a Guggenheim Fellowship.

William Luers was President of the Metropolitan Museum of Art from 1986 to 1999. He was the American ambassador to Czechoslovakia from 1983 to 1986 and to Venezuela from 1978 to 1982, and has held numerous diplomatic positions throughout his career. He was awarded the Mexican Order of the Aztec Eagle in 1992.

Carlos Monsiváis is one of Mexico's most renowned cultural and political critics. His articles have appeared in such prestigious Mexican periodicals as *Proceso* and *La Jornada*, and he has contributed to radio and television programs as well. He has received grants from Harvard University's Center for International Studies and from the Centro Mexicano de Escritores. He has been a visiting professor at Harvard and King's College, Essex. A selection of his essays has been published in an English translation as *Mexican Postcards*.

Philippe de Montebello has served as the eighth Director of the Metropolitan Museum of Art for the past twenty-two years. Among his professional affiliations are membership on the Board of Trustees of New York University's Institute of Fine Arts; and membership on the Columbia University Advisory Council of the Departments of Art and Archeology. He is also a Trustee of the American Federation of the Arts, and a member of the editorial board of the *International Journal of Museum Management and Curatorship*. He has been awarded several honors, including Chevalier de la Légion d'Honneur in 1991, the Orden de Isabel la Católica, Encomienda de Número; the Spanish Institute Gold Medal Award; and Knight Commander, the Pontifical Order of St. Gregory the Great.

Michael Palmer is a poet and translator from the French and Russian, among other languages. His books of poetry include *At Passages* (1995), *Notes for Echo Lake* (1981), *First Figure* (1984), and *Sun* (1988). He has also written plays for radio, and has collaborated with Margaret Jenkins on over a dozen dance performances.

Robert Pinsky is the thirty-ninth Poet Laureate of the United States, poetry editor of the online journal *Slate*, and contributor to *The News Hour with Jim Lehrer* on PBS. He teaches in the graduate writing program at Boston University. His book *The Figured Wheel: New and Collected Poems 1965-1995* was nominated for the Pulizter Prize in poetry. His book *The Inferno of Dante*, a new verse translation, was awarded the Los Angeles Times Book Award in poetry and the Howard Morton Landon Prize for translation. He is currently editing the *Norton Anthology of Twentieth-Century American Poetry*. *Jersey Rain* is his most recent book of poems.

Robert Rauschenberg began his career as an artist designing sets, costumes and lighting for Merce Cunningham's dance company for more than ten years. In the early 1950s, he created a series of black and white paintings, some *collage*-paintings with the paint applied over newsprint attached to the canvas. Around 1953 he began to create paintings and constructions that incorporated a range of everyday objects. His signature assemblages of painting and objects —"combines," a word he coined to describe his mixture of real and created forms, of found objects and paint— have earned him numerous national and international exhibitions. In 1997, the Guggenheim Museum in New York hosted his most comprehensive retrospective exhibition to date.

Enrico Mario Santí was born in Cuba and received his Ph.D. from Yale University. He has taught at Duke and Cornell and is currently a professor at Georgetown University. He has written five books and more than a hundred scholarly articles and is on the editorial board of more than twenty literary journals. He was recently named member of the Advisory Council of the Fundación Octavio Paz. His latest book, *The Rights of Poetry: An Intellectual Biography of Octavio Paz*, will be published by Harvard University Press and the Fondo de Cultura Económica.

Grace Schulman's poetry collections include *For That Day Only, Hemispheres,* and *Burn Down the Icons,* and she is finishing a new manuscript entitled *The Paintings of Our Lives.* She is a recipient of the Delmore Schwartz Memorial Award for Poetry and two Pushcart Prizes, and is represented in *The Best American Poetry* and *The Best of the Best of American Poetry.* A Distinguished Professor of English at Baruch College, CUNY, she is Poetry Editor of *The Nation* and a former Director of the Poetry Center, on 92nd Street. Her poems, essays, and translations have been published widely.

Richard Seaver was Octavio Paz's editor over a period of twenty years at Grove Press and Seaver Books, and published six of his works. He is now President of Arcade Publishers.

Tomás Segovia was born in Spain and emigrated in 1940 to Mexico, where he studied philosophy and literature in the UNAM. Among his publications are *Poesía 1943-1979,* three works of fiction, a play, and four non-fiction studies. He was co-editor of the *Revista Mexicana de Literatura* and was the first Editor-in-Chief of *Plural,* whose Executive Editor was Octavio Paz. He has been awarded numerous prizes, including the Xavier Villaurrutia Poetry Prize and, recently, the Octavio Paz Prize.

Guillermo Sheridan was appointed, at Octavio Paz's behest, to the position of President of the Octavio Paz Foundation in December 1997. He is a member of the Editorial Committee of the magazine *Letras Libres,* the successor publication to *Vuelta.* He has published fifteen works of literary criticism, among them *Los Contemporáneos ayer,* diaries, screenplays, a novel, and various critical editions of Mexican writers.

Jesús Silva-Herzog Márquez studied Law and Political Science in Mexico and at Columbia University. He is presently a law professor in the ITAM, Mexico City. He writes a column for the Mexico City newspaper *Reforma* and contributes to other important Mexican dailies and magazines. His works include *Esferas de la democracia* and *El viejo régimen y la Transición en México.*

Lasse Söderberg has translated Octavio Paz's poetry into Swedish. He is the author of numerous poetry collections.

Susan Sontag is a critic and writer who first gained attention with her essay, "Notes on Camp" (1964). Her essay collections include *Against Interpretation*

(1966), *About Photography* (1977), *Illness as Metaphor* (1978), and *Under the Sign of Saturn* (1980). Sontag has also written short stories and novels, including *The Volcano Lover: A Romance* (1992) and *In America* (2000) and written and directed films. Her numerous awards include fellowships from the Rockefeller Foundation, the Guggenheim Foundation, an Arts and Letters Award from the American Academy and Institute of Arts and Letters, and a National Book Critics Award.

Anthony Stanton was born in England and now lives in Mexico, where he is a Professor and Research Associate at the Colegio de México. He is President of the Octavio Paz Advisory Board and has written several books, including *Inventores de tradición: Ensayos sobre poesía mexicana moderna, Homenaje a María Zambrano: estudios y correspondencia,* and (as co-editor) *Los contemporáneos en el laberinto de la crítica.*

Mark Strand is the author of more than twenty books, which include poetry volumes, translations, children's books and collections of essays on painting and photography. He has translated volumes of poetry by Rafael Alberti and Carlos Drummond de Andrade. With Octavio Paz, he co-edited the anthology *New Poetry from Mexico* (1970). In 1990, he was chosen by the Library of Congress to be Poet Laureate of the United States. His *Selected Poems* were published in 1995. His most recent book of poems is *Blizzard of One* (1998).

Nathaniel Tarn is a poet, translator, editor and critic. He has published more than 25 books. His main titles are *The Beautiful Contradictions, Lyrics or the Bride of God, Seeing America First* and *The Architextures.* Tarn is also an anthropologist who has carried out fieldwork in Guatemala, Southeast Asia, China, Japan, Russia, Alaska, and the American Southwest, and has written many publications in the field. The latest are *Views from the Weaving Mountain: Selected Essays in Poetics & Anthropology* and *Scandals in the House of Birds: Shamans & Priests in Lake Atitlán.*

Charles Tomlinson's first book, *Relations and Contraries,* was published in 1951. His *Collected Poems* were published in 1985, and since then four shorter volumes have appeared, the latest of which is called *Jubilation* (1995). With Octavio Paz, he is co-author of *Airborne* (1979) and is one of the translators featured in Paz's *A Tale of Two Gardens: Poems from India 1952-1995* (1997). He retired in 1992 from a long teaching career at the University of Bristol.

Mario Vargas Llosa, the internationally-renowned Peruvian writer, is the author of many novels, including *Time of the Hero, The Storyteller, Aunt Julia and the Scriptwriter, The War of the End of the World,* and *The Green House.* He has been awarded the Cervantes Prize, the most prestigious literary award in the Spanish-speaking world, and the Jerusalem Prize, which is given to those writers whose work best expresses the idea of individual liberty within society. He is currently living in Europe, and his latest novel is *La fiesta del chivo*, an examination of the Trujillo dictatorship in the Dominican Republic of the 1940s and 1950s.

Nicanor Vélez is the Editorial Director of the Barcelona-based firm Círculo de Lectores, and is the editor of the Spanish edition of Octavio Paz's *Obras completas.* He is presently editing the complete works of Pablo Neruda.

Verónica Volkow is the author of several books of poetry, including *La sibila de Cumas, Litoral de tinta, El inicio,* and *Los caminos.* She has also written *Sudáfrica: Diario de un viaje,* an account of daily life under the apartheid system, and *La mordedura de la risa,* a study of Francisco Toledo's graphic art.

Eliot Weinberger's essays are collected in *Works on Paper, Outside Stories,* and *Written Reaction.* With Octavio Paz, he is the co-author of a study of the translation of Chinese poetry, *19 Ways of Looking at Wang Wei.* He is the editor of the anthology *American Poetry Since 1950: Innovators & Outsiders.* He is the editor and translator of *The Collected Poetry of Octavio Paz 1957-1987,* and most recently of the *Selected Non-Fictions of Jorge Luis Borges,* which received a National Book Critics Award in 2000. He received the PEN/ Kolovakos Award in 1992 for his work promoting Latin American literature in the United States. He was awarded the Mexican Order of the Aztec Eagle in 2000.

THIS BOOK WAS
PRINTED IN MEXICO
CITY, IN OCTOBER
2001. IT WAS COMPOSED
USING AGARAMOND TYPE.
THE EDITION CONSISTS
OF 1000 COPIES.